CONDORCET STUDIES I

CONDORCET STUDIES I

edited by

LEONORA COHEN ROSENFIELD

SUPERVISORY EDITOR: Richard H. Popkin

**Society for Study of History of Philosophy.
History of Philosophy Series #1**

HUMANITIES PRESS
Atlantic Highlands, N.J.

First published in 1984 in the United States of America by Humanities Press Inc.,
Atlantic Highlands, NJ 07716

Library of Congress Cataloging in Publication Data
Main entry under title:

Condorcet studies I.

(History of philosophy series; #1)
Includes bibliographical references and index.
1. Condorcet, Jean-Antoine-Nicolas de Caritat,
marquis de, 1743-1794 — Addresses, essays, lectures.
I. Rosenfield, Leonora Cohen, 1909-1982. II. Title:
Concorcet studies 1. III. Title: Condorcet studies one.
IV. Series.
B1997.C66 1984   194   84-686
ISBN 0-391-03006-X

MANUFACTURED IN THE UNITED STATES OF AMERICA

To
Harry N. Rosenfield
with
deepest gratitude

Table of Contents

THE QUEST FOR JUSTICE

Foreword

Richard H. Popkin

Condorcet is an extremely interesting thinker whose ideas are most relevant to present day concerns. Unfortunately, his work has not been given the attention it deserves. The last edition of his works was published in the mid-nineteenth century. Many manuscripts of his are still awaiting editing and publication.

This neglect is slowly being overcome. This collective volume of Condorcet studies brings together a varied group of scholars, who examine some of the most exciting aspects of Condorcet's thought. Condorcet was the only important *philosophe* to live until the Revolution. He was the only one of the great French enlightenment thinkers to have the opportunity to try to put his reform ideas into practice. And, as he applied his amazing liberal and rational perspective to some of the most basic problems of human existence, he finally became a martyr to the Reign of Terror. Against the background of the American and French Revolutions, Condorcet sought to work out the best constitution for modern men and women, to eliminate slavery and liberate women, to develop a truly democratic educational system, a humane hospital system, an equitable criminal law with human rights respected and torture abolished, and a just emigration policy. In addition, he backed progressive taxation with exemptions only for those at or below a bare subsistence level. He sought to create a world in which a wide variety of lifestyles could co-exist, and in which everyone would be best able to develop his or her full potential.

Readers today will be struck by how contemporary Condorcet's views seem to be. Perhaps we have not yet found as good solutions to some of the problems of organizing a just society as Condorcet had proposed almost two centuries ago. Even though Condorcet did not foresee many of the disastrous developments that have befallen Western man in the last two hundred years, he was able to focus an astonishingly modern liberal outlook on basic issues that would have to be resolved if men are to live freely and happily in a democratic world. The monumental optimism of Condorcet's final work, the sketch of the history of human progress, still provides a very important statement of an ideology of modern secular liberalism.

The late Leonora Cohen Rosenfield had long admired Condorcet's profound examination of enduring social problems. She devoted much of her great energy to encouraging other scholars to study Condorcet's views. In 1979 she brought a group of us together at a session of the American Society for Eighteenth Century Studies in Atlanta to present our findings. She then went on to put together the following volume, by encouraging the participants at that conference and others interested in aspects of Condorcet's thought to write articles on Condorcet. Before her death, Professor Rosenfield had completely edited the material. With her wealth of erudition about the eighteenth century, she brought the volume to completion. Unfortunately, finding a suitable home for the volume has taken some time, and during this period our dear friend and leader in this enterprise, Leonora Cohen Rosenfield, passed away on January 15, 1982. Her husband, Harry N. Rosenfield, then asked me to take charge of the volume and see it into print.

In so doing I have made only the minimum changes needed to reflect the fact that this is a posthumous work. One article, that by Professor Renée Waldinger, has been changed, at the author's request, from a narrow study of Condorcet's plan for public education, to a broader one placing his plan in the context of his overall philosophy. I feel sure that Professor Rosenfield would have approved this change.

Leonora Cohen Rosenfield was born in New York on February 11, 1909, the daughter of the philosopher, Morris Raphael Cohen, and Mary Ryshpan Cohen. She studied in France and America, receiving her Ph.D. from Columbia. She taught at Smith College, Brooklyn College, and the University of Maryland, where she became professor emeritus in 1979. She was very active researching and writing about the history of ideas, especially in relation to themes in French eighteenth-century thought. Her book, *From Beast-Machine to Man-Machine, Animal Soul in French Letters from Descartes to La Mettrie*, first published in 1941, remains a fundamental study. She was active in organizing and participating in a range of programs on the history of ideas at meetings of the American Society for Eighteenth Century Studies, including ones on racism, on the rights of women, and on the treatment of religious minorities. These themes all involved ones that had been seriously dealt with by Condorcet. Professor Rosenfield for years had been interested in Condorcet's innovative ideas about various social problems, and had gathered together a great deal of unpublished material. She hoped that the ensuing volume would be just the beginning of a series of volumes entitled *Condorcet Studies*, and that the series might be placed alongside *Diderot Studies, Voltaire Studies*, and others, as a way of gathering together and disseminating studies on Condorcet. At her death she was working on organizing a second volume of essays on Condorcet. Still further, she hoped that a revival of interest in Condorcet might lead to a publication program that would edit the complete works of this last of the *philosophes*—both the works previously published plus all the wealth of unpublished materials. Through this, she and the contributors to this volume, as well as other interested scholars, hoped that Condorcet's contributions would become much better known, and that some of his most fruitful ideas would help us deal with contemporary problems.

Those of us who knew Leonora, and who worked with her, hope that this volume will also provide fitting recognition of her important contribution to modern intellectual history. She stimulated us, and raised us up by her very high standards. She led us to focus on significant but often overlooked areas of interest. We hope that through her editorship, her guidance, and her concern, we have put together a volume that will lead people to reassess Condorcet's work, and to see it as throwing valuable light on many of society's present difficulties. And so, let us dedicate the completed volume to our dear departed friend and colleague, Leonora Cohen Rosenfield.

Richard H. Popkin
Washington University

Introduction

CONDORCET STUDIES I is a pioneer project, the first collection of studies devoted to him in this country.[1] It is an outgrowth of the seminar "Condorcet, from Enlightenment to Revolution" that was conducted on April 19, 1979, in Atlanta, Georgia at the tenth annual meeting of the American Society for Eighteenth-Century Studies and was their first session on Condorcet. Three of the collaborators of this book read papers there (Professors Baker, Popkin, and Waldinger) and others contributed to the discussion. Gratitude is due to the authors, as well as to the numerous other scholars who petitioned ASECS to schedule the seminar. Thanks to Professor Popkin, the venture has materialized, to be followed by subsequent studies. This first one, in English and French, has been composed, fittingly, by scholars from different disciplines, several countries, and both sexes.

Marie Jean Antoine Nicolas Caritat, Marquis de Condorcet (1743–1794) was a transitional figure, between Enlightenment and Revolution, the Age of Reason and that of the *idéologues*. Before and during the French Revolution he helped elaborate concepts that pointed the way to modern progressive society. The last of the *philosophes*, he produced innovative works on an encyclopedic range of subjects. His writings, published and unpublished, demonstrate the connections between things: from mathematics to social mathematics, from mathematics to mathematical economics, from natural philosophy to social science, from the calculus of probabilities to the political and moral sciences, from the pure to the applied sciences, from natural rights to the rights of man and woman in society, from the rights of the individual to those of society, from reform to revolution, from language to logic. Condorcet pointed out the utility of a universal language of mathematically exact terminology. Is symbolic logic a realization, at least in part, of what he was asking for?

Condorcet was an anomaly. A member of the old *noblesse d'épée* who was honored widely throughout the Republic of Letters, he was apparently never received at court. The scion of an old family from the Dauphiné, he was born and brought up in Picardy. An aristocrat who called himself Marquis (his father signed "Chevalier"), he was through his mother half bourgeois. With the traditional independence of the Caritats, he defied the family tradition whereby the sons entered the Army or the Church. Not yet twenty, with limited resources, he struck out for Paris on his own, to try to make it in mathematics. Born a Catholic and raised by an ultra pious mother assisted by an uncle who was a bishop, he became a freethinker, descended from Henri de Caritat, who had embraced Calvinism in its early days. The Condorcets reconverted to Rome only under duress, when the then head of the family was imprisoned by Louvois under Louis XIV.

A theoretician who liked to carry ideas to their logical conclusions, with neither the delivery, presence, nor timing of the politician, and never a party member, Condorcet nevertheless tasted victory more than defeat at the polls of practical politics. He was elected to the Electoral Assembly to represent the nobility from the bailiwick around his country place at Mantes. After the outbreak of the revolution his district in Paris elected him to the General Assembly of the first Paris Commune. In October 1791 he won a seat to the National Legislative Assembly, where he was elected to, and then chaired, the Committee on Public Instruction. Lastly, in the fall of 1792, he gained election to the First French Republic's National Convention, where to the envy of the defeated Robespierre, he was voted one of the nine members of the Committee on a Constitution, then made chairman. The Convention frustrated Condorcet more than the Legislative Assembly—the latter merely tabled his educational bill, the former objected to many of its features. And the Convention never even brought Condorcet's Constitution to a vote. Not a good batting average in the bill-passing league!

Condorcet grew and matured through the years as he devoted himself to "le bien public." His development was furthered through his friendly relations with leading French and foreign figures of his age, then through his marriage to the cultivated Sophie de Grouchy. She was well-connected; her brother-in-law, Dr. Cabanis, became a loyal friend. Condorcet's earliest reference to female educational rights seems to be in his *Discours sur les sciences mathématiques.* Its date is 1786, the year of his marriage. Husband and wife, with their command of English, shared an interest in translating the work of Adam Smith, who came to Paris, and they both helped Thomas Paine, whose French was inadequate to his commitments to the French revolutionary government. Prominent foreigners frequented Mme de Condorcet's brilliant salon, including Condorcet's friend Beccaria, the former mathematician whose *Dei delitti e delle pene*[2] of 1764 stirred wide interest in penal reform.

Under the exigencies of revolution, there was an evolution of such concepts of Condorcet as the necessity for a French republic, national education for all, progressive taxation, and universal suffrage. Public opinion was becoming an increasingly potent factor. To sway it, he published, launched journals, and helped found the *Société de 1789.* He proposed legislation and a Constitution preceded by its Declaration of Rights, and guided policy in the fiscal crises of the Revolution.

Professor Aldridge has evaluated the implications Condorcet drew from his study of the English Revolution of 1688. Condorcet, who knew English, studied British philosophy. At the age of twenty, he supposedly met Hume, who visited France in 1763. Professor Popkin has revealed that Condorcet at a later date purchased a book of Hume's that was being remaindered by the book seller. Other English visitors such as Adam Smith and David Williams stimulated Condorcet's thinking on economics and politics, as did Paine, the author of *Common Sense.*

But he imbibed most deeply the lessons of the American Revolution. Its state declarations of rights or constitutions, Federal Constitution, and Bill of Rights broadened his political horizons. He held an advantage over Rousseau by living to see a democratic republic become viable in a large nation, a new phenomenon in world history. Rousseau's *Contrat social* of 1762 maintained in its chapter on democracy that such a government is feasible only in a very small state where the citizens know one another and can readily assemble. To resolve the dilemma raised by Rousseau, Condorcet proposed devices whereby the popular sovereignty could exercise its general will through primary, communal, and departmental assemblies, the right to petition, referendum and plebiscite, convocation of new constitutional conventions, opportunity for constitutional revision, elections by universal suffrage for representation in the unicameral National Assembly, and the people's right to change its form of government. Finances are to be controlled by the representatives of the people, and even in the judiciary the public could exercise rights through the election of national juries.

Democracy was defined by Condorcet as:

> une Constitution où tous les citoyens, partagés en plusieurs assemblées, élisent les députés chargés de représenter, et de porter la pression générale de la volunté de leurs commettants à une assemblée générale qui représente alors la nation.[3]

The chapters of this book, as summarized below, illustrate the democratic direction of Condorcet's thought.

Rights and Revolution

Professor Rowe surveys "The Present Day Relevance of Condorcet" in a full gamut of areas, rounding out the picture of Condorcet's life and works by calling attention to his all-embracing vision of the progress of the human mind.

Professor Popkin in "Condorcet, Abolitionist," first compares Condorcet's opposition to slavery with that of Jefferson, then with that of the champion of the blacks, the abbé Grégoire.

Professor Aldridge's "Condorcet, Paine, and Historical Method," analyzing historical methods, contrasts the views of Thomas Paine and Condorcet on the Glorious Revolution of 1688, and then points out their resemblances and common international interest in revolution.

Toward the Social Sciences

In "A Note on the Problem of the Randomness of Ends," *Professor Baker* examines the relationship between Condorcet's claim that the moral and political sciences could be established on the same positive basis as the natural sciences, and his political theory based on rational principles basic to the rights of man.

In "Condorcet's *Mémoire sur les Hôpitaux*, an English Translation and Commentary," *Professor Greenbaum*, whose wife *Dr. Hilda Greenbaum* is responsible for the translation, edits it for the first time in English. Against the background of the controversy over hospitals, he delineates Condorcet's role in sponsoring the neighborhood hospice.

Professor Perkins's "Condorcet and Progessive Taxation: Theory and Practice" traces the evolution of Condorcet's views that culminated in progressive taxation (with exemptions for the poor), and explains the financial picture and Condorcet's role.

Revolution in Education

Professor Waldinger's "Condorcet: The Problematic Nature of Progress" sets Condorcet's views on education in their context, allowing us to see the relevance of his revolutionary concept of education to our present-day democratic educational philosophy.

In "Enlightenment and Revolution: the Evolution of Condorcet's Ideas on Education," *Dr. Albertone*, author of a recent book on the subject, traces that evolution, surveys the subsequent opposition to Condorcet's proposals, and finishes by noting his pedagogic legacy.

"Un Provincial Eclairé: Thomas Riboud, Emule de Condorcet" by *Professor Trénard* brings to light the role of Riboud, a colleague on the Legislative Assembly's Education Committee, who influenced its Chairman Condorcet to add some measure of moral "education" to "instruction" in his proposed national bill.

The Quest for Justice

In "Une Contribution de Condorcet à la Réforme de la Législation Pénale," jurist *Perrod* of Lyon, author of *L'Affaire Lally-Tolendal*, brings to life another miscarriage of justice, the "affaire des trois roués." He shows how Dupaty's intercession stimulated Condorcet to write his historic *Réflexions*, which proposed reformed penal legislation based on the principle that "la Justice est l'affaire de tous."

Professor Rosenblum's "Condorcet as Constitutional Draftsman: Dimensions of Substantive Commitment and Procedural Implementation" analyses Condorcet's draft of a Constitution, examined in the light of the American Constitution.

Through all these specialized studies we see Condorcet as a precursor to democratic society. The chapters of this book indicate milestones on the march to modern times. I should like to follow up with comments along these general lines.

Separation of Church and State

Like Bayle rather than Locke, Condorcet advocated toleration of all faiths or lack of faith. And like Jefferson, he held for separation of church and state. He adamantly opposed any intrusions of religion into the public schools. "Quant à la religion," he advised, "je conseille de n'en point parler."[4]

Education

Condorcet insisted the key to liberty lies in universal secular, public coeducation. In Professor Waldinger's words, education is a right, not a privilege. There must be, regardless of socio-economic status, equal educational opportunity for all, so that every youngster may realize his potential. Ignorance is an impediment to freedom.

The democratization of education has its pitfalls, as we are seeing today. Still, Condorcet realized that without it there can be no democracy. Freedom for all includes the parents' right to educate their children in religious or other private schools, but not at the public expense. Teachers have a right to academic freedom, with no political pressures. Young people have the right to vocational training, rural or urban.

For Condorcet, the educational process is rationalistic. The purpose of "instruction," to use Condorcet's term, is not to indoctrinate, but rather to train students to think for themselves. Like Descartes, Condorcet urged more emphasis on mathematics and sciences, less on dead languages and rhetoric, although he provided also for what the French call human sciences. Only in recent times is his general pedagogic blueprint being followed, in some measure, in some countries.

One of the points of contention against Condorcet's bill as proposed was that it omitted the formative educational processes, as Dr. Albertone and Professor Trénard both point out. Yet the author of the *Projet* on public instruction realized that "education" was broader than "instruction." In his words:

> l'éducation si on la prend dans toute son étendue, ne se borne pas à l'instruction positive, à l'enseignement des vérités de fait et de calcul. Mais elle embrasse toutes les qualités politiques, morales ou religeuses.[5]

Professor Trénard explains how Thomas Riboud prevailed on Condorcet to include "education," at least in elementary school. The latter's hesitancy to grant the state such powers at upper scholastic levels seems to indicate scepticism as to whether it would refrain from propagandizing.

Women's Liberation

Condorcet's drive for women's emancipation stressed civil and political rights, though it included their marital and sexual rights. The open sesame for woman's equality seemed to him via equal educational opportunity. Like Mary Wollstonecraft, who wrote her *A Vindication of the Rights of Woman*[6] in 1791–1792, Condorcet at the very same time was calling for public national coeducation at all levels. Young people thus brought together would inevitably have a tendency to choose their own marriage partners, sometimes cutting across class lines, thereby undermining the old system of arranged marriages involving family alliances and dowries. (Condorcet himself married *sans dot*.) With his final counsel to his daughter Eliza that every girl must prepare herself to earn a living, a new social order was being ushered in.

Republicanism

As early as the 1770s Condorcet evinced inclinations toward republican government. In 1775 he asked for the abolition of the *corvée*. A year later he called for liberty of the press. Before the French Revolution he drafted a plan for the abolition of feudal rights. "Une constitution, républicaine," he avowed in his *La Vie de M. Turgot* of 1786, "est la meilleure de toutes."[7] In 1788, his anonymous pamphlet, *Sentiments d'un Républicain sur les Assemblées provinciales et les états-généraux*, appeared in Philadelphia. He did not come out officially for the replacement of the monarchy by a republic until after Louis

XVI's flight to Varennes of June 21, 1791. Then in July, with Paine and DuChâtelet, he issued *Le République, ou le Défenseur du gouvernement représentatif, par une société de républicains.* For the *Cercle social* came *De la République ou un Roi est-il nécessaire à la conservation de la liberté? Par Condorcet. Discours dont l'assemblée fédérative des Amis de la vérité a demandé l'impression* (1791).

The last in date of the *philosophes*, he greatly desired to apply the lessons learned from the American experiment in republicanism.

Constitutions

Professor Rosenblum tells us how strongly Condorcet felt the need for the immediate adoption of a democratic constitution, with its preliminary Declaration of Rights, as a foundation for the new French Republic. Condorcet had read the U.S. Constitution of 1787. Paine, who served as a link between the American and the French Revolutions, was elected with Condorcet to the constitutional committee of the National Convention. The carefully drafted "Girondine" constitution (so named because the majority of the committee were members of that party), meant so much to Condorcet, its principal author, that he risked his life for it—and lost. His *Aux citoyens français, sur la nouvelle constitution*, warning the public of the dangers of the hasty substitute Constitution, "la Jacobine," stressed the advantages of his democratic provisions that allowed for constitutional review. It was a quixotic appeal. No constitution was put into effect in a country sore beset with problems, whose leaders, athirst for power or the power to survive, were draining the blood of their own revolution.

Abolition

Professor Popkin has furnished details on how Condorcet as a champion of human rights condemned slavery and the white men who profited by this immoral practice. Condorcet expressed hopes for a more equitable economy in the Antilles.

As early as 1774 he had written to Turgot:

> Il faut que je pense à nos colonies, à leurs malheureux habitants, opprimés par des gens déshonorés en Europe, et qu'on envoie chercher la fortune aux Indes; à ces nègres que Louis XIII a abandonnés à la barbarie de leurs maîtres, dans la sainte espérance qu'on pourrait les rendre chrétiens à coups de fouet? Je vois d'avance le bien que vous ferez à ces infortunés.[8]

In Condorcet's proposed constitution, slavery would not exist. Any adult residing on French territory for a year would be eligible for citizenship after registering, and after three more months of residence in a given locality could vote there.

Penal Reform

For some time jurists had been interested in codifying the laws of France, which varied from region to region. Condorcet aimed at such codification but with equal justice for all three orders. To insure democratization, he called for the "impenetrable veil" of oracular judicial secrecy to be lifted and urged distinct separation of the judiciary from the semi-legislative Parlements and from the executive. In addition, he devised provisions for citizens' rights in the courts such as trial by juries of popularly-elected jurors, in criminal and civil law, with a jury of accusation and another of judgment.

Condorcet's *Essai sur quelque changements à faire dans les lois criminelles de France*[9] proposed a new code "dicté par la raison et par la justice," under which the accused would be informed of the charges, would have the right to legal counsel with full access to the record, and would be allowed to confront his accusers. Any prisoner incarcerated for two years without trial is to be released with no future liability in the case. Torture is abolished; capital punishment resorted to solely for homicide. Some judges are "ces assassins en robe."

The above procedural guarantees, among others specified, would prevent any such miscarriage of justice, as in the case of the peasants known as "les trois roués de Champagne." Professor Perrod, the author of *L'Affaire Lally-Tolendal, Une Erreur Judiciaire au XVIIIe Siècle*, tells us in this present study how Solicitor-General Dupaty, who interested himself and others in the case, was hounded by the authorities. In his *Essai* and briefly in his *Vie de Voltaire*, Condorcet sums up the story. Then Dupaty and his detractors are compared:

> Les hommes incapables de ces actions....ignorent quelles angoisses le spectacle d'une injustice fait éprouver à une âme fière et sensible, à quel point il tourmente la mémoire et la pensée, combien il fait sentir le besoin impérieux de prévenir ou de réparer le crime; ils ne connaissent point ce trouble, cette horreur involontaire qu'excite dans tous les sens la vue, l'idée seule d'un oppresseur triomphant ou impuni...[10]

Condorcet's tribute to Voltaire's campaigns in famous cases such as this one was not accompanied by mention of his own more considerable efforts to obtain justice tempered by mercy for the victims.

Did not the coat-of-arms of Condorcet's ancestral house bear the crest CARITAS?

Social Science

Are the social sciences sciences? The eighteenth century, with its increased social awareness, witnessed the budding of disciplines that go by the name of social sciences, and the coining of the term. History in the modern sense was rediscovered by Voltaire, Montesquieu, and Gibbon. Blumenbach, who Grégoire cited as an authority on the Negro race, was creating physical anthropology. (His work was soon translated into French by Chardel.) Economics, from Boisguillebert and Vauban to the physiocrats and Turgot, was becoming a science, theoretical and statistical. Condorcet envisaged the social utility of statistics. Thus he advised comparing the accident rate in dangerous occupations such as roof tiling with those in less dangerous trades. He applied the calculus of probability to the political, sociological, and legal fields, arguing that social science is science, its data verifiable, its methods testable, its general principles rationally provable. Thus political science is a true science, founded on facts, on observation, experimentation, and calculation.[11] Bertrand Russell tells us that no investigator can be scientific unless he possesses ethical neutrality. In social problems that is difficult. Professor Baker has told us, in his book and in his chapter here, of Condorcet's insistence that social science can be real science. The question is still being debated.

Fisc and Taxation

Condorcet applied mathematical calculations toward solving the all important fiscal crises. At the same time he proposed certain legislative controls over the Treasury, to give the public a voice through its representatives. Such measures included the following:

1. Legislative control over the collection of taxes and the disbursement of public funds.
2. Complete financial figures made public at the start of the legislative session.
3. Management of the Treasury not by the Executive but by its commissioners elected by direct universal suffrage.
4. A commission of popularly-elected jurors to corroborate the auditing of state monies.

Condorcet's financial role throughout the years of the Constitutive and Legislative Assemblies and the National Convention was not only creative and original but active and influential.[12]

Professor Perkins has expatiated on Condorcet's final espousal of progressive taxation, an instance of the evolution of his ideas in the course of the Revolution. He was ahead of his times in progressive taxation, in "degressive" taxation or the exemption of the poor at or below a certain standard of subsistence, and in economic theory, leaving his impact upon modern mathematical economics.

Hospitals

Condorcet tried to make the sociology of public health care in hospitals quantitative, following the statistical approach. Professor Greenbaum's English rendition of Condorcet's *Mémoire sur les hôpitaux* with its commentary, shows how Condorcet recommended calculating how many patients should be allowed per doctor, surgeon, pharmacist, nurse, cook, service personnel, etc., and how many emergency night staff would be necessary for a given number of patients. And figures are needed for hospital morbidity rates.

But Condorcet was also an innovator in suggesting such democratic procedures as community participation in small neighborhood hospices. This community participation would include such activities as planning, patient care, and private financing of public health through appeals to philanthropists to contribute via bequests. Condorcet's suggestions are still of vital interest today to those concerned with hospital architecture, construction, financing, and maintenance, as well as to those responsible for health care, public health, and health maintenance organizations.

Revolutions and Internationalism

The Enlightenment had stressed that changes had to be made in the social order. The case of the commoner Thomas Paine and the aristocrat Condorcet shows that it was the cause of revolution that brought them together. Professor Aldridge has brought out the international outlook of these two men of different nationalities and backgrounds. Condorcet, who was honored not only by the academies of his native land, but also by those of Berlin, St. Petersbourg, Torino, Bologna, and Philadelphia, was an internationalist who applied himself to the study of comparative civilizations, historic and contemporary.

*   *   *   *   *   *   *   *

Paul Hazard once confided to us in his Columbia seminar what his fellow-Academician Bergson said to him: "Je n'aime pas vos hommes du dix-huitième siècle; ils sont trop optimistes!" One could answer Bergson, "Yes, but...." Condorcet, like Descartes, predicted man's progressive knowledge of the secrets of nature, and of how medicine would prolong life. Who can deny the strides made in these areas since the two philosophers told of their visions? The progress that Condorcet predicted has been realized in science, technology, information, and education, if not in the application of reason. What of the future? The infinite perfectability that he envisaged, like all infinity, represents only an end, approached but never attained. Perhaps Condorcet substituted for a non-existent faith in a heavenly hereafter faith in a terrestrial hereafter, aglow with science, reason, and the human mind triumphant. For all the fertility of his many useful ideas, he was upon occasion so uplifted by his ideals as to be out of touch with the reality of his times. In some ways he is closer to ours.

Yet Condorcet's complete works have not been edited since 1847–1849. As Professor Baker informs us in his indispensable *Condorcet. From Natural Philosophy to Social Mathematics*, much remains to be done in the way of revision, critical editing of texts, and filling lacunae, especially of papers in the mathematical sciences, correspondence, and *inédits* manuscripts. Even Cahen's valuable listing of these in the Bibliothèque de l'Institut is not 100 percent accurate.

May the present initiative stimulate further interest in this too-little studied pioneer figure. The field is rich with possibilities for Ph.D. and other scholarly publications, as well as for works for the general public in the many countries where Condorcet has left a legacy. It is to be hoped that the Republic of Letters will soon embark on preparing a new edition of Condorcet's *Oeuvres complètes*.

A twentieth-century rationalist, Morris R. Cohen, has confessed that to his mind:

> the spectacle of Condorcet hiding...writing this enthusiastic sketch of human progress while the Revolution which he had befriended was seeking to kill him, is a scene of the same grandeur as that of Socrates discoursing on immortality while the jailer was preparing the hemlock, or of Jesus saying "Forgive them Father," as he was nailed to the Cross.[13]

Leonora Cohen Rosenfield

Notes

1. See the recent French collection of essays, *Condorcet, Les Cahiers de Fontenay-aux Roses* (No. 5, 1976), ed. Jacqueline Bonnamour and Hugette Delavault.

2. Voltaire published Morellet's 1776 translation of Beccaria's treatise. As our contributor jurist Perrod informs us, the jurist Dupaty also worked at translating it.

3. Condorcet's note in his Kehl edition of *Oeuvres de Voltaire.* See *Oeuvres de Condorcet*, ed. Arthur C. O'Connor and Marie F. Arago, 12 vols. (Paris, 1847–1849), 4.395 (hereafter, *O.C.*)

4. Quoted from Condorcet's ms. 884, ff 46–47, in the Bibliothèque de l'Institut, by Manuela Albertone, *Una scuola per la rivoluzione, Condorcet e il dibattito sull'istruzione 1791–1792* (Napoli, 1979), 35, note 61.

5. From Condorcet's *Premier Mémoire sur l'Instruction publique, O.C.*, 7.201, quoted by Albertone, *Una scuola*, 34.

6. There are striking similarities between the educational ideas of Condorcet and Wollstonecraft, though the latter's are scattered through her loosely-written pages.

7. Condorcet, *O.C.*, 5.205.

8. Condorcet, *O.C.*, 5.242.

9. See Léon Cahen, *Condorcet et la révolution française* (Paris, 1904; Slatkine Reprints, Gèneve, 1970), Appendice I, 549–59. At the Bibliothèque de l'Institut there is an unfinished autograph *inédit* of 4 sheets, under the same title, *Essai sur quelques changements*, etc., mss. n.s. 19, dossier B, no. 6. For a listing of other writings of Condorcet critical of the criminal law of his time, see Franck Alengry, *Condorcet, Guide de la Révolution français* (Paris, 1904; Slatkine Reprints, Gèneve, 1971), 18, note 1.

10. Condorcet, *Vie de Voltaire*, in Condorcet, *O.C.*, 4.139.

11. Condorcet, *O.C.*, 8.24.

12. Alengry, *Condorcet*, 646, 728.

13. Morris R. Cohen, *The Meaning of Human History, the Carus Lectures*, 2d ed. (La Salle, Ill. 1961), 265.

RIGHTS AND REVOLUTION

1
The Present-Day Revelance of Condorcet

Constance Rowe

In few epochs was the accelerating tempo of social change more evident and challenging than in the late eighteenth century. The British colonies in America were breaking away from the mother country. In France the traditional duties of patriots to serve the king and uphold the national interests had become increasingly difficult. For it was by now unhappily apparent that the authority of the State, as invested in the sovereign, was not supporting the interests, much less rights, of the vast majority of the French people.

As the seventy-year-old Voltaire appraised the situation in 1764 from his philosophic domain at Ferney: "Everywhere I see scattered the seeds of a revolution which will come inevitably and which I myself will not have the pleasure to witness. The light has so spread from place to place that it will burst out on the first occasion, and then there will be a splendid noise. Young people are fortunate. They will see fine things."[1]

The revolution heralded by Voltaire was a revolution of ideas to be achieved by peaceful means and within existing structures of government. Of the generation to witness these "fine things" and eventually to be submerged in their raw and violent explosion was the Marquis de Condorcet.

Born in 1743, the same year as his friend Thomas Jefferson, the Marquis de Condorcet awoke to the light of day in Ribemont, a somewhat dreary town in the French province of Picardy. Soon after his birth his father, a member of the military nobility, fell in battle. His mother, a superstitiously pious woman, brought him up, aided by his uncle, a bishop.

Sent to a Jesuit college in Reims, at thirteen young Condorcet won a prize in mathematics. Two years later, he continued his education in Paris where he became a youthful prodigy in the exact sciences. At the age of twenty-two, a treatise on integral calculus won him near-celebrity status. The mathematicians, Lagrange and D'Alembert, collaborators with Diderot on the famous *Encyclopedia*, welcomed the new arrival into their midst and saw in him a man soon to become their equal.

Within four years he was admitted to the French Academy of Sciences. He then became "Perpetual Secretary" of this Academy and eventually attained honorary membership in most of the important academies of Europe. Diverted from his mathematical career, however, by the intensifying clash of ideas between the liberal reforming *philosophes* and the forces of royal and ecclesiastical absolutism, the young noble enlisted in the struggle, and chose his friends among the leaders of Enlightenment.

Toward Human Liberty

From Turgot, a man of broad philosophic vision, a genius with a temperament similar to his own, Condorcet became accutely aware of the needs of the public welfare. From D'Alembert, he learned strategies for using the academies as powerful instruments with which to create a climate of opinion favorable to social change. As for Voltaire (who in private told their mutual friend, Mme Suard, that he saw in Condorcet a philosopher whose love of liberty and justice equaled his own),[2] the shy young academician acted as a right-hand man while together they fought for a freer press, religious tolerance, a system of taxation less crushing for the poor, and more equitable law-courts, to mention only a few goals of that group of *philosophes* so aptly referred to as the "party of humanity."[3]

Triumph came to this group in 1774 when Louis XVI appointed Turgot as his Minister of Finance. To this brilliant philosophic Royal Minister fell the stupendous task of bringing order and justice to the disarrayed and disunited French kingdom. Reform, the *philosophes* thought, could at last be achieved by the enactment of laws based on those natural rights capable of ensuring the welfare of the greatest number of Frenchmen.

The new edicts, presented by Turgot to the Parlement in 1776, struck at the essential heart of the feudal system. Free trade between the French provinces, the abolishment of the *corvée* or unpaid labor on the roads by the peasantry, a single land-tax for all property-holders, not excepting the clergy, the destruction of guilds and corporations, thus allowing the laborer the right to sell freely his labor, were all measures that struck at the first two "Estates" of French society. Their vested interests they now saw attacked. The inevitable outcome was Turgot's dismissal.

Voltaire succumbed momentarily to despair: "I see only death before me since Turgot is no longer at his post."[4]

And Condorcet wrote to Voltaire: "Goodbye, dear and illustrious master, we had a fine dream, but it has been too brief. I shall return to geometry and philosophy. It leaves one cold to work only for fame when one has had the illusion of working to serve the public welfare."[5]

This pre-Revolutionary struggle to make government responsive to the elemental needs of the common man impressed upon the mind of Condorcet the indispensable relation between power and enlightenment. Turgot had hoped to transform the French political system through representative assemblies, whose decisions would be implemented by monarchical power constitutionally defined. For, as Condorcet later asserted in his *La Vie de M. Turgot*, monarchy offers an indubitable seat of power which men of good will can take possession of for the public welfare. Hence monarchy, but monarchy refined, redeemed, and sanctified by reason. Such was the eighteenth-century mirage of Turgot, Voltaire, and Condorcet, until tragic and exhilarating events forced this last of the *philosophes* to formulate his own boldly modern conception of government.

If Turgot exemplified for Condorcet the enlightened administrator, Voltaire, whose values the young mathematician largely shared, provided him a role-model of a fearless intellectual, an active humanitarian, and a relentless fighter against those forces of darkness, superstition, and fanaticism known in Voltairean terms as *"l'Infâme."*

The two men met in 1770 when Condorcet set out accompanied by D'Alembert on a visit sponsored by Frederick the Great to see the Patriarch of Ferney. Delighted with this brilliant new recruit to the *philosophe* cause, Voltaire gave him a warm welcome and Condorcet became the last major friend he made during the eight remaining years he had to live.

As regards Condorcet's write-ups of deceased academicians, a part of his function as Perpetual Secretary of the Academy of Sciences, Voltaire was ecstatic: "I received a little work in gold at my twenty-second fever-fit. I read it immediately…The work is indeed a precious monument, and you are master of all those you write about, a king, telling the story of his subjects."[6]

Voltaire likewise hoped, a hope unfulfilled in his lifetime, to see Condorcet crash the gates of the more prestigious *Académie française*. To infiltrate this body with members of the *philosophe* party would create a powerful élite whose influence could win the embattled group some support at the seats of the mighty.

In 1772, however, a blow struck. The clerical forces in the person of Abbé Sabatier published the *Dictionary of the Three Centuries*, a parody of Diderot and D'Alembert's *Encyclopedia* and Voltaire's *Philosophic Dictionary*, in which the reform-minded *philosophes* were portrayed as a vicious perverse clique who for all too long had held French letters in their octopus-like grip.

Such an attack, of course, must not remain unanswered, so an answer came. Yet this searing answer was not, as everyone supposed, by Voltaire. The anonymous author was the Marquis de Condorcet.

In his *Letter of a Theologian to the Author of the Dictionary of the Three Centuries*, the young mathematician had set aside his academic pursuits to come to the defense of the "party of humanity."

"What crimes have they committed, these philophes against whom you wish to incite the vengeance of kins and the hatred of peoples?…While you permit kings to oppress their peoples, provided that you are granted your share in the spoils, the philosophes have made known to kings the cries of the people and have not been afraid to speak to them of their rights."[7]

The word "rights," whose concrete fulfillment had consisted for Montesquieu, Voltaire, and Rousseau as the supreme criterion for social judgment, here sounded forth like a clarion call. Indeed, the concept of "rights," when used by Condorcet in this work of 1774, became explicit; the foundation on which he was to build his own original and cohesive philosophy of man.

The scathing words that animated the *Letter of a Theologian* amounted to no mere echo of Voltaire or any other Enlightenment thinker. Their fierce conviction was the author's own. To his friend, Turgot, once a man of the cloth, Condorcet confided in 1773; "When I finished my schooling, I began to reflect on moral ideas concerning justice and virtue. I believed that I perceived that the interest which I felt in being just and virtuous was founded upon the sorrow which necessarily afflicts one sentient being at the idea of the harm suffered by another sentient being."[8]

Emancipated intellectually at an early age, the prime concern of the young Marquis was the human individual as a thinking, feeling being. The dignity and freedom of this thinking, feeling being he beheld grievously threatened by the forces of organized religion, for, like all the *philosophes*, he regarded the established Church as "the most powerful and uncompromising adversary of human freedom."[9] Clerical fanatics had instigated the legalized murders of the elderly Protestant, Calas, and the young Catholic nobleman, La Barre; likewise opposition to Turgot's proposed and much needed reforms.

The anti-clericalism of Condorcet, unlike that of Voltaire, was without nuance or ambivalence. The obsessive lifelong effort of Voltaire to discover and come to terms with the invisible forces that rule the universe had made him at once a most religious and irreligious man. From his first words on superstition in *Oedipe* through his vivid appreciation of Newton's planetary system in the *Philosophic Letters*, from his analysis of the natural order in the *Treatise on Metaphysics*, to his unanswered questions in the *Unknowing Philosopher*, Voltaire sought earnestly, playfully, poetically and, above all, tirelessly, the imponderable "why" of the universe and its corresponding import for man.

Repelled by a godless universe, he felt antipathy for the naturalism of Diderot and the materialistic atheism propounded by d'Holbach in the *System of Nature*. Such views, destroying the supernatural restraint that religion provides against the passions of the populace, might well prove socially harmful and would surely discredit the *philosophe* cause.

To Voltaire (of all freethinkers the generally acknowledged "Pope"), Condorcet now had some tactful words of caution: "You are reproached with crying out too loud against the atheists. I agree that there is a danger that deism will lead to superstition; it is useless to say so, now that it is a matter of passing from superstition to deism...But the atheists are under the knife and the knife that would slaughter them would soon be plunged in the blood of the deists."[10]

The originality, or indeed the modernity, of Condorcet, is that of all the eighteenth-century philosophers, he alone dared to envision and actively plan for a totally secular state. In his *La Vie de M. Turgot* published in 1786, the author declared that since public worship is necessarily the result of religious views of which one's conscience is the sole legitimate judge, "it is evident that the expense of maintaining such worship should be voluntarily borne by those who believe in it."[11]

The disentangling of the spiritual from the temporal power, he argued, could even prove conducive to public order and stability. Since the existence of an established church implies the right of rebellion against a heretic prince, the ruler, to maintain his authority, should separate Church from State, establish civil marriage and divorce, and permit civil registration of such vital statistics as births and deaths.

Prior to 1789, Condorcet judged France to be unready for so daring an innovation. Yet when the Revolution broke out he allowed his stand in favor of separation of the spiritual from the temporal power to become public, even militant. For governments to infringe upon individual property by taxing citizens to support a faith toward which they might be indifferent or inimical he now condemned as contrary to the "rights" of man, according to which an individual "is as free not to pay for any religion as not to believe in any."[12]

Hostile to clerical power, Condorcet looked with particular disfavor on convents and monasteries. The irrevocable vows required by such religious organizations seemed to him a violation of natural rights. For on the strength of a promise often given in early youth, individuals were committed to a service within monastic or convent walls for life. The administration of such human resources as well as the land they occupied, he believed, should be regulated by the state, and for the public good.

Condorcet attacked religious orders, not their individual members. These persons he saw as inviolable and possessed of individual prerogatives that must be fulfilled. When the French Revolution suppressed religious communities, leaving monks and nuns homeless and bereft of a livelihood, Condorcet demanded for these persons compensation in the form of pensions. "When a corporation is destroyed," he argued, "what is left are the individuals who compose it…having the same rights as other men, who should be treated according to the same principles of justice and humanity."[13]

In the decade before the outbreak of the French Revolution no event did more to confirm his belief in the practical efficacy of political democracy than the American Revolution. In a France where discontent with the government was widespread, liberal-minded Frenchmen and Frenchwomen were reading *Collections of the Constitutions of the English Colonies*, a compilation of American state constitutions originally presented to Louis XVI by American Ambassador Benjamin Franklin, and translated into French and published in 1778. This work, which the royal censorship tried to suppress, had wide circulation and acclaim. Among the readers most influenced was the Marquis de Condorcet.

The Marquis called the Declaration of Independence, "A restoration of humanity's long-lost title-deeds."[14] Here clearly formulated, as in the Declaration of Rights of the state constitutions, he found the doctrines of "natural rights" and national sovereignty. Such philosophic preambles to documents of state were unknown to public law at that time.

True, the ideas therein expressed stemmed from the seventeenth-century English Bill of Rights. Yet the entire tone of the English document remains concrete and pragmatic, not universal and philosophic. The words merely define the specific rights of subjects and the members of Parliament. The Declaration of Independence, however, as formulated by Jefferson, abruptly captured the French imagination. For it amounted to a brilliant application of those liberal philosophic ideas European thinkers had been toying with or propounding for more than two centuries.

To Condorcet, written constitutions, state and federal, were America's most unique and innovative contribution to the science of government. The objectives of government, he believed, should be so clearly spelled out and defined that they could be read by all men, including the lowly. Furthermore, after a revolutionary upheaval, a constitution could serve as an indisputable instrument in stabilizing conditions; likewise as a legal guarantee to all reasoning beings of rights gained by their revolt.

Once the Declaration of Independence was accepted, America formulated state constitutions by means of conventions, then submitted the constitutions for ratification by the voting public. Thus began the procedure that culminated in the famous federal Constitution of 1787.

The spectacle of a people forging a government by the use of reason and zeal for the public good, rather than allowing themselves to be governed by force, fate, or intrigue, seemed to Condorcet a unique phenomenon. Rousseau's "social contract" between the government and the people was no longer the far-fetched metaphor of a philosopher, but a concrete reality. "Here," said Condorcet, "is something which had not grown, but was planned; which gathered no prestige from the weight of the centuries, but was put together mechanically in a few years; which had no foundation in sanctifying legend, and the appeal to some vastly distant heroic time, but reposed on the known debates, arguments and votes of recent men."[15]

When France, in turn, broke with the past and declared a Republic, Condorcet, inspired by the American example, drew up a Declaration of Rights and devoted his major energies to a formula for implementing these rights in a written constitution. His action, the outcome of which was that excellent though ultimately rejected document known as "La Girondine," he judged momentous. The most enlightened monarchies of Europe, despite such rudimentary documents as the Magna Charta and the British Bill of Rights, had allowed themselves to be governed by custom, precedent and history. Yet the aristocratic mathematician, Condorcet, by his clear understanding of the role of a precisely worded constitution and how to amend it peacefully through constitutional review, referendum, and popular ratification, showed his evolving concept of democratic principles and laid the principles for modern constitutional law.

However, not all Condorcet's comments on the American government were laudatory. In his *Letters of a Gentleman of New Haven to a Citizen of Virginia*, he judged the American Senator's six-year term as too long; equal representation of the states in the Senate he opposed, preferring a system of representation in proportion to the population of the states. Also, uncannily prophetic, he warned of encroachment by the power of the Supreme Court and possible abuses from judicial review.[16]

As an observer of the British Houses of Parliament, and as a Frenchman experiencing clashes between the three Estates of French society, Condorcet based his political thinking on the individual. To insure national cohesiveness, he preferred a unicameral system of government to a bicameral one. The abstract-minded philosopher-mathematician tended to think of the voting public as individual reasoning units, who, without party pressures, would express not so much the "general will" as the general public reason.

The separation of the legislative, executive, and judicial powers warmly advocated by Montesquieu and adapted by the United States, he also criticized. "Why, for instance," he asked, "is the simplicity of these constitutions, federal and state, disfigured by the system of separation, and why is identity of interests rather than equality of rights adopted as the principle?"[17]

Such criticism has validity even today. True, there is what Woodrow Wilson called the "literary" or theoretical government of the country in contrast to the ingenious if imperfect practical system that welds together the separate powers and sets them in operation, such as political parties and an efficient well-integrated party machine.

Primarily, however, Condorcet admired the American nation for having peaceably put into practice the hitherto unattainable ideal of religious liberty. This basic liberty, which stems from the "natural right" of freedom of thought and expression, remained non-existent in a Europe torn and split by centuries of bitter religious strife. True, some enlightened governments in Europe had attained religious toleration. Yet such tolerance consisted of a privileged established Church with freedom of worship for dissenters, a condition leading to flagrantly un-Christian discrimination, both social and economic.

So weak a compromise, said Condocet, the Americans rejected as an "outrage against human nature." In the Virginia law of 1785 which erected what Jefferson was pleased to call the "wall" separating church and state, and in the provision of the American constitution forbidding Congress to establish a national form of worship, the Americans, so Condorcet believed, had set up the political machinery to put into safe effect entire religious liberty. On the influence of this liberty, he proved a perceptive critic. In a land where, untroubled by outside coercion, each man remained free to follow his individual conscience, tranquility is assured, with the result, said Condorcet, that "Americans are the most religious people on earth."[18]

His view, even after two centuries, remains surprisingly valid. For in a country where clerics remain without dominating power, that peculiarly European state of mind known as "anti-clericalism" has remained non-existent. Instead of the state influencing religious worship, the reverse has been more prevalent. The vitality of the religious spirit has become in early America and even into the opening decades of the twentieth century sufficiently pervasive to have produced a pious secularism.

Though Condorcet never visited America, he enjoyed the friendship of such élite Americans as Ambassadors Benjamin Franklin and Thomas Jefferson. For his pseudonymous comments on the American government in *Letters of a Gentleman of New Haven to a Citizen of Virginia* (possibly Jefferson), the French Marquis was made "Honorary Citizen of New Haven, Connecticut," a title in which he took great pride. His enthusiasm for the "new Land of Liberty," however, did not blind him to one serious deficiency. In Negro slavery, he beheld, like his friend, Thomas Jefferson, an obvious crack in the American "Liberty Bell." The flaw admittedly was deep-seated, yet could not be expected to endure in the liberty-loving climate of America. Slavery, Condorcet felt optimistically, would be phased out in another fifty years.

The reduction of human beings to the level of commodities, and their shameless exploitation for material profit, revolted the humanitarian conscience of the late eighteenth century. Though in England and France the slave trade was a long-established vested interest, in both countries anti-slavery societies kept springing up. Condorcet leveled his first attack against the evil institution in *Reflections on Negro Slavery*, a devastating pamphlet of 1781. Later, while campaigning for the Estates General, he may have forfeited his seat by impolitically calling upon the voters to outlaw African slavery in Saint-Domingue, a territory then under French rule. Again, when the National Assembly was in the process of organization, he issued a plea to the members to exclude the representatives of Saint-Domingue. These men, mostly planters, were masters, and as such could not represent such political non-persons as slaves.

Ever a consistent libertarian, Condorcet judged the fulfillment of those "inalienable liberties" (or in twentieth-century terms, "human rights"), as a world-wide imperative, at all points of the compass the sole object and purpose of any government worthy of the name. His opinion he based on the fact that "men are thinking, feeling beings, capable of moral ideas and reasoning from these ideas." As woman hold these qualities in common with men, they of necessity are entitled to the same rights. "So," he concludes, "either no one truly has any rights or all have the same ones. And he who is against the rights of another because of religion, color, or sex abjures his own."[19]

The Rights of Women

The inevitable corollary of man's rights was, of course, woman's rights. In his *Letters of a Gentleman from New Haven to a Citizen of Virginia*, Condorcet advised the emergent United States of America to break with Old World prejudice and grant women legal and social equality, full voting rights, and equal access to any position in the land. As Regents and Queens, women in Europe had ruled, at least as well, and in some cases better, than men. Why not then, he reasoned, in a Republic, a citizeness as President? A suggestion which with possible help from ERA awaits fulfillment in our land even today.

Again, in Revolutionary France, when a new government presumably based on individual liberties was being set up and organized, Condorcet made a vigorous attempt to convince the National Assembly that the so-called natural rights of Man belonged also and equally to women. In *On the Admission of Women to the Rights of Citizenship*, which was published in 1790 in the prestigious *Journal of 1789*, he warns of the power of habit and custom to win acceptance even for injustice. By just such dulling of ethical perceptions, philosophers and even the liberty-loving legislators had callously excluded women from the rights of citizenship, thus depriving half the human race of political expression. "Is there," he challenged, "a stronger proof of the power of habit even among enlightened men, than to hear the principle of liberty invoked in favor of 300 or 400 men, deprived of their rights by some absurd prejudice, and forgotten in the case of 12 million women?"[20]

To those who would object that women's anatomy, their child-bearing function, and periodic disabilities incapacitated them mentally as well as physically, Condorcet had an answer. "Should men be deprived of their rights as citizens because many among them suffered from gout every winter and catch cold easily?"[21]

True, women, as everyone seemed to agree, were ruled not by reason, a damaging charge in the "Age of Reason," but by emotion. This feminine tendency Condorcet attributed to their ignorance, their inferior status, and their total domination by men. Yet women, too, were rational. They reasoned, however, from different premises, their priorities, values, and occupations being different from those of men. Concluded the author of *On the Admission of Women to the Right of Citizenship*: "It is as reasonable for a woman to be concerned about her physical charms as it was for Demosthenes to be concerned about his voice and gestures."[22]

To the argument that extending the franchise to women would ruin the nation's home life, Condorcet countered that enfranchised women would no more abandon their children and domestic duties than the enfranchised farmer would abandon his plow or the enfranchised artisan his shop. Instead, women who participated in the larger life of the community would necessarily become more intelligent mothers as well as more helpful and understanding wives.

In expressing these opinions, Condorcet stood out even in the liberal eighteenth century. Only his rank as a French Marquis and his reputation as a brilliant academician saved him from scorn and ridicule for advancing the feminist cause.

He retained an unshaken belief, however, that both sexes are equal in intelligence and character, with the possible exception of a small percentage of male geniuses, whose accomplishments stand unsurpassed. "Female inferiority" was therefore a myth and a misconception, and like most myths, the product of force and guile. Feminine faults there were. Yet these Condorcet attributed to the false and inadequate education of women and their lack of the disciplined intellectual training received by men. His remedy would consequently be to offer women educational opportunities equal with men from the grade school level to the universities and beyond. Even so, there remained invisible barriers to feminine development. By treating the entire female sex as the obvious inferiors of men, society inflicted upon women a pervasive and paralyzing discouragement. "The kind of constraint," concluded Condorcet, "imposed upon women by traditional views concerning manners and morals has influenced their mind and soul almost from infancy, and when talent begins to develop this constraint has the effect of destroying it."[23]

Such sensitive insights into the female experience may have been offered Condorcet by his personal history. For, according to most of his biographers, his twice-widowed superstitious mother had dedicated him to the Virgin, extending the schoolboy period of "skirt and pinafore" from the customary age of six until eight. Such constraint upon a growing male child may serve to explain his personal shyness, and his later hatred of the superstition that had imposed upon him this early frustration.

His wife, the beautiful and accomplished Sophie de Grouchy, no doubt appeared to him as the epitome of female wit and brilliance. As translator of the English economist Adam Smith, and herself the author of some much admired *Letters on Sympathy*, she inspired his ideas, and throughout their marriage contributed to his writing her useful comment and advice.

It is piquant to note that Condorcet, the devoted husband and father, who never kept a mistress, remained of all the *philosophes*, the one most critical of the family, as this institution was known in the eighteenth century. The indissoluble character that the Church had conferred upon marriage appeared to him as a veritable seedbed of such evils as adultery, prostitution, and bastardy. Marriage, he insisted in his *Sketch of a Historical Tableau on the Progress of the Human Mind*, should be a civil, not a religious contract. Divorce should be permitted upon the recommendation of an advisory council made up of the relatives of the marriage partners. The same council would spell out the terms of child custody, deciding upon the education of the children and the rigid upholding of their rights. In a notable step toward a single moral standard, he would grant alimony to either wife or husband depending on the circumstances.

Marital infidelity, an inescapable commonplace in the eighteenth century, resulted, Condorcet contended, from archaic laws that maintained the despotic authority of parents to arrange the marriages of their children. The frequent outcome was illegitimate births which left children outside the structure of organized society, deprived of their basic liberties by inhuman laws that had sprung into being in the class division of society, "in the great inequality of wealth, in the system that prevents children from marrying without their parents' consent, and above all in the indissolubility of marriage."[24]

To ease the stigma of illegitimacy, Condorcet advocated the founding of special hospitals and homes where unwed pregnant women could bring their children into the world in discreet privacy. Then after the birth of their babies, they would be taught a salable skill. Illegitimate children too should be taught a trade in institutions designed for that purpose. He would even allow those born outside wedlock to claim rights to property from both their parents, a measure which for practical purposes would render illegitimacy almost obsolete.

To grapple with these social problems in the eighteenth century was rare. Yet rarer still was the attempt to blame both sexes for such evils in anything like equal measure. For, genially permissive as was French society toward the sexual misdeeds of men, toward any lapses by women both public opinion and the laws could often prove merciless, because, concluded Condorcet, "men punish severely the evils of which they themselves are the instigators and accomplices."[25]

Neither a Puritan, nor a hedonist, Condorcet believed that relations between the sexes would grow in beauty, affection, and disinterestedness only when men and women could stand together as equals in education, political expression, and full participation in professional life. Every woman, married or single, he maintained, should be equipped to earn her livelihood, even if she belonged to the highest aristocracy of the realm. Such was the counsel he bequeathed to his three-year-old daughter in that noble and moving testimonial written under the lengthening shadow of the guillotine during those last days in his precarious hide-out off the rue des Fossoyeurs (today's rue Servandoni). This personal message addressed to his own individual posterity and dated 1794 was published in the O'Connor and Arago edition of the philosopher's works under the title, *Advice of Condorcet to his Daughter*, (1, 611).

Less a feminist than a logically consistent liberal, whose human ideal was for the rational mastery by each person of his individual destiny, Condorcet openly advocated birth control. As enlightenment advanced, and with it, a corresponding emancipation from superstition, men, he declared, would understand that to their children they owed more than the elemental gift of life. They owed them well-being. Before bringing children into the world they should take into consideration the welfare of humanity, the society in which they lived, and the family of which they were a part.[26]

Should the food supply ever prove unable to support the population, this emergency would be met not by what Malthus was to call "prudential restraint" but by population control. Among the unpublished manuscripts of Condorcet, Frank Manuel claims to have found some remarkably modern proposals for research on this subject.

The coming equality between the sexes that Condorcet envisioned elicited from the eighteenth-century thinker some thought-provoking psychological insights into what might be the quality of their love for each other resulting from women's new emancipation. "Everything," declared Condorcet, "which can contribute to rendering individuals more independent also increases the happiness they can reciprocally bestow upon each other; their happiness will be greater when the individual action is more voluntary."[27]

Thus equality ignites progress. And progress in turn generates more equality, more happiness, more freedom. Such was the high-powered rocket that propelled the mind and imagination of Condorcet through the continuum of time in search of that nether-nether point where past merges with future.

Man's Progress Toward Equality

"Long since persuaded that the human species is infinitely perfectible, and that this perfection...cannot be arrested but by physical revolutions of the globe, I considered the task of hastening progress to be one of my most precious occupations, one of the first duties of a man who has strengthened his reason by study and meditation."[28]

So Condorcet summed up his lifetime mission in his *Fragment of Justification* of 1793, while hiding from the Terror, under sentence of death, separated from wife and daughter, and awaiting stoically his secular martyrdom.

His political failure had set him on the path of his ultimate glory. Unable to deal as a politician with the violence, corruption, and urgency of the present, like an early Christian martyr he set his sights on the future; not, however, on the welfare of his individual immortal soul, but on the terrestrial happiness, in the centuries to come, of all humanity. Consoled not by faith in any deity, but in the collective perfectibility of mankind, he compiled his *Sketch of a Historical Tableau on the Progress of the Human Mind*, a work which, by both its virtues and defects, lives on today as the final testament to posterity of the Age of Enlightenment.

"We pass," said Condorcet in his masterwork, "by imperceptible gradations from the brute to the savage and from the savage to Euler and Newton."[29] The dynamic propellent of these successive transformations was progress, a progress he conceived as manifested in the increasing ability of man to tame and ameliorate his life circumstances. A capacity for such creative innovation is inherent in the growth of rational intelligence, and hence an identifying mark of moral man.

Condorcet's *Sketch of a Historical Tableau on the Progress of the Human Mind*, the prospectus of a longer work that fate denied him the opportunity to write, is admirable in its concision and intellectual impact. His history, divided into nine epochs, ranges from seemingly static tribal society to the discovery of agriculture and the alphabet; continues through the flowering and decline of Greek genius, to be followed by a long retrogressive medieval period. A renewal of creative energy produces the Renaissance and that most crucial of inventions, the printing-press; all of which makes possible a gradual liberation of science from the fetters of Church and government. The ninth Epoch, from Descartes to the French Revolution, has culminated, so the author believes, in a veritable explosion of progress. For in separate hemispheres, two nations, the United States of America and France, have adopted governments based on the natural and inalienable rights of man.

As so new and vital a point of departure opens to humanity, Condorcet adds to his work a tenth Epoch devoted to rational prophesy, his own logically deduced forecast of the limitless progress and perfectibility to be attained amost inevitably by man.

The use of history to prove or illustrate ideas was not without precedent in the eighteenth century. In his *Essay on the Manners and Morals of Nations*, Voltaire had used the spectacle of world history, not so much to measure the dynamics of progress (he was much too skeptical for that) but in hopes of stirring French society to a change of values; an appreciation of rationality versus superstition; humanity versus brute aggression; culture versus pious ignorance.

Speculations on these successively favorable developments of humanity called "progress" had become even in the mid-eighteenth-century a sort of intellectual obsession. Turgot, elaborating on this theme in two addresses delivered before the Sorbonne in 1749 and 1750, declared that "the human race from its origins appears to the eye of the philosopher as one vast whole which like the individuals composing it has had its infancy and development. "Even the fierce passions of men become leading-strings by which Providence draws them on to new challenges and creative innovations,"[30] hence "progress."

By the closing years of the century, however, it remained for Turgot's friend and disciple, Condorcet, to raise the word "progress" to both a banner and a battle-cry, building upon the idea a social system and a philosophy.

Condorcet's summation of history, in contrast to such earlier presentations by Bossuet and Turgot, remains fearlessly secular. To the guiding hand of a benign Providence he assigns no role. Man he sees as entirely autonomous—for good or ill, his own determinant. Enlightened, he has the power to tame events and wrest from them a future of progress and happiness.

Since man is part of the natural order, Condorcet identified human history with the natural sciences. Though absolute prediction as in mathematics is not entirely possible, the findings of his study he called "truths with a high degree of probability." By rigorously testing his historical hypotheses, he hoped to integrate historical and social studies with the natural sciences.

Condorcet had forged a powerful intellectual implement. To measure social progress or the increasingly productive control of one's own life by the individual, and individual ability to work wisely and effectively with groups for the public welfare, the historian now had a scale, the whole historical process. The highest point on this indicator was human rights and their fulfillment. Thus the task of the philosopher-historian was to determine what forces tipped the scale in favor of progress and which others caused it to descend in the direction of darkness.

Such an approach resulted in an inevitable Manicheanism, inspiring often arbitrary judgments on what constituted darkness and light. Obsessively Condorcet presents the somber god, religion, and the healing god of light, philosophy, as engaged in a titanic struggle for the mind and emotions of man. Throughout nine epochs the contest continues, while the author charts the major defeats and victories. The longest defeat for reason occurred, he believed, during the medieval centuries when a greedy priesthood, invested with full powers of theocracy, held mankind in a superstitious and unrelenting grip. Their psychological levers of control were two ideas, both products of the primitive imagination, and in their effects inimical to progress. One was fixation on rewards and punishments allotted the soul after death; the other, the worship of man-made gods too viciously reflective of the human image. Sanctified and enthroned by the medieval church and state, these ideas found expression in that fossilized feudalism that had endured in some degree until 1789.

No mention is made of the vast humanitarian and cultural benefits of the medieval convents and monasteries; how in an age of violence and tumult these institutions had served as almshouses for the sick and orphaned; a means of employment for land-workers, and, in the case of learned orders like the Benedictines, safe storehouses for classical culture where precious manuscripts were copied and conserved. A whole epoch of history was dismissed as unproductive, if not anti-human. With time running out for both the anti-clerical author and his century, he contined his Voltairean battle against those so-called forces of darkness, fanaticism and superstition, indeed *l'Infâme*, until the last.

To Condorcet progress is inexorably linked with liberty and the spirit of free inquiry. In the unfettered search for truth and the urge to perfect his environment, the historian perceives the natural motivation of man. Tools useful in the struggle for survival represent the first triumph of human ingenuity. Yet in his pursuit of utility, called "happiness" by some, man moves on. From chance discoveries come conscious innovations, each embodying a consensus of rational minds. As time passes and such inventions multiply they have the power of transforming man's world and even man himself.

That the effects of technology might actually modify human character is interestingly touched upon by Condorcet in his account of the discovery of cannon and gunpowder. As judged by the humanitarian, peace-loving morality of the Enlightenment, these deadly weapons gravely threatened and obstructed progress. Yet from their long-term effects he paradoxically discerned several beneficial results. Warriors, he believed, became less brutal and more humane when they fought at a distance, when the horrors of hand-to-hand combat were rendered obsolete. Furthermore, the exorbitant cost of military expeditions made warfare unprofitable, acting on even the most belligerent nations as a potent argument for peace.

A modern reader may wonder how Condorcet, the rational forecaster, would judge the prospects for peace and progress in our own atomic present. Will fear of global destruction and the astronomic cost of nuclear weapons outlaw war in the modern world? Or will an uneasy armed truce, neither war nor peace, signal a return to the Dark Ages with such Dark Age violations of civilized justice as political kidnapping, and the seizing of hostages, amidst an utter breakdown of international law?

Again technology pulls the lever of progress in the eighth epoch by making possible the invention of the printing-press. This discovery Condorcet judges as the most revolutionary event in intellectual history. Thereafter knowledge, no longer the possession of a few, "became the object of an active and universal commerce." An informed public opinion could now come into being, thanks to the printed page, which effected a meeting of minds between people far apart from each other and scattered over a wide area. Formerly, a clerical or lay tyrant, by burning a few manuscript pages, could make a book disappear forever. As of now, said Condorcet, such destruction is impossible so long as a "corner of the earth exists which holds on its territory a free press."[31] So the pace of progress was infinitely accelerated.

In the tenth Epoch, as he deduces the future from the present, Condorcet speaks of the tremendous accumulation of knowledge that will be won by man, with the aid of man's particular creation machines. "As facts multiply man learns to classify them and reduce them to more general formulas; while instruments used to observe and accurately measure them acquire, at the same time, new precision." Condorcet goes on to say that the more relationships are discerned between a multiplicity of objects, and as these relationships are defined in clear and understandable formulas, then truths, whose discovery cost the most effort, and which until then could be understood only by profound thinkers, will be brought within range of the average intelligence.[32] Thus the democratization of learning will have become irreversible.

For Condorcet, more than any of his eighteenth-century predecessors, equated progress with such intellectual and material advantages as are enjoyed by the mass of society. Turgot had favored the fostering of an élite of geniuses who represented, so he believed, a small but fixed percentage of the population. Condorcet, however, would require the State to provide a universal secular education for all its citizens, male and female. In his Constitution (tabled and finally rejected by the National Convention in 1793), he had added to the basic "rights of Man" still another, the right of the individual to, at the least, an elementary education, secular, of course. His remarkably forward-looking *Report and Project of a Decree on the General Organization of Public Instruction*, presented to the Legislative Assembly in the Spring of 1792, and tabled, had contained a detailed plan of national secular instruction for both sexes from elementary school to the university, providing scholarships for the gifted poor, and devices to safeguard the independence of the teachers from undue state control. Productive scientists, Condorcet realized, could come only from the ranks of persons who had received a rational education. With the advent of mass schooling, the number of these creative innovators must increase astronomically.

As enlightenment spreads and the "rights of Man" philosophy wins increasing acceptance, people everywhere, Condorcet believed, must recognize that the goal of progress is equality of rights; equality between individuals within the nation; equality between nations, and also, races in underdeveloped areas of the world. For the ultimate promise inherent in the human condition is the perfectibility of mankind. Absolute equality remains, due to differences in ability, neither possible nor desirable. The evil to eliminate is *artificial* inequality imposed throughout history by force and deceit.

The lessening of inequality between individuals within the nation could be brought about by legislation that would no longer favor the concentration, but the distribution of wealth. A policy of free trade and industry would serve as a key to this desirable spreading of resources; likewise fewer marriages for financial ambition, and the establishment of equal inheritance, though in advancing this last proposal, Condorcet seems unaware of conflict with the fundamental right of the individual to dispose freely of his property. In the Declaration of Rights that had preceded his personally crafted Constitution ("La Girondine"), he had added not only the right of the citizen to an elementary education, but a program of "welfare." "Public Assistance is a sacred debt of society; laws should determine its extent and application."[33] An eighteenth-century ancestor of the modern Social Security system is clearly apparent in the *Sketch of a Historical Tableau on the Progress of the Human Mind* as the author advocates a plan for old age and widow's pensions and child support funded by public tax money, to be distributed to persons whose only assets remain what they earn.

Of progress, and hence, equality, the pace-setting standard should be the level of intellectual and material well-being attained by the élite of France and the Anglo-American nations—indeed, the "Atlantic Community," and Condorcet was one of the first to use the name. Inequalities between civilizations remain flagrant. Yet certain questions must be asked, and should be answered empirically. Are certain nations or races condemned to inferiority? Or can they be improved and corrected by the "social art" (by which he meant the science of government and sound administration)?

This last question Condorcet could only answer in the affirmative, convinced as he remained that the egalitarian principles of the French Revolution must inevitably prevail and transform the globe. Equality between Europeans and their colonial dependents will yet become a reality, a happy outcome of the abolition of slavery and those unfair trade monopolies so impoverishing to colonial lands. Then, into these newly independent nations will come a new population of Europeans, no longer venal petty officials and parasitic agents of a "home government," but industrious settlers and prosperous homesteaders from whom the native inhabitants can learn new technical skills and useful means of self support. So, exulted Condorcet, "The day will come when the sun will shine on free men only, who will regard reason alone as their master, and tyrants and slaves...will exist only in the pages of history or on the stage of a theater."[34]

In such a climate of equality, war will be outlawed as "the greatest of plagues and the greatest of crimes."[35] Yet even among the most exemplary of international equals, to maintain universal peace and with it, the independence of each nation, some means must be found. Condorcet offers a solution with startlingly modern overtones. Almost one hundred and fifty years before Woodrow Wilson, he recommended a permanent "League of Nations" (*confédérations perpétuelles des nations*) to arbitrate quarrels, to arrange plebescites, and to act as a bulwark of collective security in case of outside aggression or attack. Only thus would the rule of reason and humanity prevail against those sanguinary violations that demean not only one nation or nations, but indeed the entire family of mankind.

The bizarre destiny of Condorcet, his passionate belief in the "perfectibility" of imperfect man, who seems capable, at best, of slow amelioration; the extravagant work projects sketched in the *New Atlantis*; his dream under the shadow or the guillotine of a medical plan to prolong life indefinitely, as if to win thereby a secular immortality; such seeming extravagances have too often blinded later generations to the good sense and practicality of much of his thinking. To this same man, nevertheless, France owes a system of free coeducational public education, fully realized only in the second half of the twentieth century; universal suffrage, proportional representation, social security legislation, progressive income taxes, and such eminently practical contributions as hydrodynamic experiments to determine engineering principles essential to canal construction, in twentieth century terms, a "feasibility study."

So in perilous hiding back of the rue Servandoni, with the conclusion in sight not only for his book, but for his own personal life-span, Condorcet reached out with exquisite sympathy to the future generations of mankind. Despite the injustice and cruelty he suffered at the hands of the French Revolutionaries, he felt proud to have served and helped formulate the universal and transforming principles on which this Revolution was founded. Then, as he concluded his masterwork, the philosopher dares to link his own efforts in behalf of reason and liberty to the "eternal chain of human destinies; it is there that he finds the true reward of virtue, the pleasure of having accomplished a lasting good...This contemplation is for him a refuge, where the memory of his persecutors cannot pursue him...It is there that he truly exists in company with his equals, in an Elysium that his reason has been able to create for him, and that his love of humanity enhances with the purest joys."[36]

Notes

1. Voltaire, *Oeuvres* ed. Moland, 52 vols. (Paris 1883-1885), 43, 256.

2. Janine Bouissounouse, *Condorcet. Le philosophe dans la Révolution* (Paris, 1962), 39.

3. Voltaire, *Lettres Philosophiques*, ed. Garnier. (Paris 1964), chap. 25 "Sur les Pensées de Pascal." 141: "I presume to plead the case for humanity against this sublime misanthropist."

4. Janine Bouissounouse, *Condorcet*, 82.

5. Condorcet, *Oeuvres de Condorcet*, ed. Arthur C. O'Connor and Marie F. Arago, 12 vols. (Paris, 1847-1849), 1.115. (Unless otherwise stated, subsequent references will be translated from this edition.)

6. Condorcet, *Oeuvres*, 1.12-13.

7. Condorcet, *Lettre d'un Théologien*, 5.335-36.

8. Condorcet, *Oeuvres* 1.220.

9. J. Salwyn Schapiro, *Condorcet and the Rise of Liberalism*, (New York, 1963), 178.

10. Condorcet, *Oeuvres*, 1.86.

11. Condorcet, *La Vie de M. Turgot*, 5.144-45.

12. Condorcet, *Idées sur le despotisme*, 60.169.

13. Condorcet, *Réflexion sur l'usufruit*, 10.20.

14. "Restoration of Humanity's Title-deeds," Voltaire's comment on Montesquieu's *Spirit of Laws*, applied by Condorcet to the American Declaration of Independence, 8.11.

15. J. Salwyn Schapiro, *Condorcet and the Rise of Liberalism*, 223; Condorcet, *Esquisse*, 6.198.

16. Condorcet, *Lettres d'un Bourgeois de New Haven...*, 60.33–34.

17. Condorcet, *Esquisse*, 6.198.

18. Condorcet, *Religion Catholique*, 10.99.

19. Condorcet, *Sur l'Admission des Femmes au Droit de Cité*, 10.122.

20. Condorcet, Ibid., 10.121.

21. Condorcet, *Selected Writings*, ed. Keith Michael Baker. (Indianapolis, Ind., 1976), 99–100; Condorcet, *Oeuvres*, 10.122.

22. Condorcet, *Sur l'Admission des Femmes*, 10.125.

23. Condorcet, *Lettres d'un Bourgeois de New Haven...*, 60.19.

24. Condorcet, *Esquisse*, 6.523.

25. Condorcet, *Réponse au Plaidoyer*, 7.43, 45.

26. Condorcet, *Esquisse*, 6.258.

27. Manuel, Frank, *Prophets of Paris* (Cambridge, Mass., 1962), quoting Bibl. Natl. ms. N.a. fr4586, fol. 18.

28. Condorcet, *Oeuvres*, 1.574.

29. Condorcet, *Esquisse*, 6.346.

30. Turgot, *Tableau Philosophique...*, *Oeuvres* (Paris, 1913), 1.215.

31. Condorcet, *Esquisse*, 6.142.

32. Condorcet, Ibid., 6.252.

33. Condorcet, *Projet de Constitution Française*, 12.421.

34. Condorcet, *Esquisse*, 6.244.

35. Condorcet, *Esquisse*, 6.265.

36. Condorcet, *Esquisse*, 6.276.

2
Condorcet, Abolitionist

Richard H. Popkin

Marie Jean Antoine Nicolas Caritat, Marquis de Condorcet (1743–1794) was not only a very important mathematician, philosopher, and social scientist, but also one of the leading humanitarians of the latter part of the eighteenth century, fighting for causes, some of which are just succeeding in our own time. Condorcet was one of the first modern advocates of women's rights and equality. He also struggled for the rights of Protestants in Catholic France (though he did not seem to be particularly concerned about the rights of Jews, which became a significant issue in the last years of Condorcet's career). He was about the only public advocate of social rights for homosexuals and prostitutes, as long as they did not engage in physical violence against unwilling persons. In addition, and what is crucial for this study, Condorcet was one of the strongest advocates of his day in France for the abolition of African slavery, first in French colonies like Saint-Domingue and next throughout the world.[1]

Of all the philosophers, Condorcet alone came out unequivocally against almost all forms of discrimination. As he put it near the start of his *On the Admission of Women to Voting Rights* (1790), "he who votes against the right of another, whatever be his religion, color, or sex has from that moment on abjured his own rights." Condorcet was the most important Enlightenment figure to live on to the Revolution. He, could therefore try to implement the abstract radical solutions that he had developed out of discussions with the other famous Enlightenment figures, in the new political arena that developed after 1789.

Condorcet's interest in radical reform concerning slavery seems to have been greatly influenced both by British abolitionists and events in America. He was a fellow Masonic lodge member with Benjamin Franklin,[2] and he knew Thomas Jefferson well. He also read the Abbé Raynal's account of the Revolution in America and the controversy surrounding it.[3] One of the strongest and earliest statements of his abolitionist views is in his "Remarques sur les pensées de Pascal," from Condorcet's edition of Pascal of 1776.[4] In discussing the misery of men, Condorcet devoted four pages to the situation of the blacks. He spoke of "slavery, that horrible violation of human rights." He demanded the abolition of slavery in a letter of June 7, 1777 to the *Journal de Paris*. His *La Vie de M.*

Turgot (1786) called the slave trade "cet infâme trafic." Only an entente among all the European countries could stop the slave trade, he pointed out in an unpublished manuscript now at the Bibliothèque de l'Institut. His best known statement of his position on slavery, and his proposed solution to the problem, appears in his *Réflexions sur l'esclavage des Nègres*, dated 1781.[5] He made several further statements, one in his address on election to the French Academy in 1782, another after he joined the Société des Amis des Noirs in 1788, then when he was its president and principal spokesman. A circular letter of his to all the bailiwicks of France as they were preparing to vote for delegates to the Estates General urged them to demand the destruction of the slave trade and preparations for the ultimate abolition of slavery (*Au corps électoral contre l'esclavage des nègres*, 4 février, 1789). The next month, as one of the electors of the nobility from Mantes, he was able to insert in their *cahier* a recommendation to the Estates General to "examine the means of destroying the slave trade and preparing for the destruction of black slavery."[6] Later, as a member of the revolutionary assembly, he advocated bills to eliminate slavery in the French colonies.[7] Condorcet continued his activities as a polemicist for the liberation of slaves, as a politician trying to bring that about, until he had to flee in 1793 for opposing the Jacobin proposal for a new constitution. (In the nine months that he was in hiding before he was caught and died, he wrote the final version of his most famous work, *Sketch of a Historical Tableau on the Progress of the Human Mind*, in which he again attacked slavery.)[8] Condorcet's unfortunate need to hide prevented him from taking part in the crucial events in France's march toward abolition of slavery—the rebellion in Saint-Domingue, the establishment of Haiti, the first black republic, the French acceptance of Haiti, and the final outlawing of slavery. Condorcet's place as the leading advocate of the blacks was taken over by the great egalitarian, the abbé Henri Grégoire.

What I shall deal with in this study is first the examination of Condorcet's view about the slavery of Africans. His reasons for condemning slavery will be considered, as well as his program for abolishing slavery. This then will be treated in terms of the American context in which Condorcet saw it. Briefly, I will then touch on the similarities and differences in the views of Condorcet and of Thomas Jefferson. Lastly, I shall look at how Condorcet's views compare with those of his successor as "chief abolitionist" of France, the abbé Grégoire.

Condorcet's major statement of his objections to African slavery, the *Réflexions sur l'esclavage des Nègres* of 1781, was published pseudonymously, with the work attributed to a pastor, one Joachim Schwartz. (He used this name also in his unpublished essay of 1776.)[9] In the dedicatory epistle of the Negro slaves, Condorcet-Schwartz began by insisting that he and all other whites and the slaves had the same "esprit," the same reason and the same virtue.[10] Then, as the body of the writing begins, "To reduce a man to slavery, to buy him, to sell him, to keep him in servitude, all these are real crimes, and crimes that are worse than stealing." The slave is deprived not only of all his property, but of the very means of acquiring any. He is also deprived of the control of any of the faculties that have been given him for preserving his life, or satisfying his needs; or of controlling his own being. Even if the crime of slavery were approved by public opinion and by laws; even if "the human race by unanimous vote approved, the crime would still remain a crime." Condorcet pointed out that "les moralistes" are silent about the crime involved in reducing men to slavery.[11]

It is often claimed that the Africans benefit from being made slaves. It is said that those who are enslaved are either condemned criminals about to die, or prisoners of war who would be killed if they were not bought by the Europeans. So, it is made to appear that the enslavement of blacks is a humanitarian act. To this Condorcet expressed great disbelief. Is it possible, he asked, that before the Europeans arrived each African tribe killed all their prisoners of war? Isn't it more plausible that the fighting tribes exchanged prisoners after a while? The only evidence offered to the contrary comes from those engaged in the slave trade. And besides, even if we suppose that the life of an African is saved by his being bought, is it not the case that one crime is being substituted for another? The African is saved from situations only to be dragooned into another totally unjustified and immoral one. In addition, one has to consider that the European slave dealers are aiding and abetting the African tribal wars (and sometimes fomenting them) so that there will be a continuous source of supply of prisoners of war to be purchased.[12]

Next Condorcet pointed out that the excuse offered by the European buyer of slaves in Africa does not provide any justification for the colonist who buys the slaves in America. He is not rescuing the poor slave from any threat of death. And this excuse has even less applicability to the blacks on the plantations who are born into slavery.[13]

Enslaving criminals who are legitimately condemned is not itself legitimate, since for a punishment to be just, it must be determined by law as to its duration and as to its form. Punishing someone by making him someone's slave does not make the penalty precise, since the master can do what he likes with the slave. Then Condorcet added, bringing this back to his subject, who can believe that Africa actually had so many criminals?[14]

It is claimed that the colonies cannot be developed without black slaves. Even if this is true, Condorcet said, it does not make slavery legitimate. Why do people have to make a fortune in the colonies? Why do they have to commit a crime to do it? To get to the heart of the matter, can people buy other people? If someone offers to sell himself to me, he cannot in so doing sell me his descendants. Everyone, Condorcet insisted, is born free. In just about all of his statements opposing slavery he maintained that freedom is a natural right that cannot legitimately be taken away. A person can sell his services, even for life, but he cannot be made a slave. The sale contract would give each party rights in the matter. Thus, the person who sold himself would still retain his natural rights. The contract could be abrogated under various conditions, and the person would regain his or her freedom. Hence, "There is then no case in which slavery, even voluntarily entered into, is not contrary to natural rights." (Condorcet here cited Rousseau's *Contrat social* as his authority for this claim.)[15]

Having argued his general philosophical theses (1) that liberty and the rights of men are everywhere the same regardless of the color or nationality of the persons involved, and (2) that a crime is always a crime regardless of what else is happening, Condorcet then went on to deal with the practical considerations involved with slavery, especially the economic ones. The claim was being made by French, English, and Dutch colonists in the Caribbean that sugar and indigo cannot be cultivated without Negro slaves. But has this been proven? The way the white colonists live makes them incapable of doing the work. The work habits of the whites and the blacks develop from the economy of the islands, and are not the cause of it. Condorcet also claimed that the actual production of sugar and indigo would probably increase if carried on by free labor. If the blacks were free they would become a flourishing nation. They are now burdened with the vices of their corrupters, but they are naturally a gentle (*doux*) people who are industrious and sensitive.[16]

From this it follows, according to Condorcet, that slavery has to be destroyed. Condorcet, who was a great mathematician, frequently claimed that arguing against defenses of slavery was like arguing against those who believe $2 + 2 = 5$, or those who believe they can square the circle. All three views can be logically demolished, but the latter two, the mathematical absurdities, are morally harmless, whereas the pro-slavery view is extremely dangerous morally.[17]

Having said all this, it must also be recognized that though the institution of slavery be unjust, illegitimate, illogical, and immoral, nonetheless the practical problem of dismantling it is not simple. Here Condorcet may have been influenced by the attitude of his friend, Thomas Jefferson. Condorcet, in his writings in the 1780s on abolition kept discussing what was happening in America, which he saw as the beginning of the slow process of eliminating slavery. There is a work of his, *De l'influence de la Révolution de l'Amérique sur l'Europe*, dedicated to the Marquis de Lafayette, and written in 1787-89, in which in the first chapter we are told that though slavery still exists in some of the United States, nonetheless all of the enlightened persons are ashamed of it and it will soon be eliminated. In the postscript to the *Réflexions*, Condorcet listed some American laws that would lead to the end of slavery and said that slavery was universally regarded as a crime in the thirteen colonies, as a splotch on the glory of liberty.[18]

But the problem of abolishing such an institution involving so many people and so much property needs to be considered very carefully. The first step

Condorcet proposed (along with many English and American abolitionists) was the legal forbidding of any further trade in slaves. Such trade should be treated as criminal, as a form of kidnapping. Such a law would have the effect also of ameliorating the situation of those in slavery, since their owners would have to treat them better since there would be no new source of supply of other slaves.[19]

Next Condorcet proposed that children born of slaves be freed at age thirty-five and given a stipend and a pension by their former masters. If a master doesn't want to commit himself to this, then the child should be freed at birth, and the mother will decide how it shall be raised. (And Condorcet, who was extremely careful in his proposals, also offered precise conditions as to how the mother would be enabled to do this.) As for children who were slaves when Condorcet's law would have gone into effect, those aged fifteen or below should be freed at age forty, and those aged over fifteen when the law goes into effect should be freed at age fifty. Condorcet also proposed conditions that should exist for the freed slaves and arrangements to prevent people from being mistreated while they are still slaves. He also would set up a public office to defend the interest of the blacks. Further a tariff scale would be announced stating how much a slave of age X would have to pay, or have paid for him, in order to be free.[20]

Condorcet claimed that the slow effect of his proposed legislation should allow it to operate successfully. Slavery would disappear little by little while other economic ways of running the colonial societies developed. What would these societies be like, with two free peoples with customs and habits that are quite different? After a few generations, Condorcet asserted, the differences would disappear, except for skin color. Condorcet, in several of his writings insisted, in addition, that the cost of a society of free blacks is not necessarily greater than that of a slave economy. He tried to show that there would be more interest on the part of the blacks in cultivating the land if they were free than under present slave conditions. As to what might happen in the white world, Condorcet foresaw first that the decadent planter culture would be replaced by the sort of stable family society of the British colonies in North America. Second, he saw an ideal opportunity to solve some other European problems. Protestants could be encouraged to develop the colonies. And next Jews could be told that they could practice their religion freely in the colonies. Religious quarrels could be overcome and the industry and ability of the persecuted groups could be channeled into fruitful endeavors.[21]

Having presented his arguments for abolition, and having offered his gradual plan for ending slavery without too much economic or culture shock, Condorcet next considered possible objections to his views. One such objection is that the mistreatment of blacks is exaggerated. The slaves don't really care about the loss of liberty, and they are actually happier than the "free" peasants of Europe.

Also the slave owners have an interest in protecting them and so guard them against dangers.[22]

Condorcet contended that all these points are false. The testimony of slaves who have escaped gives ample evidence that they are mistreated. Only the supporters of slavery seem to be unaware of the mistreatment. Secondly, everyone, black or white, wants to be free, and suffers when he cannot exercise his freedom. People will only choose slavery over freedom when the free state would lead quickly to their death from starvation or exposure. Next, is the Caribbean slave better off than the European peasant? Condorcet was willing to admit that it might be the case for the poorest peasant, but for the rest, the slave, he maintained, was obviously worse off. Since both the slaves and the European peasants were suffering, both needed to be helped. "One injustice doesn't cease being one just because it can be proven that it is not the only one taking place on the surface of the earth." Lastly, slaves are treated like animals. Both are grossly mistreated, so it is obvious that slave owners don't really take care of the slaves.[23]

The next objection Condorcet considered was that he was treating some of the finest Europeans, the colonial slaveholders, as if they were criminals. Condorcet insisted they they *were* criminals, since a crime, as he said at the outset of his presentation of his case, is always a crime. The European colonists don't see this because they are guided by a false conscience. Condorcet was struck by this point very early in his abolitionist crusade. In 1773 he had published his *Sermon sur la fausse conscience* about the slaveowner's view of himself. If he really was a good person, he would want to change his slaves into free, productive, and happy men. If it were brought about, everyone involved would be restored, rejuvenated, and redeemed, and slavery would be over. There is a slight Messianic flavor in Condorcet's finale, somewhat like that in his last work, *The Sketch.*[24]

Condorcet's *Réflexions* were written in 1781. He added a postscript to the 1788 edition surveying the state of affairs regarding slavery in the newly established United States of America. Condorcet saw great hope in the Constitutional possibility that the importation of slaves could be forbidden after 1808, and in the abolitionist provisions in the constitutions of the northern states. He also believed that the freedom that existed in the U.S. with regard to expression would soon lead to the end of slavery. In England, Condorcet believed that the anti-slavery movement was so strong that sooner or later it would prevail. In France, the abolitionist movement had just organized itself into the Société des Amis des Noirs. So far, Condorcet admitted the Society had not accomplished much, but he hoped (in 1788!) that the then present French government, of which none other "had shown a more enlightened spirit of humanity" would do something about the problem.[25]

An unpublished fragment of Condorcet's in the Bibliothèque de l'Institut pokes ironic fun at the *Déclaration des droits de l'homme:* "tous les hommes blancs naissent libres et égaux en droits; donner une méthode pour déterminer le degré de blancheur nécessaire!" Condorcet's view, thus, boils down to a few points: (1) Freedom is a natural right and cannot be abrogated. (2) Enslavement is both a legal and moral crime, and remains a crime regardless of the circumstances before, during, and after. (3) Slaves are usually mistreated. (4) Slave economies would probably fare better if they were turned into free ones. (5) Abolition should take place quite gradually over about 40 years. (6) The resulting culture will be very much better qualitatively for both slaves and masters, blacks and whites. All will thrive and create a rich society for everyone.

Condorcet was a good friend of Thomas Jefferson, who was our ambassador in Paris in the 1780s. Jefferson had purchased two copies of Condorcet's *Réflexions sur l'esclavage des Nègres* in 1788, and apparently in early 1789 was preparing a translation of it.[26] And it was apparently partly through Jefferson that Condorcet got his information about American developments. Jefferson's *Notes on Virginia* were first issued in France in 1784-85, (and were in fact written in 1781-82 in answer to a query by a French diplomat stationed in Philadelphia).[27] Jefferson was anti-slavery most of the time, though he had a great fear of the possible effects of abolition. Like Condorcet, Jefferson felt that the rights of man are applicable to all, black or white, and that slavery is a violation of the natural rights of human beings. His repeated efforts against the entrenched system were, in the *realpolitik* of his time, seldom successful, but they were more so as time went on.

In the *Notes on Virginia*, Jefferson raised a problem that was usually central to the pro-slavery theories, namely the possibility that the black Africans, the brown Indians, and other people of color are naturally inferior in some important mental or spiritual sense to European whites. After considering the physical differences between blacks and whites, Jefferson discussed the evidence that the blacks were mentally inferior to the whites, concluding, "Comparing them by their faculties of memory, reason, and imagination, it appears to me that in memory they are equal to the whites; in reason much inferior, as I think one could scarcely be found capable of tracing and comprehending the investigations of Euclid; and that in imagination they are dull, tasteless and anomalous."[28] Later, our third President concluded his examination by saying, "I advance it, therefore, as a suspicion only, that the blacks, whether originally a distinct race, or made distinct by time and circumstances, are inferior to the whites in the endowments both of body and mind."[29] Slaveholders used this view, plus a stronger one offered by the Scottish philosopher, Dave Hume, to justify keeping the mentally inferior blacks in bondage.[30] Condorcet did not use arguments about human equality (as Grégoire later did) to bolster his case. However, he apparently indicated his disapproval of Jefferson's view to the author. Therefore, in 1791, Jefferson was glad to tell Condorcet the good news that he, Jefferson, had met an intelligent Negro, Benjamin Banneker, who was "a very respectable mathematician." "I have seen very elegant solutions of Geometrical problems by him. Add to this that he is a worthy and respectable member of society."[31] Banneker had written an almanac, and later offered a design for the U.S. Capitol. His case was to come back and haunt Jefferson. Condorcet's successor as leader of the French abolitionist movement, the abbé Grégoire, wrote a work early in the nineteenth century, *La Littérature des nègres*, to refute the theory of Jefferson and Hume on Negro inferiority. Grégoire gave some case histories of intellectual Negroes, including Banneker, to show that blacks were capable of the same levels of intellectual achievements as whites.[33] Grégoire sent Jefferson a copy. Jefferson wrote to their mutual friend, Joel Barlow, that Grégoire's cases did not amount to much, including Banneker's. "We know he had spherical trigonometry enough to make almanacs, but not without the suspicion of aid from Elicot, who was his neighbor and friend, and never missed an opportunity of puffing him. I have a long letter from Banneker, which shows him to have had a mind of very common stature indeed."[33]

In the middle of 1789 it seemed that the French abolitionist movement might achieve its goals as a result of the Revolution. Condorcet, on behalf of the Société des Amis des Noirs, issued an address, which began "We hold that all men are born free and with equal rights, regardless of their color, their nationality, or their condition of birth. We hold that no man can give up his freedom, that no man can seize the freedom of his fellow man, and that no society can legitimate such crime."

"We hold that, regardless of contrary laws, customs, and practices, the slave is always free, since the law of nature cannot be annulled. Accordingly, the restoration of a slave's freedom is not a gift or an act of charity. It is rather a compelling duty, an act of justice, which simply affirms an existing truth."[34]

The Society unfortunately was unable to generate much enthusiasm for abolition in the Revolutionary governments in spite of the fact that very influential figures like Mirabeau, Lafayette, Brissot, Pétion, and Condorcet were leaders of the group. This sad result was partly due to the political ineptness of the Society's members in the government, and mostly due to genuine French lack of interest in, or antagonism to, abolition. The planters and those engaged in the slave-trade prove to have more clout than the members of the elite Société des Amis des Noirs.[35] Thomas Clarkson, the English abolitionist leader, described the negotiations to get a resolution voted on condemning slavery and the slave trade. Clarkson was in Paris, continually in touch with the French abolitionists, including Condorcet. Clarkson's account shows how hard it was to get the leading abolitionists together because they were each busy with some phase of the Revolution. The rush of events kept pushing the abolitionist resolution aside. And the close relationship between the English abolitionist movement and the French one, which at first was a real benefit, became a detriment. Clarkson was suspected of being a spy, and his allies in Paris also became suspect. There were also direct threats of physical harm made against Clarkson and the members of the Society. Under all of this pressure, the Society began to disintegrate. Lafayette retired. Mirabeau died. Condorcet was engrossed in working out a new constitution. The abolitionist resolution never came to a vote, though it would seem that it was a simple consequence of the Declaration of the Rights of Man.[37]

The first genuine progress in passing any measures benefiting the blacks was due to Condorcet's successor as leader of the abolitionist movement, the abbé Henri Grégoire, 1750-1831. He was a priest from a small town in Alsace. Prior to the Revolution he was slightly known for his only public achievement, his prize-winning essay in answer to the question posed by the Academy of Metz in 1787, How to make the Jews happy and useful in France. His essay was published in early 1789. On the strength of this he became a member of the First Estate at the meeting of the Estates General. He couldn't stand the pomposity and vanity of his fellow Churchmen, and he led the famous walkout of the clergymen, who then joined the Third Estate and thereby formed the critical mass for developing the Revolution. Grégoire at the start of the Revolution was pushing his two favorite reform plans, one to make the Jews citizens, the other to reform the Church by putting it under state control. Up to this point in his life he seems to have been oblivious to the problems of the blacks.[37] Through meeting Clarkson in 1791 he became aware of the horrors of slavery.[38] At this time a tangential problem arose. A small group of mulattoes, offspring of wealthy planters in the colonies, lived in Paris. They petitioned the National Assembly to recognize them as citizens. The abolitionists at first feared that the mulattoes would support their fathers' views on slavery. At a dinner with them, the mulattoes agreed to denounce slavery.[39] Grégoire, who by this time was a major figure in the Assembly, took on the cause of the mulattoes, then the cause of ending the slave trade and slavery. Next he moved on pressing for the recognition of Haiti as an independent black republic. Grégoire wrote polemics for forty years arguing the black cause.[40] His last great one, *De la noblesse de la peau*, (1826), is a minor masterpiece.[41] Almost as soon as Grégoire was converted to the black cause, he was swept into the world of the abolitionists. He was made an honorary member of the Société des Amis des Noirs. (Ruth Necheles suggests "honorary" because he could not afford the dues, which were about $100.00.) Soon after he was the president of the organization.[42] He also took on Condorcet's role of being the chief arguer for the cause. Grégoire's argument was somewhat different than Condorcet's because Grégoire's case was based on his millenarian theology, rather than on naturalistic philosophy. Grégoire made the equality of men, because they are all created by the same

God, the basis of his view. Then, because men are all created equal, no man can justly enslave another. Further, and what was probably most important to Grégoire, the liberation of Jews, blacks, and everyone else would have monumental millenarian significance, setting the stage for the final redemption of all mankind.

It has been said by the excellent historian of eighteenth-century American racism, Winthrop Jordan, that, "It seems certain that it was the specifically religious impulse in anti-slavery, in contrast to the natural rights philosophy, which provided the energy and vision necessary to think and act beyond abolition of slavery, notably in the direction of "improvement by education.""[43] This may well have been true in France as well as America. This, however, is not the time to argue such a vast claim. Grégoire did, however, manage to accomplish a lot more than Condorcet, in advancing the equality and rights of the blacks. In evaluating their respective contributions, one has to take account of their contexts. Condorcet's was the strongest voice in France for the abolition of slavery before the Revolution. He wrote the basic statement of the case, providing both a natural rights justification and a practical plan. His leadership of the Société de Amis des Noirs made it the voice of the most important liberals in the country. Yet Condorcet, Clarkson, and others could not get sufficient political support to get a bill on slavery voted on at that time.

From July 1793 until March 25, 1974, Condorcet was in hiding at Mme Vernet's house. A fellow boarder there was the Montagnard deputy Marcoz. A former professor of mathematics from Chambéry, he not only kept mum about Condorcet's presence, but also kept him informed of political events. In all probability he would have told his fellow-mathematician that the Convention's president issued a decree for the French Republic on February 4, 1794 abolishing slavery in the French overseas empire. Ironically the move was inspired less by abolitionist pressure than by expediency. After the mulattoes rebelled on Saint-Domingue, Spain and England invaded the island. Its commissioners, hoping the slaves would rally to defend Saint-Domingue, emancipated them on August 23, 1793.[44]

Starting from the equality of man, Grégoire went on to lead the fight against slavery. The establishment of Haiti in 1794 made the issue of black freedom central in France. Grégoire saw Haiti as the beacon light to all oppressed peoples. In terms of the actual situation, he carried on the abolitionist struggle. The developments in the Caribbean colonies and in the United States made it possible to achieve some of the goals that had been set forth by Condorcet, by the Quakers, by the American and British liberals, etc. Hence Grégoire and his allies were able to make significant strides in the early nineteenth century.

Then, to conclude, Condorcet was obviously a major figure in the abolitionist world. He was the most philosophical of the pre-Revolutionary French opponents of slavery, and published probably the best statement of their case in his

Réflexions. He was able to learn of important American developments, and to pass on French abolitionist views to America through his friendship with Franklin, Jefferson, and others. Condorcet saw immediately that the French Revolution opened the door to making all men free. It was left to his successors to abolish slavery, the transference of Condorcet's theories into practice.

In the light of the current interest in the rise and fall of slavery as a major economic, social, and political institution, Condorcet deserves much more study in terms of both what he had to say, and the effect his views had in France and elsewhere.[45] He was the only major figure of the Enlightenment to play a role in the actual movement to eliminate slavery. His brilliant mind, applied to this topic, made crystal clear what the issues were, and what some of the basic problems of resolving them in practice were to be.

Notes

I wish to thank Leonora Cohen Rosenfield for her assistance in this paper, especially in bringing my attention to some unpublished or little-known material concerning Condorcet's views on the abolition of slavery.

1. See J. Salwyn Schapiro, *Condorcet and The Rise of Liberalism*, (New York, 1934).
2. Ibid., 79, 218.
3. Ibid., 219–22.
4. Reprinted in Condorcet, *Oeuvres de Condorcet*, ed. Arthur C. O'Connor and Marie F. Arago, 12 vols. (Paris, 1847–1849), 3:635–62.
5. Condorcet, *Refléxions sur l'esclavage des Nègres*, in *Collection des Principaux Economistes* (Paris, 1847), 14:505–43.
6. *Archives parlementaires*, Art. 7, 662, cited in Léon Cahier, *Condorcet et la révolution française* (Paris, 1904), 112.
7. See Keith M. Baker, "Condorcet's notes for a revised edition of his reception speech to the Académie française, *Voltaire Studies*, vol. 169 (1977) esp. 23; and Léon Cahen, "La Société des Amis des Noirs et Condorcet," *La Révolution française* (1906), 50:481–511, where some of Condorcet's statements about slavery are included.
8. Condorcet, *Sketch of a Historical Tableau on the Progress of the Human Mind*, trans. June Barraclough (New York, 1955), Eighth Epoch, 114.
9. See Cahen, "La Société des Amis des Noirs et Condorcet," 498–503.
10. Condorcet, *Réflexions*, 502. A postscript follows the twelve chapters. Their titles are instructive:

> "1. De l'injustice de l'esclavage des nègres, considérée par rapport à leurs maîtres.
> "2. Raisons dont on se sert pour excuser l'esclavage des nègres.
> "3. De la prétendue nécessité de l'esclavage des nègres, considérée par rapport au droit qui peut en résulter pour leurs maîtres.
> "4. Si un homme peut acheter un autre homme de lui-même.
> "5. De l'injustice de l'esclavage des nègres, considérée par rapport au législateur.
> "6. Les colonies à sucre et à indigo ne peuvent-elles être cultivées que par des nègres esclaves?
> "7. Qu'il faut détruire l'esclavage des nègres et que leurs maîtres ne peuvent exiger aucun dédommagement.
> "8. Examen des raisons que peuvent empêcher la puissance législatrice des Etats où

l'esclavage des noirs est toléré, de remplir, par une loi d'affranchissement général, le devoir de justice qui l'oblige à leur rendre la liberté.
"9. Des moyens de détruire l'esclavage des nègres par degrés.
"10. Sur les projets pour adoucir l'esclavage des nègres.
"11. De la culture après la destruction de l'esclavage.
"12. Réponse à quelques raisonnements des partisans de l'esclavage."

11. Ibid., 505.

12. Ibid., 506–7.

13. Ibid., 507.

14. Ibid., 507.

15. Ibid., 508–9.

16. Ibid., 512–16.

17. Ibid., 516; and Condorcet, "Lettre de Condorcet à un Marquis (La Fayette?) in Cahen, "La Société des Amis des Noirs et Condorcet," 498 and 502–3.

18. Condorcet, *De l'Influence de la Révolution de l'Amérique sur l'Europe*, in *Collection des Principaux Eonomistes*, 14:548, and *Réflexions*, 542-43.

19. Condorcet, *Réflexions*, 519-21.

20. Ibid., 521–24.

21. Ibid., 525–32.

22. Ibid., 532.

23. Ibid., 532–35.

24. Ibid., 536–40. Condorcet's *Sermon sur la fausse conscience* (Yverdan, 1773), is discussed in Condorcet's note, 536–37.

25. Condorcet, *Réflexions*, 542-43.

26. Thomas Jefferson, *The Papers of Thomas Jefferson*, Vol. 14 (Princeton, 1958), note on 498. Only four pages of the translation exist. They are reproduced on 494-98.

27. See Winthrop D. Jordan, *White over Black* (Chapel Hill, 1968), 432.

28. Thomas Jefferson, *The Writings of Thomas Jefferson*, ed. H. A. Washington (Washington, 1854), Vol. 8, Query 14, 382.

29. Ibid., 386.

30. See R. H. Popkin, "Hume's Racism," *Philosophical Forum*, 9 (nos. 2-3, 1977–78), 211–26.

31. Jefferson's letter to Condorcet is cited in Jordan, *White over Black*, 452. On Aug. 30, 1791 Jefferson wrote Banneker that he was sending the latter's almanac to "Monsieur de Condozett (sic)."

32. Henri Grégoire, *De la Littérature de Nègres* (Paris, 1808). Banneker is discussed on 211–12.

33. Jefferson's letter to Grégoire, Washington, February 1809, and Jefferson's letter to Joel Barlow, Monticello, October 8, 1809, in *The Writings of Thomas Jefferson*, ed. H. A. Washington, 5:429 and 475–76.

34. Cited from Condorcet's *Adresse de la Société des Amis des Noirs, à l'assemblée nationale, à toute les villes de commerce, à toutes les manufactures, aux colonies, à toutes les sociétés des amis de la constitution de 1791*, in David Brion Davies, *The Problem of Slavery in the Age of Revolution, 1770-1823* (Ithaca, 1975), 328 and note 73.

35. See Davis, *Slavery*, 94, 112; and Ruth Necheles, *The Abbé Grégoire, 1789-1831, The Odyssey of an Egalitarian* (Westport, Conn., 1971), 53-109.

36. Thomas Clarkson, *The History of the Rise, and Accomplishment of the Abolition of the African Slave-Trade by The British Parliament* (Philadelphia, 1808), vol. 2, chap. 2.

37. On Grégoire's background and development, see Necheles, *The Abbé Grégoire*, chap. 1-3.

38. This is described by Clarkson in *History of the Abolition of the Slave Trade*, Vol. 2, 122–23.

39. See Necheles, *The Abbé Grégoire*, chap. 3 and 4.

40. All of this is dealt with in great detail in Necheles, *The Abbé Grégoire*.

41. It was also published in English, entitled *Essay on the Nobility of the Skin or the Prejudice of White Persons against the Colour of Africans and their Progeny, Black and of Mixed-Blood* (Paris, 1826), trans. Charlotte Nooth.

42. Necheles, *The Abbé Grégoire*, 60–66 and 69 n. 23 (where the question of the dues was discussed).

43. Jordan, *White over Black*, 361–62.

44. In 1802, Napoleon, whose wife Josephine came from a family of planters on Martinique, reinstated slavery in the French Antilles.

45. For an earlier study, see Edward Derbyshire Seeber, *Anti-Slavery Opinion in France during the Second Half of the Eighteenth Century*, The Johns Hopkins Studies in Romance Literatures and Languages, extra volume 10 (Baltimore, London and Paris, 1937).

3
Condorcet, Paine and Historical Method

A. Owen Aldridge

When the scholarly method of the history of ideas emerged in the 1930s as a research technique based in large measure on the example of A. O. Lovejoy, the traditional approach then being utilized in the study of both literature and history was that which has since been pejoratively described as positivism. Even as late as the 1950s, despite the growing influence of formalist criticism, it was still considered respectable and desirable to study both literature and history by arranging relevant facts in a narrative order based on chronology or theme and drawing various general conclusions from the process. The method of history of ideas was accepted as supplementary and in no way antagonistic to that based on *rapports de fait.*

The method is particularly applicable to the study of Condorcet and Paine, individually or jointly as representatives of the Englightenment. Although the word *idéologue* did not attain common usage until early in the nineteenth century, the concept certainly fits the two revolutionary intellectuals. Each is the prototype in his own culture of the purposeful dedication to the theories and goals of a radical sociopolitical program. In France, the organ of the *idéologues*, the journal *La Décade philosophique littéraire et politique* (1794-1807), drew its political doctrine from Condorcet's *Esquisse d'un tableau historique des progrès de l'esprit humain.* In England and the United States, Paine is generally associated with the goal of establishing religion and politics upon reason and is, rightly or wrongly, the symbol of abstract theorizing in the political realm. Among the many parallels that can be drawn between Condorcet and Paine, the most significant is this attachment to the realm of ideas.

In an article on the intellectual relations between Condorcet and Paine that I published during the 1950s, I observed that in comparing the ideas of two men of letters belonging to different milieux, one could follow Plutarch in drawing attention to analogies in their lives or works, even in the absence of any direct contact or mutual influence—as one could, for example, underline various superficial resemblances between Rousseau and Franklin.[1] I then described the alternate method of bringing to light the specific relationships between the two men—either in their actual day-by-day careers or in their intellectual development and determining whether these direct contacts had any influence on their own lives or ideas. In regard to Condorcet and Paine, I affirmed that the Plutarchan method had only a limited utility and that the broad affinities between the two men had already been fully explored by Franck Alengry in his *Condorcet guide de la révolution française* (1904). The second method (that combining history of ideas with *rapports de fait* or positivism, which I did not label as such), I affirmed, was more efficacious in the interpretation of the literary works of the two men, and it was this method that I proceeded to use in my article.

Since that time both positivism and the history of ideas have come under attack by both historiographers and literary critics. In general, literary critics have aimed the hardest blows against positivism, and the historiographers have been most vehement against the history of ideas. The quest for facts and verifiable details was the first to come under fire. In 1958, René Wellek, at a conference of the International Comparative Literature Association, defined the continuing vogue of positivism as a major detriment to literary scholarship while Gilbert Chinard at the same meeting strenuously advocated the extension of the history of ideas method to the area of French-American relations. In the 1960s the study of ideas became associated with the then highly modish enterprise of American intellectual history, although the two methods are fundamentally different. Vernon L. Parrington can be considered the originator and apostle of intellectual history in America, performing much the same role for American studies that Lovejoy occupied for the history of ideas. Parrington and his disciples through their tracing of main currents of thought looked not so much for the action of particular events or ideas or the function of particular institutions, but rather for "more general patterns of meaning which were presumed to guide all the particulars."[2] Historians of this stamp tended to concentrate on major writers and thinkers and, therefore, opened themselves to the charge of intellectual élitism. In this sense, they were following a direction completely opposite from Lovejoy, who argued that key ideas were likely to find sharpest expression in writers of the second or third class rather than in original thinkers or major authors.

Despite this fundamental difference separating the history of ideas and intellectual history, the two methods have recently been jointly condemned for concentrating on élitist groups and neglecting social and economic forces. The true focus of historians, certain critics maintain, should be the activities of the common man rather than the ideas of the privileged. According to a particularly severe denunciation, "The infatuation with consensus; the vogue of a disembodied 'history of ideas' divorced from considerations of class or other determinants of social organization; the obsession with 'American studies' which perpetuates a nationalistic myth of American uniqueness—these things reflect the degree to which historians have become apologists, in effect, for American national power in the holy war against communism."[3] According to this rather politicized analysis, the preoccupation with "disembodied" ideas improperly leads historians "to confuse intellectual values with the interest of intellectuals as a class."[4] In my opinion, the charge that ideas are "disembodied" is misleading or even fallacious. All ideas are the product of particular minds, and as such they have as much historical reality as events which have taken place and belong to the past. Indeed, in one sense ideas have a more substantial reality than events since they are constantly being refreshed by new minds that embrace them. They are no more "disembodied" than are literary plots or even entire literary works whose authors are dead. Even those ideas that have been rejected or proved false, for example, that angels participate in human affairs or that some biological species are generated spontaneously, have as much historical relevance as do artistic representations of purely mythological notions. It is paradoxical, moreover, that objection should be made to the study of disembodied ideas in the same time segment that has produced formalists and structuralists who maintain that it is legitimate to treat literary works completely abstracted from their authors and even to "decompose" and reconstruct them.

Another contemporary view considers that history, instead of concerning itself with either particular ideas or the climate of opinion in specific regions and segments of time, should reverse its perspective by studying men in relation to their social classes and institutions, thereby concentrating on the lower levels of the social strata (for example, slaves, sailors, small farmers and industrial workers). The new breed of historian, however, shows little more concern than did the old guard with the housewife.

The most recent book on Thomas Paine, published during the Bicentennial year, falls into the pattern of portraying "history from the bottom up." It argues that Paine's republican doctrine grew out of his humble birth and his continuous association with the working class, particularly with the artisans of Philadelphia. In effect this joins the new social history with ideology.[5] There is a great deal in Paine's biography to expose the fallacy of ascribing intellectual patterns to class origins,[6] and the notion becomes absurd when applied to aristocrats such as Condorcet who adopted extreme egalitarian doctrines. If the theory had any substance at all, Paine and Condorcet would have been political opponents instead of collaborators in spreading revolutionary propaganda. I have no intention to deny, however, that there exists an interreaction between life and ideas. Events shape ideologies, and ideologies bring about events. But this does not mean that social status determines whether any person's political attitudes toward society are radical or conservative.

Nothing could illustrate this more forcefully than the careers of Condorcet and Paine. Paine was born in Norfolk, England of humble parents, had no formal education after the age of thirteen, adopted for a time the trade of his father as a corset-maker, and became a poorly-paid outrider in the excise service before emigrating to America. Condorcet, in contrast, was born into an aristocratic family and was well educated. Not in the least embarrassed by this environment of privilege, he insisted on his title of *marquis*. The only major circumstances that the two *idéologues* seem to have had in common was exposure to scientific knowledge, which inspired the phrase of Paine, the "science of government" and that of Condorcet, "social science." According to the theory of social influences on ideology, Paine should have become, as he did, a spokesman for the rights of the common man, and Condorcet should have developed into a zealous apologist for privilege, social distinction, and wealth. To the contrary, the two men developed social and political ideas that were almost identical. Paine, if anything, was less radical than Condorcet, particularly in regard to women's rights.

The similarities we note in their careers have absolutely nothing to do with class origins or the social institutions to which they belonged. Each played a major and active role in the political upheaval of his own country; each interested himself, moreover, in the revolution of the other's country and wrote on its problems. Paine became an honorary citizen of France and Condorcet a citizen of New York and New Haven. Both professed unorthodox religious opinions and both cultivated science as well as literature. The greatest contribution of each man consisted in the continuing influence of his thoughts and writing. Although each symbolized the spirit of revolutions in his milieu, the tremendous value of their services went largely unrecognized during their lives; both died ignored and abandoned by the mass of their fellow citizens, Condorcet in prison and Paine in a cottage attended only by the widow of Nicolas de Bonneville. To be sure, such friends as Cabanis and M. J. Chenier remained loyal to Condorcet, and Jefferson and Monroe still held Paine in esteem, but it is within recent years that the two men have been given the full recognition that is their due.

At this time I have no desire to withdraw my approbation of the method of studying the relations between Condorcet and Paine based on *rapports de fait*. I am not aware of any new documentary evidence discovered since the publication of my original article nor am I prepared to offer any now. What I propose to examine at this time is their approach toward history, a purely intellectual subject that has nothing to do with the social background of either man, but which is related to the climate of opinion in which they wrote. I shall show that they adopted contrary points of view on a topic of major significance in international relations of the time, but that these diverse opinions were, nevertheless, based upon an identical ideology. Since the two men emerged from completely different social backgrounds, this ideology cannot logically be attributed in the thought of either man to a particular social class or environment.

No scholarly attention has hitherto been devoted to their diverse treatment of the specific topic to which they addressed themselves, that of the relationship between the revolution which took place in England in 1688 and that which began in France in 1789. Condorcet in his *Réflexions sur la révolution de 1688 et sur celle du 10 août 1792* (1792), argued that the two movements had much in common; Paine that they were essentially different. As historians they offered contrary interpretations of specific events; yet their reasoning was based on identical principles and ideals. They agreed completely that a good government should be based on the notions of natural rights and equality, that it should be simple, and that its legislative body should function democratically.

The parallel between the English and French Revolutions was forcibly drawn in England by Richard Price in a sermon delivered before the Revolution Society in London on November 5, 1789 to celebrate the anniversary of the Revolution of 1688. In the course of the latter upheaval James II was forced to abdicate and was replaced on the throne by William and Mary. Price declared in his sermon that the kings of England after that time were the only lawful kings in the world because they were the only ones who owed their crown to the choice of their people. This principle, which suggested perpetual accountability on the part of the monarch or the ruling family, naturally appealed to political reformers such as Paine and Condorcet, but it alarmed those who advocated a static social order. One of the latter, Edmund Burke, who had, nevertheless, supported the American Revolution, feared that the principle of popular sovereignty, if applied to France, would lead to unchecked social unrest on the continent, which might spread to England. He published, therefore, his *Reflections on the Revolution in France* (1790), an attack on both Price and the French political innovations. He charged that the members of the Revolution Society "in all their reasonings on the Revolution of 1688, have a revolution which happened in England about forty years before, [the Commonwealth] and the late French Revolution, so much before their eyes and in their hearts, that they are constantly confounding all the three together."[7] Burke made no other formal statement disassociating the English and French revolutions, but his entire work was devoted to contrasting the two systems, arguing that the English, based on precedent, was legal and stable; whereas the French, based on the theory of natural rights, was illegitimate and anarchistic.

Paine, in replying to Burke in his *Rights of Man*, agreed that no similarities joined the English and French Revolutions, but, contrary to Burke, praised the French at the expense of the English. *Rights of Man* appeared in two parts, the first (1791) devoted to theory or principle, and the second (1792) devoted to practice. In the first part, Paine concentrates on refuting Burke and defending the principles of the French Revolution; in the second, he draws illustrations of bad government from England and of salutary reforms from France and the United States. The parallels to Condorcet all appear in the first part, which is, nevertheless, much longer than the twenty-page *Réflexions*. In form, *Rights of Man* is essentially a treatise on government; *Réflexions*, a document for international consumption. Paine accused Burke of applying "the poison drawn from his horrid principles, not only to the English nation, but to the French Revolution and the National Assembly" as well, and he consequently proceeded to place another system of principles in opposition to Burke's.

First of all, he denied Burke's contention that the English people in 1688 had the authority to submit themselves, their heirs, and their posterities forever to the house of William and Mary or to renounce for themselves and all their posterity their right to choose their governors. To the contrary, he maintained that the people always retain this right. The basic distinction between the risings in England and France was that the first was merely a change in governments, the second a true revolution based on principle. "In the case of Charles I and James II of England, the revolt was against the personal despotism of the men; whereas in France, it was against the hereditary despotism of the established government."[8] The revolts in countries other than France were inspired by hatred of individuals, but in France *"principles* and not *persons,* were the meditated objects of destruction."[9] As a firm believer in the efficacy of ideas, Paine affirmed, moreover, that the Revolution occurred as "the consequence of a mental revolution previously existing in France," and he gave a brief survey of the spirit of liberty in the writings of the major French *philosophes.*[10]

In response to a remark by Burke that he would in the future compare the constitutions of England and France, Paine replied that Burke could not produce an English constitution, for the "constitution of a country is not the act of its government, but of the people constituting a government."[11] He denied that Burke's notion of prescription or "precedents drawn from authority" comprised a constitution and contrasted the British system with the written document on the basis of which the Constituent Assembly of France was organized. Among the differences in government between the two countries, Paine pointed to the bicameral legislature in England and the unicameral one in France. He described the House of Lords as a form of aristocratical tyranny and listed in detail the reasons why the French constitution eliminated such a house. Paine's emphasis throughout his work, as the title indicates, was on the concept of natural rights, which he maintained had been the guiding spirit of the French Revolution, but was completely lacking in the English Revolution of 1688.

Condorcet presumably read Paine's *Rights of Man* soon after its publication, for he referred to it immediately in the columns of the *Bibliothèque de l'homme public.* (9 (1791), 3). In the following year Condorcet wrote his own *Réflexions sur la révolution de 1688, et sur celle du 10 août 1792* in which, as I have said, he came to conclusions completely opposite from Paine's. In his words, the two revolutions "offer comparisons in the motives which brought them about, in the principles which guided them, which in spite of the differences in times, in enlightenment or in circumstances, show that the cause of the French people is that of the English nation, as of all free people or of those with the hope of becoming free."[12] To be sure, Paine was dealing with the French Revolution only up to 1791; whereas Condorcet covered the period through August 1792, but the decree of the National Assembly calling for the people to hold a national convention, which took place on the 10th of that month, did not change in any way the general situation or principles that Paine was discussing. (Condorcet probably wrote his *Réflexions* between August 10 and September 21, 1792, the latter date marking the declaration of the French Republic, and, therefore, subsequent to Condorcet's *Réflexions* which does not mention it.) Paine emphasized for the most part intellectual relationships; whereas Condorcet established, in addition, parallels in events and circumstances.

Paine accepted Burke's opinion that the British and French Revolutions were disparate in character since he wished to emphasize the differences between the two governments and to draw the French people further in the direction of democracy. Condorcet was as firmly committed to liberal ideals as was Paine, but he felt that he could more successfully promote democracy in France by stressing resemblances rather than differences between the British and French political systems.

According to Condorcet's reasoning, both James II of England and Louis XVI of France were constitutional monarchs who reigned by the will and consent of the people. The English accepted James because their fear of the disorder consequent to civil strife outweighed their repugnance toward a papist imbued with authoritarian ideas, and the French tolerated Louis XVI because they also feared civil disorder despite the dangers to liberty in his previous use of power. James II had two policies; a public one, which pursued his projects of usurpation moderately, and a secret one, which urged on his tyranny with precipitation. Louis XVI also had twin policies, a moderate one of seeking to destroy liberty through the constitution and a more energetic one of preparing to deliver France to the aristocrats and foreign armies. James II prorogued Parliament and relied on the army and navy; Louis XVI interfered with the legislative body and built up support in the army and national guard. Both monarchs fled, although Louis was recaptured at Varennes. The British Parliament invited William of Orange to reign as a constitutional monarch, and the French Assembly ordered the holding of a national convention. By this parallel with England, Condorcet sought to impart legitimacy to the actions of the French Assembly. At the same time he criticized the power of the British House of Lords, which made it possible for about two hundred wealthy nobles to oppose the will of the entire people.

According to Condorcet, the friends of liberty held conflicting opinions concerning government. A small number (including Condorcet and Paine) believed that sovereignty resides only in the people from whom all authority emanates. A larger number believed that a contract existed between the people and the king that could not be dissolved unless it were violated by the king. The contract theory dominated English opinion in 1688, and it was clear that since James II had violated the contract with his subjects, a successor could be chosen. Condorcet explained the problem, which was still unresolved. If the contract bound all generations to the descendants of an original leader, the question remained whether the invalidating of it by an individual king meant that the contract was dissolved for the rest of his family as well: in other words, did the people merely possess the right of divesting merely the culpable individual, or did they have the right to choose a leader from an entirely different family or to establish another form of government. Paine in *Rights of Man* analyzed a similar dichotomy: the right of a particular family to establish itself and the right of a nation to establish a particular family. He argued that although the second heading seems less despotic than the first, the two circumstances are actually equivalent since "the preclusion of consent is despotism."[13] Condorcet, in continuing his line of reasoning, pointed out that the plurality in England wished in principle to conserve the order of succession, but this would have meant accepting the son of James II, who was then an infant. If the latter were passed over, the next in line would have been James's sister, Mary, but her husband, William of Orange, was not willing to reign morganatically. In deciding to declare him king, therefore, the English people were violating the order of succession. In so doing they affirmed the right of adding new conditions to the original contract and thereby sacrificed hereditary right to the national interest. Condorcet then affirmed a parallel with the situation in France. He maintained that if the Convention then in session were to adopt—not the enlightened principle of public right—but merely the legalistic one of the English Parliament, the Convention could not be denied the authority of acting for the public interest. If the English were to accuse such a step as illegitimate, they would be impugning their own government; they would be saying that the British royal family ruled by hereditary power alone—not through the authority of the people—and admitting that all of the arbitrary pretensions of monarchs before 1688, including divine right, passive obedience, and right to suspend the laws, had been transmitted to the subsequent dynasty and were still in force. The same would be true of the governments of the Dutch and the Swiss cantons, which had cast off the yoke of hereditary sovereignty by the same process as the British. According to Condorcet's reasoning, the French resolution calling for a national convention should be approved not only by those who believe in the complete equality of all men, but also by those who accept the more limited principles of the English Revolution, that is, those moderates who do not recognize in the sovereign a power independent of the people, and who do not wish to be slaves, in short, all those who do not wish to lose their rights, but to retain those conserved in their laws. Earlier the French people had called on the other nations to support the original rights of man. Without retreating from this noble principle, Condorcet affirmed that the French were now appealing on other and vastly more limited grounds—merely that Europe not support tyranny or regress to the conditions of the fourteenth century.

Condorcet next entered a plea for the unicameral legislative system, a section of his document in which his private opinions came strongly to the fore. There are, he maintained, two kinds of constitutions, one embodying a single power of decision-making, as in part of the United States; the other, with a double or triple power, as in England, in which lack of agreement may disrupt the entire process. Condorcet must have realized that the federal constitution of the United States, which was then in force, had established a bicameral system and that the only state with a unicameral legislature (the justification for his reference to a "part" of the United States) was Pennsylvania. According to Condorcet, the English system (the bicameral) would not be bad if its members were to adhere at all times to the sentiment of the majority, but if those who have a negative vote in the assembly abuse their right, then the people would be forced to engage in a series of revolutions until the necessary unity could be attained. The double system that France had recently tried as an experiment could not work, as experts had predicted, for the body which had been given the right of opposition saw the right merely as a means of suspending action and destroying the constitution itself. After the new unicameral system came into effect, however, (the National Legislative Assembly, in October 1791) France became strong and unified and functioned as the only guarantee of the independent states of Europe against the great monarchies.

Along with the unicameral assembly, the French people had established an elective council to exercise the executive power in place of the king. Condorcet maintained, therefore, that for the European powers to recognize in France the elective council in place of the king would be equivalent to their having recognized William of Orange as a substitute for James II. He asked in addition why the people of France could not do in regard to Louis XVI what the "nations of America" had done for George III.

Anticipating the work of the National Convention, Condorcet asked his readers to suppose that this body develop and propose a constitution; that it be contaminated by no principle of heredity or personal inviolability, no great power dangerous to liberty, no counter-balances, "these mutual oppositions of powers, so injurious to the simplicity and activity of governmental operations"; that it unify the expression of national will; that no resistance be able to halt it; that the people immediately name their representatives; and that wise management overcome the inconveniences of the two previous attempts to form a government. Would the European powers, he asked, refuse to recognize this national body because it had been established on the immutable principles of natural rights? Would they affirm by their attitude that principles which are true in America are false in Europe "and that the same maxim is true or false, criminal or virtuous, according to the requirements of their insidious politics?" By this conclusion Condorcet seemed to have changed the parallel from that between the English and French revolutions to one between the American and the French, but it was, nevertheless, the form which represented his main thesis.

It is apparent that Paine and Condorcet were using history to support their own ideologies. What they were writing was interpretative history in the broadest sense, that is, metahistory or the "speculative philosophy of history."[14] Since their theses were contradictory, they could not both be right, but their underlying ideologies were, nevertheless, identical. Both considered the French Revolution to be a more satisfactory resolution of political problems than the English Revolution and they gave essentially the same reasons for their opinion.

An important phrase in Condorcet's final paragraph concerns "the simplicity and activity of governmental operations." Simplicty is a concept that both Paine and Condorcet felt should be reflected in government. Paine made no specific declaration in *Rights of Man*, but in his earlier *Common Sense* he stated that he had drawn his "idea of the form of government from a principle in nature which no art can overturn, viz. that the more simple anything is, the less liable it is to be disordered, and the easier repaired when disordered." John Adams even believed that Paine's views on simplicity had brought about Condorcet's infatuation with the notion of unicameralism.[15] Actually, Paine was not inexorably committed to unicameralism, and he changed his mind about it a number of times throughout his life. In *Rights of Man*, Part 2, he suggested a unicameral system that would avoid the objection that a single house acted too quickly and impulsively: there would be but a single governing body or representation, but this representation would be divided by lot into two or three parts. Every proposed bill would be debated in each part by succession, each part listening to the other, but without voting.[16] Paine suggested the same system in a French publication that Condorcet translated at about the same time that he was writing his *Réflexions*.[17] Condorcet was much more devoted to unicameralism than was Paine, but even if he were under Paine's influence, the latter's proposal could hardly be considered an example of simplicity.

Paine's *Rights of Man* is one of the most influential works of political propaganda in western literature. By the end of 1792, two hundred thousand copies had been sold, and in subsequent years over a hundred pamphlets were published in polemics about it. It is almost impossible to estimate, however, the impact of Condorcet's less ambitious work. There appear to have been only three separate printings of the *Réflexions* in France, all in 1792, two of them in Paris and one in Dunquerque. It was translated, not in any continental language, but in English, and published, also in 1792, in London and in the rising industrial city of Manchester. Here it was issued as the appendix to a pamphlet[18] concerning the suspension of the powers of Louis XVI in June 1791, which was attributed to J. B. d'Aumont about whom nothing else is known. What is significant about the pamphlet is that it was edited by Thomas Cooper, a prominent member of the radical Constitutional Society of Manchester and one of Paine's outspoken admirers. Cooper was in Paris in the spring of 1792, and it is quite possible that he obtained Condorcet's *Réflexions* from the hands of Paine himself.[19]

The main reason why Paine and Condorcet upheld opposing theses concerning the similarity of the English and French revolutions is that they had different readers in view. *Rights of Man* was written for the people of both France and England, and for their benefit Paine wished to make the governments of the two countries seem as different from each other as possible—to maintain in France the dedication to the principles of equality and democracy and to bring about in England changes in the direction of these principles. Condorcet nowhere discloses his intentions for writing the *Réflexions*, but he undoubtedly intended them also for European countries other than France and England, and as such, parallel to other tracts he had openly addressed to the people of various other countries in the same year, *Avis aux espagnols, Adresse aux bataves, Aux germains*, and *Lettre à M...., magistrat...en Suisse.* In these short tracts, he was obviously not unmindful of French public opinion, but he was primarily concerned with persuading the people of neighboring nations to accept and to promote the revolution in France. His appeal was in large measure to the governments of these other countries to accept the French experiments and his tone was, therefore, moderate. This is why he attempted on the surface to portray the revolutions of England and France as similar rather than contrasting. But the principles and ideals he expresses are exactly the same as Paine's—the rights of man, equality, and the solidarity of the French and the English people. Condorcet and Paine may have been defending contrary theses, but they advocated the same system of government. Attracted by the example of the American Revolution, they sought to create in France a more rational world dedicated to the rights of man on this earth. The French Revolution served as a magnet to bring them together along with other idealistic minds whatever their country of origin or class.

Notes

1. A. Owen Aldridge, "Condorcet et Paine: Leurs rapports intellectuels," *Revue de littérature comparée*, 32 (1958): 49–65.

2. Gene Wise, "The Contemporary Crisis in Intellectual History," *Clio* 5 (1975): 58.

3. Quoted by Gene Wise, *Clio* 5: 59.

4. Gene Wise, *Clio* 5: 61.

5. Eric Foner, *Tom Paine and Revolutionary America* (New York, 1976).

6. I have developed this position more fully in "The Problem of Thomas Paine," *Studies in Burke and His Time* 19 (1978): 127–43.

7. Peter J. Stanlis, ed., *Edmund Burke: Selected Writings* (New York, 1963), 431.

8. Philip S. Foner, ed., *Complete Writings* (New York, 1945), 1:257.

9. *Complete Writings*, 1:259.

10. *Complete Writings*, 1:298.

11. *Complete Writings*, 1:278.

12. Condorcet, *Oeuvres de Condorcet*, ed. Arthur C. O'Connor and Marie F. Arago, 12 vols. (1847–1849), 12:197. This is a verbal echo of Paine's *Common Sense* written in 1776: "The cause of America is in a great measure the cause of all mankind." [Foner, 1:3] In a *letter* to the French people in September 1792, Paine shifted locale and proclaimed with Condorcet "the cause of France is the cause of all mankind." [Foner, 2:538]

13. *Complete Writings*, 1:323.

14. Hayden White, "Interpretations in History," *New Literary History* 4 (1973):282.

15. Aldridge, "Thomas Paine and the idéologues," *Studies on Voltaire and the Eighteenth Century* 151 (1976): 112–13.

16. *Complete Writings*, 1:390.

17. *Réponse de Thomas Paine à quatre questions sur les pouvoirs législatif et exécutif* in *Chronique du mois ou les Cahiers patriotiques* (mai, juin, et juillet 1792). The journal affirms "traduit sur le manuscrit par Condorcet." See: Aldridge, "Condorcet et Paine," *Revue de littérature comparée* 32 (1958): 57.

18. The Manchester pamphlet, *A Narrative of the Proceedings relating to the suspension of the King of the French, etc, 1792* had an appendix, *Reflections on the English Revolution, 1688, and that of the 10th of August, 1792*. The title of the London edition was *Reflections on the English Revolution of 1688, and that of the French, August 10, 1792*. By Condorcet, Tr. from the French. Printed for J. Ridgeway.

19. Apart from their journalistic ventures in France, the only example of the joint publication of a work by Condorcet and one by Paine consists of a pamphlet of 29 pages printed in New York in 1793 which combines Condorcet's letter to a Swiss magistrate [O'Connor and Arago, 12:169–77] with Paine's letter to the people of France acknowledging the honor of being made a Citizen of France and elected to the National Convention [Foner, ed. *Complete Writings*, 2:538–40]. Condorcet seeks to persuade the Swiss people to ally themselves with France rather than with Austria and to discard ancient charters as the foundation of their governments in favor of the constitutional principle based on the sovereignty of the people. Paine affirms that the cause of France is the cause of all mankind and predicts that the struggle for human rights will be extended to the other countries of Europe. The two letters have little in common except the notion that despots who actively work against revolutionary principles in France are hastening the importation of these principles into their own dominions.

4
Condorcet and the Problem of Emigration in 1791

Carol Blum

In the summer of 1791 Condorcet, the only *Encyclopédiste* who survived to participate in making the French Revolution, looked forward to the *Assemblée législative* and the role he would play in it. He described his vision of the legislator's function with admirable lucidity: "Je crois l'espèce humaine indéfiniment perfectible," he said, "et qu'ainsi elle doit faire vers la paix, la liberté et l'égalité, c'est à dire vers le bonheur et la vertu, des progrès dont il est impossible de fixer le terme. Je crois aussi que ces progrès doivent être l'ouvrage de la raison, fortifiée par la méditation, appuyée par l'expérience. D'après ces principes, ma philosophie doit être froide et patiente....Je ne dirai point: 'Tout est bien,' mais 'Tout sera bien,' et, par là, je déplairai aux deux partis" (quoted in F. Buisson, *Condorcet* [Paris; 1929], p. 48).

His foresight proved remarkably accurate in the first test of his new status as legislator when he proposed, on October 25, 1791, a series of decrees intended to stem the mounting tide of emigration from France. As he had predicted, he was denounced on the right for having "cherché à entraver la liberté des émigrés" (*Mercure de France patriotique* [5 nov., 1791], 14-15), and on the left for his wish to "s'appuyer sur le principe d'égalité" (*Journal universel* [no. 709], 249).

Emigration was not new in 1791. Frenchmen had been leaving their country in reaction to the Revolution since its very inception. The brother of Louis XVI, the Comte d'Artois, had led the procession by fleeing Versailles two days after the fall of the Bastille, having deduced better than the King the logical consequences of that event. Emigration continued during the Revolution and in its wake, reflecting the changing fortunes of contending political groups. Jacques Godechot distinguishes three great waves before 1792: the one prompted by the fall of the Bastille and the "great fear" of 1789, the second wave of 1790, provoked by the decrees abolishing feudal rights, and the third which took place during the summer of 1791 in response to the royal family's aborted attempt to flee the kingdom (*La Contre-Révolution: Doctrine et action* [Paris; 1961], pp. 161-173).[1]

The émigrés numbered some one hundred-fifty thousand, of which only around sixteen thousand belonged to the nobility. The aristocrats loomed larger than their numbers would warrant, however, for they carried off with them much of the prestige of old France, and still more of its gold. Their presence in England, Italy, Russia, Switzerland, Belgium, and especially the German states was a source of continuing irritation, and their indiscrete conspiracies, threats, and denunciations only exacerbated tensions in France.

When Condorcet proposed his decrees in the fall of 1791 the problem was assuming special urgency because of several converging factors. The government found itself in a position so uncomfortable that it eventually became intolerable. By its newly-approved constitution, France was a monarchy uneasily coupled to a legislative assembly, and this bi-polarity of authority, what Condorcet referred to as "l'alliance contre nature du trône et de la liberté," might well alone have sufficed to undo the constitution. In addition, after the flight to Varennes, Louis himself was a captive king.

Varennes, of course, had not been the royal family's destination in June of 1791. It was widely understood in France that Louis and his queen had been attempting to reach Belgium and eventually Coblenz, where the princes and the elite of émigrés were congregating. Their arrest made them, in effect, *émigrés manqués*, and this circumstance caused Louis's subsequent contributions to the debate to seem, according to one's sympathies, either pathetic or provocative.

Marie-Antoinette's brother, Leopold II, Emperor of Germany, although a pacifist and not overly fond of his sister, was goaded by the princess into issuing a circular on July 10 which "demanded" that the royal family be set free. Not long after, he put his seal to the unfortunate Declaration of Pillnitz, by which he and the King of Prussia threatened in a vague way to "use the most efficacious means to put the King of France in a state to affirm...the bases of a monarchical government."

This distant saber-rattling of the despised queen's relatives was seized upon by the Gironde at the beginning of the *Assemblée législative*, and used to advance the cause of war. War, for Brissot de Warville, Vergniaud, Isnard, and other leaders of their party, was the means to revitalize a Revolution that seemed to have sunk into a kind of frozen lethargy with the acceptance of the unsatisfactory constitution. The threat from the outside served to energize nerves drained by internal doubts. By deliberately exaggerating the dangers from émigré conspiracies with foreign powers and demanding a belligerent posture against the other European nations, leaders of the Gironde hoped to consolidate their own strength in the new assembly.

Historians and other scholars of the period have often acquiesced in the Gironde's espousal of war in 1791. Alengry, for example, comments: "Le rassemblement des émigrés sur la frontière du Rhin avait, avec raison, alarmé l'Assemblée Législative. Elle se proposait de prendre et elle prit bientôt des mesures de rigueur."[2]

To Jean Jaurés, on the other hand, the war was not an inevitable consequence of emigration and foreign provocation, but an artificial crisis, created and, for a time, controlled by the Gironde. "La Gironde voulait faire de la guerre une formidable manoeuvre de politique intérieure. Terrible responsabilité! Quand nous pensons aux épreuves inouies que la France va subir, quand nous songeons que cette surexcitation d'un moment sera payée par vingt années de césarisme sanglant et qu'ensuite de 1815 à 1848, on peut dire de 1815 à 1870, la France aura moins de liberté qu'elle n'en avait sous la Constitution de 1791, quand on songe que la propagande armée des principes révolutionnaires a surexcité contre nous le sentiment national des peuples et créé le formidable état militaire sous lequel plient les nations, on se demande si la Gironde avait le droit de jouer cette extraordinaire partie de dés."[3]

The opportunities offered by the warmongering were, however, too tempting for most leaders of the Gironde to resist. By linking emigration to the fear of foreign attack, the Gironde was able to threaten not only the monarchists but all moderate elements still bent on integrating the old régime into the new by compromise, rather than extirpating it by repression.

Multiple ironies invested the situation in 1791. While aristocratic emigration was described as a menace to the Revolution, implicit in the Revolution since its beginnings was the notion that the aristocracy should consider itself a caste without a country. As the author of a widely-read *Cathéchisme d'un peuple libre* had put it as early as 1789: "Qu'est-ce que la Noblesse? C'est un peuple à part, mais un faux peuple, qui ne pouvant, à défaut d'organes utiles, exister par lui-même, s'attache à une nation réelle, comme ces tumeurs végétales qui ne peuvent vivre que de la sève des plantes qu'elles fatiguent et dessèchent" (Londres, 1789, p. 11).

This totally negative definition of the nobility only reversed the Second Estate's own claims to being a Germanic race, separate from and superior to the Gallo-Roman *roturiers* its ancestors had conquered.[4]

Sieyès posed the question even before the *Etats généraux*, asking of the *Tiers état* "pourquoi ne renverrait-il pas dans les forêts de la Franconie toutes ces familles qui conservent la folle prétention d'être issues de la race des conquérants et d'avoir succédé à leurs droits?" (*Qu'est-ce que le Tiers Etat?* reprint [New York, 1979], p. 32).

But however ardently some patriots wished to rid France of its useless cream, as the ci-devant aristocracy and its followers streamed back into the "forests of Franconia" from which it claimed to have once issued, the Revolutionaries registered more unease than jubilation. Popular journalism echoed the question: if this "noble race of conquerors" had once established hegemony over France by force of arms, would it not attempt to do so again? Laden with their country's gold and connected with foreign sovereigns, the knots of émigrés forming on France's northeastern borders mobilized, not entirely without reason, the fears and hatreds of long generations.

Thus for certain elements in the Gironde the surge of emigration following the acceptance of the constitution was an opportunity to press for war and in so doing to re-establish control over the government and over a restless population. Belgium and the German states were to be punished for admitting French nationals deserting their country.

To those Revolutionaries who still in some sense identified themselves with the philosophic tradition, on the other hand, not only was an offensive war difficult to accept, but even the notion of restricting emigration was antithetical. The followers of Diderot and Voltaire, deeply imbued with the principles of individual freedom, could not easily reconcile a Revolutionary government prohibiting emigration with the belief they shared with Candide, that 'c'était un privilège de l'espèce humaine, comme de l'espèce animale, de se servir de ses jambes à son plaisir" (Voltaire, *Romans et contes* [Paris; 1960], p. 141).

Restrictions on travel belonged to the era of despotic sovereigns; it was with the greatest mistrust that the heirs of the *Encyclopédie* saw a government, free at least in principle, promulgating them.

To the financially pressed Revolutionaries, however, the prospect of protecting abandoned estates for disloyal absentee landlords was scarcely attractive, and if the *philosophes* had defended the freedom of the individual, they had also certainly displayed ambivalence toward the ownership of vast lands by a privileged few. Great empty châteaux and fallow fields invited comandeering in a time of economic and social unrest, when the debate on the redemption of feudal rights had veered dangerously near challenging the legitimacy of private property altogether, and the word "usurpation" had been pronounced by more than one delegate (March–July 1791).

Thus when the question of decrees against the émigrés was raised in the fall of 1791 it was against a background of political, economic, and intellectual turbulence. The issue was exploited variously to advance the cause of war, to humiliate the King, to placate the restless poor, and to attempt to repair the battered financial structure of the state.

On October 14 Louis XVI made an effort to anticipate severe decrees by issuing an appeal to discontented subjects. He urged them to remain in France but did so in terms so equivocal that despite himself he provided the best reasons for monarchists to leave: "Le roi n'ignore pas," he wrote, "que plusieurs citoyens, des propriétaires surtout, n'ont quitté leur pays que parce qu'ils n'ont pas trouvé dans l'autorité des lois la protection qui leur était due: son coeur a gémi de ces désordres. Ne doit-on rien pardonner aux circonstances? Le roi lui-même n'a-t-il pas eu des chagrins?" Having reminded his aristocratic readers that he too had dreamed of Coblenz, Louis went on to exhort: "Français, qui avez abandonné votre patrie, revenez dans son sein. C'est là qu'est le poste d'honneur, parce qu'il n'y a de véritable honneur qu'à servir son pays, et à défendre les lois" (Buchez et Roux, *Histoire parlementaire de la Révolution française* [Paris; 1834], 12:161).

So couched, using the offensive expression "poste d'honneur," the letter could only heighten suspicions, and when debate opened in the newly-created *Assemblée législative* the following week, Brissot de Warville's beginning words constituted a deliberate affront to Louis XVI. He denounced the Princes of the blood in terms which applied equally to the King himself, saying that they had "le coeur corrompu de naissance; ils se croient les souverains nés du peuple" (Buchez et Roux, 12:164). After this excursion into *lèse-majesté*, Brissot's discourse went on to the issue of emigration, utilizing it adroitly to announce the pressing necessity for war. It was not the average émigrés who were the problem, according to him, but their leaders, that is, the King's brothers, the Comtes de Provence and d'Artois, fostering counter-revolution, who must be struck down. Brissot called for a bellicose stance: France should demand that her neighbors expel the emigrants and if they refused, they would be told "si vous préférez à l'amitié d'une grande nation vos relations avec quelques rebelles, attendez-vous à des vengeances. La vengeance d'un peuple libre est lente, mais elle frappe sûrement" (Buchez et Roux, 12:173). Brissot's address, like the less important ones of Kock, Rougier la Bergerie, Pyro and others that followed, was only secondarily focused on the realities of France's situation. It was primarily designed to further the political ambitions of the speaker. Brissot, a talented demagogue, heated his speech to just that level the active majority of his listeners found agreeable, advancing his war interests in a warm soup of patriotism. The enthusiastic response to his invocation of a "free people's vengeance" encouraged him and his fellow Girondists to utter increasingly specific incitements to arms in the months that followed.

Condorcet's contribution to the debate and the decrees he recommended might appear at first reading merely politically maladroit, were we unaware of how deliberate and conscious his choices were. Condorcet, as cognizant as his friend Brissot of the political stew, its ingredients, and its temperature, elected to transcend the accidental circumstances of the moment and to address himself to the issue in its largest context.[5] He did not ignore the specific problems posed by the emigrants in the fall of 1791, but he subordinated them to the principles of a free nation, as he conceived it. Realizing, perhaps more clearly than any other Revolutionary figure, that expediency and opportunism posed greater threats to the integrity of the Revolution than Pitt and Pillnitz, he placed the burden of his argument squarely on timeless principles.

"C'est une grande erreur," be began, "de croire que l'utilité commune ne se trouve pas constamment unie avec le respect pour les droits des individus, et que le salut public puisse commander de véritables injustices. Cette erreur a été partout l'éternelle excuse des attentats de la tyrannie, et le prétexte des menées artificieuses pour l'établir" (*Oeuvres complètes* [Paris: ed. O'Connor-Arago, 1848], 10:225).

The aloofness, the chilly rectitude of this introduction, were purposeful on Condorcet's part. He did not wish to move his fellow-legislators, but to enlighten them. As he explained in his *Lettre aux amis de la liberté*, "ma philosophie doit être froide et patiente." Like the unyielding pedagogue he never ceased to be, he began by demonstrating to his colleagues that they were mistaken in their efforts to respond quickly and passionately to the situation. The whole import of Condorcet's discourse was that the pace and heat of events should be lessened, that a colder, slower, more reasoned approach should be employed. Condorcet was describing a Revolution for the centuries to an audience whose mental and physical life was, unfortunately, ordered largely day-by-day.

Injustice to the individual could never serve the common interest seen under its eternal light, of this Condorcet was serenely assured, and for the momentary advantage envisaged by his colleagues, he had more distrust than regard. He pointed out, the weight of history in his words, that tyranny never fails to beg the common weal as its first excuse for injustice.

"Dans toute mesure proposée comme utile," he continued, "il faut d'abord examiner s'il est juste. Ne l'est-il pas, il faut en conclure qu'elle n'avait qu'une vaine et trompeuse apparence d'utilité" (*Oeuvres complètes*, 10:225). Having thus firmly subordinated considerations of expediency to those of justice, he went on to examine the phenomenon of emigration in relation to the *Droits de l'homme* just adopted as part of the Constitution, and embodying, for his purposes, immutable rights of the individual. He began with the assertion: "La nature accorde à tout homme le droit de sortir de son pays; la Constitution le garantit à tout citoyen francais, et nous ne pouvons y porter atteinte" (226).

In this trinary phase, he moved with almost geometrical precision from Nature, the timeless and immutable law, to the French Constitution of 1791, derived from Nature but temporal and therefore more particular in its objects, to the Legislators themselves, mere agents subject to the higher powers from which they drew their authority. Seen in this somewhat awesome perspective, the Legislators, far from being free to pass laws according to the impassioned impulse of the moment, were but trustees of eternal truths, empowered to act only in accordance with them.

Condorcet, however, was not blinded by his abstractions to the realities of the situation. He saw quite clearly that emigration posed problems both as a dangerous social phenomenon and as an occasion for inflammatory demagogic excesses. After having carefully spelled out the individual's right to leave his country, he went on to define the distinction between a simple émigré and a traitor. The latter was identified as he who "emploierait ses richesses, ses talents contre ses anciens compatriotes" (227).

Condorcet believed that the vast bulk of emigration was caused, not by treachery or counter-revolutionary intrigue, but by class prejudices that would eventually disappear. With his profound conviction of the gradual improvement of mankind, implemented by the French Revolution, Condorcet saw emigration as a momentary aberration, a transitory mistake that time alone would correct: "Dans cette multitude de Français, les uns ne sortent de leur pays que pour des motifs légitimes, les autres le quittent parce que sa nouvelle constitution blesse leurs opinions, et surtout leur vanité. Citoyens égarés, mais paisibles, ils sont plus malheureux que coupables; car c'est un malheur que d'avoir placé ses jouissances dans de vains préjugés que le jour de la raison a dissipés. Nous devons les plaindre…" (228-229). And further: "Un grand nombre d'émigrants n'a, pour la constitution française, qu'une aversion fondée sur d'anciens préjugés,…il faut y joindre le désagrément passager d'un changement dans leur importance personnelle. Presque tous, une fois assurés de la stabilité de la constitution française désireront d'en partager les avantages…" (236-237).

Against those, however, who were irrevocably hostile to their country's new fundamental premises, those who "forment un corps armé, une espèce de nation sans territoire," Condorcet proposed that France take "précautions pour sa sûreté." He proposed that émigrés be classified, not according to their titles or civil functions, as others had suggested, but exclusively as to their *will*. Those who wished to abandon their country were to be distinguished from those who merely wanted to leave it. France had the right to "connaître ses ennemis," Condorcet insisted, and to that end set forth a complicated series of proposals by which those who resided abroad would be obliged to make a formal declaration, before the French consul, of their adherence to the French Constitution. He who refused to make this declaration, or, alternately, to pronounce the "serment civique inséré dans l'acte constitutionnel," could promise not to enter the service of any foreign power for a period of two years.

To those persons declining the opportunity to make any of the foregoing promises or declarations would be imputed "une intention ennemie," for which they would be punished. Their assets would be frozen and they would be deprived of income from France.

Condorcet went on to justify the utility of these measures in the light of what he clearly felt to be France's greatest problem: its floundering sense of itself as a nation. He envisaged the appropriate way for France to address her recalcitrant citizens, not as a howling mob pursuing refugees from its violence, but as a mighty nation, serene in its righteousness, wisely but firmly recalling its misguided members to their duties. French morale depended on the Revolutionaries' conviction of the legitimacy of their government. To the extent that the new order incarnated a morally superior society and could be so regarded by its neighbors, the image would in turn be cherished by the French people as a representation of themselves. Condorcet was aware of how powerful the question of moral superiority had been in precipitating actions againt the corrupt *ancien régime*, and how precarious and ambiguous was the moral authority of the new government.

"C'est de notre conduite envers cette lie de la nation, qui ose encore s'en nommer l'élite," he remarked, in the speech's only playful allusion, "que dépend l'opinion des nations étrangères, si nécessaire au succès de nos travaux. Soyez modérés et justes, mais fermes, vous serez respectés par elles..." (236). Condorcet then proposed eight articles in which were detailed the complicated procedures by which French citizens residing abroad were to declare their patriotism, and the penalties to be imposed if they failed to do so.

The Assembly applauded Condorcet's speech, ordered it to be printed, and gave it first priority for consideration, over those of Brissot, Couthon, and Vergniaud.

On October 31, however, when debate began, the tide ran strongly against Condorcet's ideas. Isnard objected that "le projet de décret de M. Condorcet peut satisfaire à ce que nous devons à la prudence; mais il ne satisfait point à ce que demande la justice, à ce que réclament tous les français." He denounced the civil vow in sanguinary rhetoric, "c'est souiller la sainteté du serment que de le placer dans des bouches affamées de notre sang" (Buchez et Roux, 12:203).

The carefully modulated system Condorcet had elaborated was swept aside contemptuously. For the following speaker, Xavier Girardin, "les mesures qu'il contient sont d'une exécution lente et difficile,...inutiles sous plusieurs rapports, et dangereuses sous beaucoup d'autres" (Buchez et Roux, 12:203).

Condorcet attempted, somewhat flounderingly, to defend his project, pointing out that 'c'est précisément parce que j'ai cru qu'il fallait commencer par s'assurer invariablement des dispositions des Français émigrés, que j'ai proposé des mesures qui paraissent un peu lentes" (206). He was interrupted by repeated murmurs of disapproval and his project was quickly voted down by a large majority. The Assembly, a few days later, approved a plan by which emigrants who continued to congregate together would be "déclarés coupables de conjuration, poursuivis comme tels, et punis de mort" (219). Their property was to be confiscated.

This aggressive proposal was vetoed by Louis XVI on November 12, exacerbating the friction between the monarch and the representatives of the nation.

The subsequent history of the controversy over emigration becomes inseparably entangled with the twisting strands of regicide, Republic, and war.

At this point it is legitimate to attempt to evaluate Condorcet's role in events during the Fall of 1791. Although under vicious attack from both the left and the right, he appears to have enjoyed a considerable authority at the beginning of the *Législative*, as the priority given his discourse demonstrates. Yet it is clear from the rapidity with which his proposals were jettisoned that his thinking did not correspond to the mood of the majority. As Michelet put it, "Vergniaud, Isnard, répondant mieux à la pensée du moment, déclarèrent (ses) mesures insuffisantes" (*Histoire de la Révolution fr.* [Paris, 1868], 4:106).

Is Condorcet therefore to be blamed for having failed to seize leadership when the opportunity presented itself? Shoud he have tailored his project to the temperament of his constituents, lending formal representation to their fluctuating impulses? Had he been capable of doing so consistently, he might have ended his days, like a Sieyès, or a Tallien, or a Talleyrand-Périgord, in comfortable retirement under a restored Bourbon monarchy, rather than suffering that terrible exile within France, the "internal emigration" of 1793-94, which led to his death.

Yet it was never Condorcet's intention to "represent" those who had elected him to the *Assemblée législative* in that sense; he did not see himself as the formulator or spokesman for his constituents' wishes. Still less did he see his function as manipulating the masses in the interests of a political party. On the contrary, Condorcet envisaged the legislator as a guardian of truth against attempts to subvert it through the political process. He would propose and favor legislation that most closely approximated the principles of justice and reason that he, the standard-bearer of the Encyclopedic tradition, upheld.

As he explained his position to his constituents the day after his election, he believed he had been chosen because of his association with the *philosophes* and he would serve by submitting all questions before the *Assemblée législative* to the scrutiny of philosophic reasoning: "Vous avez voulu sans doute honorer en moi la mémoire des hommes illustres dont j'ai eu le bonheur d'être l'ami et les récompenser, dans un disciple qu'ils aimaient, de tout ce qu'ils ont fait pout préparer, pour accélérer le règne de la raison et de la liberté. Fidèle à leurs principes, c'est en conservant l'indépendance absolue de mes opinions, c'est en mettant tous mes soins à chercher la vérité, toute ma politique à la dire, que je m'efforcerai de répondre à cette marque si glorieuse de votre confiance" (quoted by J. Bouissounouse, *Condorcet, Le Philosophe dans la Révolution* [Paris, 1962], p. 183).

It was not, therefore, in resisting a popular Draconian approach to emigration that Condorcet fell short of his own ideals. Rather it was in December of that year when he finally did succumb to the mounting pressure for war being brought to bear by the Gironde, and accepted, at least provisionally, the concomitant nationalism and violence, that Condorcet strayed furthest from Encyclopedic principles. He did so, however, in a speech which, although in support of the war, expressed his deepest wishes for peace. The soldiers of France, he said, "se conduiront sur une terre étrangère comme ils se conduiraient sur celle de leur patrie s'ils étaient forcés d'y combattre. La France présentera au monde le spectacle nouveau d'une nation vraiment libre, soumise aux règles de la justice au milieu des orages de la guerre et respectant partout, en tout temps, à l'égard de tous les hommes, les droits qui sont les mêmes pour tous" (Jaurès, 3:152).

That Condorcet was capable of such an unrealistically endearing description of the war to come is perhaps a measure of how terrible he must have found the strain of accepting France's commitment to hostilities. His profound attachment to peace makes itself felt in the atypical illogic of these statements where Condorcet, only human, momentarily falters.

In every political sense he may be said to have lost: the émigrés were definitively ostracized by the Revolution, cutting off any possibility of the reconciliation that he had so hopefully seen on the horizon. France was embarked on a war that was to last twenty years, one which unfortunately did note dazzle the world with the spectacle of a "truly free nation,...respecting rights which are the same for all."

He himself saw the standards of "cold and patient" philosophy for which he stood rejected by the politicians, the journalists, and the public, who preferred the emotionally steamy and intellectually mediocre discourses of the Gironde or the radical left.

And yet, paradoxically, despite Condorcet's seeming failures, it was his set of principles which could have saved the French Revolution from its debasement through Terror and Imperial aggrandizement.

Today we are trying to survive in a world where only a few nations even attempt to provide the individual liberties enumerated in the *Droits de l'homme* of France's 1791 Constitution. We are surrounded by nations where dissident citizens are neither tolerated and integrated into the whole nor permitted to seek their happiness in another country. The impotence of governments to resolve internal conflicts is still the occasion for foreign aggression. It is to Condorcet's principles, just as ungratifying to the baser emotions now as they were in 1791, and just as prodigiously difficult of application, that we must turn if we are to have any hope of realizing the human progress of which he spoke so luminously. If his discourses did not vibrate in harmony with popular passions as did those of Brissot or Isnard, nevertheless, it is to his doctrine of "cold and patient" philosophy, as applied to political action, to which posterity could with profit aspire while theirs are long forgotten. Condorcet summed up in 1777, eleven years before the convocation of the Etats généraux, the philosophy which was to carry him, with only minor lapses, through his career as Revolutionary spokesman and legislator: "si l'on me demande quelle est la première règle de la politique? *C'est d'être juste.* La seconde? *C'est d'être juste.* Et la troisième? *C'est encore d'être juste. (Journal de Paris* [22 juin, 1777], no. 173).

Notes

1. Godechot's work remains the authoritative study of the ideologies and political repercussions of emigration (1789-1804). Donald Greer has applied modern statistical techniques to the analysis of patterns and frequencies of emigration (*The Incidence of Emigration during the Fr. Rev.* [Cambridge, 1951]). Many interesting memoirs and correspondences are to be found in which the adventures of individual émigrés are recounted. Ernest Daudet, in a curious three-volume compendium of these stories, provides a good anecdotal survey of the movement (*Histoire de l'émigration* [Paris, 1898]). In a study called *The Fr. Exiles* (London, 1960), M. Weiner describes in detail the fortunes of those who settled in London, particularly the circle which formed around the Comte d'Artois and Louise de Polastron.

2. Franck Alengry, *Condorcet, Guide de la Révolution française* (Paris, 1904), 130.

3. Jean Jaurès *Histoire socialiste de la Révolution française* (Paris, 1922), 3:96.

4. In *The Aryan Myth, A History of Racist and Nationalist Ideas in Europe* (New York, 1971), Léon Poliakov traces the political implications of the "Germanic" origins of France's aristocracy (see chap. 2, "France, the Controversy about the Two Races").

5. It was at this point, as Léon Cahen points out, that Condorcet clearly established his political independence from any party led by Brissot. (*Condorcet et la Rév. fr.* [Paris, 1904], 283).

5
Condorcet: A Note on the Problem
of the Randomness of Ends

Keith Michael Baker

My aim in this paper is to take up the relationship in Condorcet's thinking between his social science (or, more precisely, his claim that the moral and political sciences could be established on the same positive basis as the natural sciences) and his political theory (which he regarded as based on rational principles issuing in such universally valid conceptions as the rights of man). One very acute reviewer of my book on Condorcet felt that in my analysis of this relationship I had succumbed to the constant temptation of intellectual historians to discover consistency where none exists, giving an artificial coherence to ideas that are contradictory, unsystematic or simply not thought through.[1] Since this raises interesting questions of approach for the intellectual historian, as well as of interpretation regarding Condorcet's ideas, I should like to return to it here.

Let me therefore try to state the problem more directly. Condorcet wanted, on the one hand, to argue that the moral and political sciences were positive sciences, based no less securely than the physical sciences on empirical fact. He wanted, on the other hand, to appeal to certain universal principles of right and justice, which he regarded as providing the rational foundation for individual action and social organization. Was he necessarily inconsistent in making both these claims? Does the attempt to construe them as reconcilable, at least within the terms of Condorcet's own discourse, involve the construction of an artificial coherence where none exists? Is the effort to discover some consistency on this point therefore misdirected, in the sense that disclosure of inconsistency would open up more fundamental historical considerations regarding the reasons for its existence? I shall try to touch on these questions in the course of the following discussion.

Condorcet's program for the moral and political sciences was first stated in summary form in the reception speech he gave at the *Académie française* in 1782. "In mediating on the nature of the moral sciences," he argued there:

> one cannot indeed help seeing that based like the physical sciences upon the observation of facts, they must follow the same method, acquire an equally exact and precise language, attain the same degree of certainty.[2]

This conviction, he admitted in the supplementary notes he prepared for a second edition of his reception speech, was necessarily contrary to accepted ideas. Indeed, there were powerful vested interests in its remaining so. For if reason alone was adequate to teach man his nature and the means of assuring happiness for himself and his fellows, then priests were unnecessary. And if politics and administration were sciences with fixed, rational principles, then nothing would remain arbitrary or obscure in government, and the claims of those whose power depended on its remaining an esoteric art would wither away.[3]

For this reason, Condorcet devoted a special section of the supplementary notes for his reception speech to developing the arguments for his claim that the moral and political sciences could indeed attain the certainty of the physical sciences. In doing so, he sketched a distinction between what he called the *évidence* (rational demonstrability, or truth) of scientific propositions, and their *realité* (empirical grounding), that is to say, the distinction between their status as analytical truths and their status in relationship to the world of experience. As analytical truths, Condorcet argued, the propositions of the moral and of the physical sciences depend for their certainty upon the validity of a chain of reasoning in which each successive idea has been precisely and exactly analyzed. In this respect, their conclusions can be regarded as equally certain and precise, though Condorcet was careful to point out (with Hume) that this certainty (like the certainty of mathematics) was itself a kind of cognitive probability "founded on the constant order that I have observed, that every time I re-examine a proposition that I remember having seen rigorously demonstrated, I still find it evidently true."[4]

As statements regarding empirical reality, however, the validity of the propositions of the moral (as of the physical) sciences also depends upon a constant order of facts and experience, "fortified by the observation that the fact which was observed yesterday will be observed today if no circumstance has changed."[5] In this respect, all the truths of observation are but probabilities: their reliability (or "degree of certainty") depends upon the greater or lesser probability of the order of facts observed, the greater or lesser probability that these facts have a common cause, the greater or lesser probability that the fact regarded as a cause is indeed the cause. This is no less true of the moral sciences, Condorcet argued, than of the physical sciences. "Thus it is from the more or less constant order of facts observed in moral as in physical matters that the kind of certainty derives that pertains to reality."[6]

Having made this point, Condorcet found it necessary to distinguish two further aspects of "the kind of cerrainty that pertains to reality": the more or less constant order of facts; and the certainty that one knows this order of facts. These two factors, he maintained, influence on the one hand, "the real and absolute certainty of a science," and on the other hand, its "actual certainty."[7]

The force of this distinction can be illustrated as follows. My expectation that a phenomenon that has occurred 999 times out of a thousand will recur in the same circumstances is less than it would have been if the phenomenon had occurred 9999 times out of ten thousand. But while the probability of the event's occurrence is different in two such cases, Condorcet wished to argue, the mathematical precision with which these probabilities can be expressed is equivalent. "The science in general is as certain since I know exactly in the same manner the degree of certainty that I obtain, but the degree of certainty of the result is not the same." Thus since "the moral sciences are founded on facts and reasoning, their certainty will therefore be the same as that of the physical sciences."[8]

Thus seizing upon the calculus of probabilities as the essential link between the moral and the physical sciences, Condorcet aimed to integrate them within a mathematical model of science theoretically applicable to the whole realm of human knowledge and experience. If the observation of facts is more difficult in human affairs, and their order consequently less easy to elicit, the moral sciences may in given cases acquire fewer precise truths. If the order of observed facts is itself less constant than that revealed by the physical sciences, then their actual results will be less probable:

> But if we examine the small number of facts necessary to establish the first foundations of ethics, of political, civil or criminal legislation, or of administration, and even of the facts that can further be necessary to establish the most important general truths [i.e. in politics] ...we shall see that these facts are as general and as constant as the facts of the physical order.[9]

But in what sense can these first principles of social organization be thought of as grounded in fact? And if (as Condorcet suggested in the supplementary notes to his reception speech) the political sciences consist, "human nature being given, the ideas of right and justice being well established, in deducing the consequences of those principles,"[10] how can the existence of such universally valid propositions be justified within the positivistic and probabilistic framework of knowledge we have been discussing? Whatever the answer to this question, I do not think that it can simply be said that Condorcet was contradictory or merely incoherent on this point. Whether or not we find the solution he gave to this problem convincing, it was indeed a problem that he attempted to address within the terms of his theory of knowledge, and not simply a contradiction in his thinking awaiting a historian to disclose it.

To understand his position, we need to turn to a brief note appended to the Kehl edition of the *Oeuvres de Voltaire*, in which Condorcet discussed the issue of the "reality" and the "truth" of moral propositions in terms that parallel the discussion in the unpublished notes for his reception speech at the *Académie française.*[11] Condorcet argued there that "The idea of justice, of right, forms necessarily in the same manner in all sensitive beings capable of the necessary combinations to acquire those ideas." As a result, Condorcet stated, "They will therefore be uniform."[12] It is of course true, he admitted, that rational beings can reason erroneously regarding such matters, just as they can regarding other matters:

> But since every being reasoning precisely will be led to the same ideas in morality as in geometry, it is no less true that these ideas are not arbitrary, but certain and invariable. They are in effect the necessary result of the properties of sensate beings capable of reasoning; they derive from their nature; from which it follows that it is sufficient to suppose the existence of these beings for the propositions founded on these notions to be true; just as it is sufficient to suppose the existence of a circle to establish the truth of the propositions which develop its different characteristics.[13]

Not surprisingly, Condorcet never explicitly spelled out the logic by which the first principles of morals and politics could be regarded as analytical truths derivable from the very definition of man as a sensate being capable of reasoning. But it seems clear from this—as from other passages of his work—that he regarded such propositions as enjoying the same analytical certainty, or precision, in respect to their "truth," as mathematical propositions. This truth, it must be remembered from our earlier discussion, was itself a probability "based on the constancy of the laws observed in the operation of our understanding."

But what of the "reality" of such moral propositions, that is to say their status in relationship to the world of experience? On this point, Condorcet argued that if it was enough to posit the existence of sensate beings capable of reasoning to demonstrate the "truth" of these propositions, it was enough further to establish empirically the existence of such beings to prove their "reality":

> Thus the reality of moral propositions, their truth relative to the state of real beings, of men, depends entirely upon this truth of fact: that men are sensitive and intelligent beings.[14]

This argument explains, I think, why in the supplementary notes to his reception speech Condorcet linked his case for the equal validity of the moral and of the physical sciences with an argument regarding our belief in the existence of the body, the basic fact of man's physical nature. This belief, probable though it may be, is nevertheless as reliable and as constant as the most certain truth of the physical sciences: the fact that the sun will rise tomorrow. It would seem to be in this sense, then, that "if we examine the small number of facts necessary to establish the first foundations of ethics, of political, civil or criminal legislation, or of administration...we shall see that these facts are as general and as constant as those of the physical order."

This does not present itself as a felicitous argument to modern, post-Kantian, eyes. Since it depends upon an assertion that is never demonstrated (i.e., that moral principles are analytically implied in the very definition of man as a sensate being) it can hardly be regarded as an argument that is thought through in any systematic or sustained way. But neither does it appear to be contradictory within its own terms, inconsistent with other aspects of Condorcet's thinking, or incoherent in the sense that we cannot recognize what he was trying to do on the contrary, it seems to represent a response (within the terms of Condorcet's scientific discourse) to a fundamental problem in the approach to social science that Talcott Parsons has called the "positivist theory of action."[15] The distinguishing feature of this approach—and I would argue that no one exemplified it better than Condorcet, though he is not in fact discussed by Talcott Parsons in this context—is, that it is concerned with individual conduct and rational choice. The individual actor is considered as if he were a scientific investigator; and the aim is to introduce into the realm of social and political decision-making the cognitive rationality and precision of scientific reasoning. The theory of probability upon which Condorcet attempted to base such a sicence of social action was, in his understanding of it, explicitly individual and subjective. The calculus of probabilities afforded a scientific model for evaluating the validity of individual opinions and determining the probable outcomes of individual action. Epistemologically, it was the key to the rational understanding of the relationship between individual knowledge and external phenomena. Sociologically, it operated at the level of the interrelationship between an individual's choices and actions and those of other individuals. It was therefore the appropriate scientific model for a conception of social science oriented toward a view of society as the field of purposive action between rational individuals.

The difficulty inherent in such a positivist theory of action, however, lies in establishing the positivistic aspects of the theory—its claim to rely on facts as the basis of scientific reasoning—without subverting its status as a theory of action. This is the difficulty that Parsons has called the problem of "randomness of ends."[16] Either action implies choice of ends as an independent factor in the social situation, in which case the choice of ends seems to fall outside the positive range of the theory and there is no "scientific" basis for choosing among them, or the choice of ends is dictated by positive scientific knowledge of the social situation, in which case action seems to lose its independent status as the expression of rational choice and becomes a function of determining social conditions. It was exactly this difficulty that Condorcet sought to evade. He wanted to argue that the principles of the moral and political sciences—the ends of social action—could be defined no less certainly and precisely than those of the physical sciences, on the basis of positive fact. But he also wanted to avoid the implication—into which he was convinced that Montesquieu, for example, had fallen—that a scientific approach to society reduced social action to a function of determining social and historical conditions. He therefore attempted to bring the principles of social action within the framework of his scientific model as enjoying the same status, analytically, as mathematics, while also attempting to tie them down empirically to the fact of man's existence as a sensate being. His aim, in other words, was to give a positive, naturalistic basis for the principles of social organization, while avoiding any implication of the social or psychological determinism that would undermine their status as rational principles of social action.

This is why, as his thought matured, Condorcet came to distinguish what he called the "social science" strictly speaking—that is to say the principles of social organization derived from the nature of man by the method of the analysis of sensations and ideas—from the "social art" intended to implement these principles through the rationalization and mathematicization of social choice. This is why he wrote the *Equisse d'un tableau historique des progrès de l'esprit humain:* not to demonstrate "the entire system of the social science" (for that could not be demonstrated historically) nor to establish "the rules of the art that must realize its principles,"[17] but precisely to show the power of the social art to effect rational social choice in the face of historical conditions. Thus the idea of progress—the idea, that is, of the power of humanity to realize the principles of a rational social order through the cumulative actualization of rational social choice—was the matrix of Condorcet's conception of the social art, but it did not define its principles by reducing them to functions of a deter-mined historical development. Quite the contrary, it was intended to sustain the status of Condorcet's social science as a theory of rational action, by demon-strating man's power to secure freedom from determining conditions. "I have merely wished to show," Condorcet stated in the preface he drafted for the *Tableau historique*, "how by dint of time and effort [man] has been able to enrich his mind with new truths, perfect his intelligence, extend his faculties, and learn to employ them for his own well-being and for the common happi-ness."[18]

As I have tried to suggest elsewhere, this particular solution to the problem of the "randomness of ends" did not long survive.[19] In fact, it disappeared almost immediately, as Saint-Simon and Comte undertook to rewrite Condorcet's theory of progress in different historical circumstances and for different purposes. The transformation is virtually complete in one of the earliest frag-ments of the young Auguste Comte, his review of Thouret's *Abrégé des révolutions de l'ancien gouvernement français* (1819). Comte's interest in that review was to argue a position he attributed to Condorcet, namely, that historical knowledge must "furnish the only solid basis and the only positive point of departure that political research can have."[20] But while he credited Condorcet with discovery of the proper relationship between historical knowledge and political theory, it is quite clear that his understanding of that relationship was altogether different from that set forth in the *Esquisse d'un tableau historique des progrès de l'esprit humain*. "For the route that civilization must take is predetermined," the young Comte insisted:

> no human power can know how to enforce the slightest change. We can only choose whether or not to march along like blindmen, and such choice is the object of real politics. Only the observation of the path already travelled can give us some understanding of that which remains to be traversed.
>
> Conceived of in this spirit, history...takes on the character of a real science, as positive as the others and, like them, perfectible.[21]

With this argument, social science may perhaps have become more fully positive, as Comte proclaimed. But it had ceased to exist as a science of social action.

Notes

1. Keith Michael Baker, *Condorcet. From Natural Philosophy to Social Mathematics* (Chicago, 1975), reviewed by Alan Charles Kors, *Journal of Modern History* 48 (1976): 718–23.

2. *Oeuvres de Condorcet*, ed. Arthur C. O'Connor and Marie F. Arago, 12 vols. (Paris, 1847–1849), 1:392.

3. Baker, "Condorcet's Notes for a Revised Edition of his Reception Speech to the *Académie française*," *Studies on Voltaire and the Eighteenth Century* 1969 (1977): 43.

4. Ibid., 44. For the relationship of Condorcet's epistemology and Hume's, see *Condorcet. From Natural Philosophy to Social Mathematics*, 138–94.

5. "Condorcet's Notes," 44.

6. Ibid.

7. Ibid.

8. Ibid., 44–45. I should point out here that the translation of the first sentence of this passage previously given in *Condorcet. From Natural Philosophy to Social Mathematics*, 182, is not quite accurate, owing to an error of transcription from the manuscript.

9. Ibid., 45.

10. Ibid., 43.

11. *Oeuvres*, 4:540. Since the Kehl edition was published betwen 1784 and 1789, this note is roughly contemporaneous with the notes for a revised edition of Condorcet's reception speech, which appear to have been written between 1782 and 1785, the year in which Condorcet published his broadest statement of his probabilistic theory of knowledge, the *Essai sur l'application de l'analyse à la probabilité des décisions rendues à la pluralité des voix* (Paris, 1785).

12. *Oeuvres*, 4:540.

13. Ibid.

14. Ibid.
15. Talcott Parsons, *The Structure of Social Action*, 2 vols. (New York, 1968), 1:60-69.
16. Ibid., 1:60.
17. *Oeuvres*, 6:282.
18. Ibid., 6:282-83.
19. *Condorcet. From Natural Philosophy to Social Mathematics*, 371-82.
20. A. Comte, *Ecrits de jeunesse 1816-1818*, ed. Paolo E. De Barrêdo Carneiro and Pierre Arnaud, (Paris, 1970), 454.
21. Ibid.

TOWARD THE SOCIAL SCIENCES

6
Condorcet's *"Mémoire sur les hôpitaux"* (1786):* An English Translation and Commentary

Louis S. Greenbaum

On the eve of the French Revolution the Marquis de Condorcet urged in a *Mémoire sur les hôpitaux* that the thousand-year old municipal hospital of the city of Paris, the Hôtel-Dieu, be closed down, and that it be replaced by a more effective health-delivery system in the form of small neighborhood hospices. His confidential memoir, translated here for the first time, remained *inédit* until 1977.[1] Condorcet's perception of the large urban hosptial led him to reject it as an instrument of therapy. His call to transfer the main burden of health-care from the hospital—long associated with indigence and Christian charity—to a network of local, democratically-organized health centers added strength to the pre-Revolutionary movement to nationalize and laicize medical care. Condorcet's hospice, an institution of rationally-determined size, organization, and services, and a harbinger of modern conceptions of hospital management like cost-efficiency, helped shape contemporary scientific thought that developed the new pavilion form of hospital design. The memoir takes its place as part of Condorcet's long-time preoccupation with the calculus of probability. It reflects his attempt to formulate a rational science of decision-making, to quantify costs, risks, and benefits of alternative courses of action, and to reduce events of life and human conduct to probable degrees of certainty. The treatment of the sick within the hospital environment Condorcet subjected to what he termed "precise and measured calculation." Hospital organization, administration, and mortality were susceptible to statistical and mathematical evaluation based on precise observation of facts and rigorous analysis of their relationships.

Memoir on Hospitals*

The investigation entrusted to the members of the hospital commission [of the Royal Academy of Sciences] is so important, and their decision can have such a great influence on the administration of assistance for the poor sick, in Paris or elsewhere, that all members of the Academy have a duty to support

*Translation by Dr. Hilda B. Greenbaum

them in this investigation. But, since the Academy has confided in them, I believe myself obliged to follow its example by communicating to those persons only my ideas on the subject before them.

The first question to try to resolve appears to be the following: what is the proper size for a hospital in which the greatest number of patients can be treated at the least possible expense.

There are many degrees between an institution where each patient, like a rich man, can enjoy a room for himself with a nurse who would care for him alone, and an Hôtel-Dieu where all the sick of a city like Paris are taken. It is reasonable that there exists between these two extremes a middle ground which presents the greatest possible advantage.

This middle ground appears to me not impossible to determine. To be specific:

1) Hospital specialists may well know how many patients a single person can tend in one night without excessive fatigue and without depriving any patients of necessary care. This number would then determine how many patients can be housed in a single ward and at the same time determine the minimum number in the same building.

2) The number of patients for whom a single pharmacist with an assistant can prepare the necessary medications, the number of patients for whom a single attendant can prepare broths and other beverages in the kitchen will determine the number of beds below which one cannot go in an institution without increasing costs that would have no observable benefit to patients.

3) I am not considering here physicians and surgeons. Since they can see other patients [outside the hospital] it would be easy to determine their salary by the number of beds. But it would be well to have available to the patients a doctor who could be awakened at night for emergencies; and it is possible for hospital specialists experienced in the healing art to determine how many patients a single man can treat without the fatigue of night duty disrupting his regular duties.

For example a man who would be awakened two nights in a row only once or twice a year would not have to interrupt his customary service, and it is possible to determine the number of patients for which this would apply.

These numbers once given, not only for these kinds of service but also for all others, we would have a kind of minimum number of beds. Here no one would be appointed solely as director or administrator. Consequently there would be no further expenses to cut and everything to lose by reducing the size of the building.

The minimum number having been determined, we could see what degree of patient salubrity and comfort we could provide in a hospital having this number of beds for a given initial cost and a given annual expense per bed. And it would be necessary to determine what we would gain or lose by increasing the number of beds but retaining the same benefits. I believe the method least susceptible of inducing error is to seek to reduce all calculations to money, since with five, six or eight thousand patients in the same structure, it would be physically possible to obtain for them all the advantages of a small hospice providing enough money were spent. Excessive costs not only confirm the existence of abuses within these large institutions, but also provide a kind of scale which can serve to measure them.

Since there are hospitals having a great many patients, and hospices with few, the comparison of mortality in these different institutions can yield useful information. But I believe the foregoing method would yield greater probability and more precise results.

1) It is very doubtful, either at the Hôtel-Dieu of Paris or in the hospices which have been built there, that abuses and mismanagement do not exist independent of the size of these institutions.

2) The observation that a very large portion of the patients of the Hôtel-Dieu are brought there in advanced stages of illness alters and weakens the conclusion that could be drawn from a comparison of mortality rates.

3) Comparison should be made from tables where the type of disease is identified, because it is possible that the excessive mortality of the Hôtel-Dieu, for example, may be due to certain particular diseases found there or perhaps to the effect of hospital air on other diseases. This would again alter the conclusions drawn from this observation and render them very much less telling against large institutions. M.... [Poyet] has stated as one reason for preferring the large hospital over the hospice that it is easier to find one man capable of managing a large hospital than fifty men capable of managing the hospices. This opinion seems contrary to general experience in all particulars. In addition the director of an immense institution would have under him sub-directors just as difficult to find as directors of small hospices. Finally it is almost as difficult to evaluate such an extensive organization as to manage it. The administrator in charge would not have any real judges. Praised or blamed at random by public opinion, he would wind up by becoming indifferent to it.

If, on the contrary, there were several administrations, then competition, emulation would be established among them. It would be much easier to evaluate them, at once because they are smaller and because they would serve each other as a standard of comparison. Public opinion would become for each director a brake, all the more powerful in that it would not be an absolute judgment but a judgment of comparison more humiliating for him whom public opinion places below his colleagues. This competition, this emulation would occur equally among the heads of each house and among the residents of the neighborhoods where they would be situated.

Further, mismanagement in a large institution is for the most part serious and very difficult to overcome even when, with good fortune, it is detected. And it is detected too late. Reform is very difficult. Abuses find powerful protectors. Setting out to make improvements can only be embarked on with great difficulty. In small institutions, on the contrary, each one enlightening the other, where each can profit from the experience of all, error would be more readily detected, more readily corrected. Improvement would be more prompt.

I do not know any argument whatsoever in favor of the very large and nearly unique hospital which can counterbalance the advantages I have just enumerated.

Regarding the means of execution, it appears to me that all the advantages would be again in favor of the parish hospice. There is not in Paris a single parish, even an ordinary one, where we cannot find some rich men, a few architects, mathematicians capable of evaluating architect's plans, doctors, surgeons, physicists, jurisconsults, merchants, men employed, or having been employed, in management, and men who have studied the theory of political science. Every curate could gather the men of his parish from whom he might expect the most knowledge and help. He would ask them to choose from their ranks a committee which would be responsible for preparing designs for a hospice most suited to the needs of that parish. This plan would then be discussed, examined by the parishioners and drafted in accordance with their views. Having been presented to them, it would then become in a certain sense their creation. Laying aside all vanity, assuming men to be animated by a very pure beneficence, in order that this beneficence will occasion sacrifice, in order that it be launched with dispatch, we must join the feeling of satisfaction at doing good to the pleasure of working for its realization, of being involved. As a result assistance will be more prompt and of greater magnitude. From another point of view, the plans will have the advantage of being the product of bringing together enlightened men widely scattered in one of the cities where there have never been more. This enlightenment is lost in the case of large hospitals, because, given the extent of detail which they entail, people cannot get involved except by devoting themselves exclusively.

It is very likely that the forty hospices that could replace the Hôtel-Dieu of M. Poyet would together not cost any more than this single edifice. They would be completed more promptly and put into operation more easily.

It should be observed moreover that in the case of small institutions, cash donations can be received as well as pledges payable at the death of donors, personal estate, and life and term annuities. The conversion into cash of all these donations would be very easy for sums like 200,000 francs or 100,000 crowns, but would be very difficult for sums like twelve or eighteen millions. Finally the hospices could be founded at no cost to the government and without the inhabitants of the provinces having to pay for assistance intended for the Paris poor, a tax which in some ways may be considered unjust.

Condorcet and the Hospitals of Paris

The transition of the hospital from an essentially confessional house of confinement, charity, and relief, to a public curative institution, organized and operated in accordance with innovations in science, medicine and public health, can be seen at work in France during the last two decades before the Revolution. The principal reform impulse focused on the Hôtel-Dieu of Paris. A disastrous fire at that hospital in 1772, which burned for eleven days and took a grisly toll of life and property, aroused the anger and resentment of Parisians against the horrors that prevailed there. Perhaps its most important consequence was to unite an impressive group of physicians, scientists, architects, philanthropists, philosophers, social reformers, and journalists into a protest movement that nearly succeeded in closing down the antediluvian "temple of death" at the end of the reign of Louis XV. Turgot and Necker later embarked on similar projects that foundered on opposition of powerful groups within the Hôtel-Dieu and within the magistracy.[2]

The most serious and promising attempt to reform the hospitals of Paris and the kingdom before the Revolution occurred between 1785 and 1788. The government, under the initiative of the Minister of the Royal Household, the Baron de Breteuil, and with the direct support of Louis XVI, acknowledged that no more time should be lost in ending the sacrifice of lives at the Hôtel-Dieu and to meet the health needs of the people in a new city hospital. It appointed a committee of nine distinguished scientists of the prestigious Royal Academy of Sciences whose initial charge was to evaluate the merits of proposals for a new Hôtel-Dieu. Chief among these was the architect Bernard Poyet's and C.-P. Coquêau's plan of a round edifice designed after the Roman Coliseum to accommodate 5,400 patients and to be built on the Ile des Cygnes (where the Eiffel Tower now stands).[3] The committee's authority was subsequently extended to the planning and construction of a new hospital system. Among its most active members were the astronomer and future Mayor of Paris, Jean-Sylvain Bailly, chairman, the brilliant chemist, farmer-general and humanitarian, Antoine Laurent Lavoisier, and the anatomist-surgeon and hospital specialist, Jacques Tenon.[4] These men and their colleagues had an extensive experience in Academy committees dealing with questions of public health including experience on a committee appointed by Necker to reform the prisons of the capital.[5] Their three reports embodied a conception of the sick man as citizen, equally entitled to the enjoyment of life, dignity, and health for his own sake and for society. The scientists affirmed the hospital as the key to an effective system of health provision, an instrument of medical instruction and study, and a model of hygienic improvement. They recommended abandoning the immense and abuse-ridden Hôtel-Dieu, at the doorstep of Notre-Dame Cathedral on the Ile de la

Cité, and the construction of four smaller hospitals in outlying sections of Paris. Enjoying wide publicity, their recommendations were enthusiastically received by all segments of public opinion and culminated in the law of June 22, 1787, which authorized the new Hôtel-Dieu and public subscriptions that raised 2.3 million livres in two months to defray building costs.

One of the responsibilities of the Academy committee was to solicit reform proposals. Condorcet's paper figured prominently among them.[6] The Marquis de Condorcet, permanent secretary of the Academy of Sciences, was well known for the broad sphere of his humanitarian concern and projects of social reform.[7] The opening sentence of his "Mémoire sur les hôpitaux," directed to his Academy colleagues, is a strong endorsement of their work for the success of future programs of medical care in France.

The Hôtel-Dieu, founded around 660, the oldest continually operating hospital in the world, was reviled by eighteenth-century Parisians as a house haunted by death. Far from being cured, the entering patient might perish from epidemics of typhus and puerperal fever which raged in that institution.[8] Huddled together in the same bed with two or three others afflicted with various communicable diseases, he was subjected to intolerable conditions of filth, stifling air, and neglect. Space and hygienic resources were woefully inadequate. The mortality of surgical and obstetric patients was terrifying.[9] The tiny medical staff of 131 physicians and surgeons (of whom 90 were surgical assistants) and 90 nurses[10] was grossly inadequate to the needs of 3,000 patients, a population larger than 84 percent of the towns of France.[11] With whatever crude medicine the teeming sick might be lucky enough to receive, and with the discovery of aseptic surgery and modern diagnostic methods still well in the future, little promise was held out for the cure of most ailments. The municipal hospital of Paris was thus reduced to an essentially custodial institution. To those who sought admission—the sick, disabled, homeless, unemployed, malnourished, ill-clad—the Hôtel-Dieu was the last refuge of desperation and despair.[12]

The terrible conditions that prevailed in the large hospitals of Paris and the provinces, and the need to reform them, were widely broadcast by 1789 by a mass of writings of *philosophes*, physiocrats, the *Encylopédie, traités de police*, legal dictionaries, royal edicts, crown commissions, prize-winning dissertations, the *commissions intermédiaires* of Provincial Assemblies, and the *cahiers* to the Estates General. Not surprisingly, the question whether hospitals should be done away with altogether was hotly debated. The mortality rate of 25 percent at the Paris Hôtel-Dieu, reputedly the highest in Europe,[13] shocked contemporaries.[14] The insalubrity of large hospitals was seen not only as a source of disease to those inside but a peril to the public health of the whole city.[15] Enjoying huge revenues from the inalienable holdings of the Church, they were held by critics to be expensive to operate, subject to enormous financial and administrative abuse, secretive, insensitive to criticism, and hostile to reform.[16] Hospital

wealth, economists like Du Pont de Nemours held, was also a wasteful, unproductive use of capital which in turn bred non-productivity, for instead of being
used to create work and relieve the suffering of families, it only multiplied
laziness and poverty.[17]

Out of dissatisfaction with the hospital, contemporaries settled on at least
two alternatives: home care and parish hospices. From the 1760s on, numerous
writers had advocated the elimination of hospitals altogether and the dehospitali-
zation of disease and poverty by medical assistance at home.[18] Common to all
these proposals was the affirmation that home care was more humane, healthier
and chapter than care at the hospital, promised greater therapeutic success free of
cross-infections, restored familial and social relationships in the natural domestic
environment, facilitated return to work (thereby discouraging beggary), and
involved the local citizenry in the responsibility of aiding their neighbors, as in
England and Holland.

As for parish hospices, the 1770s and 1780s saw the establishment of several
prominent institutions. The most notable, the Hospice de Charité, was founded
in 1778 by Mme Necker, wife of the Director-General of Finances, in the largest
parish of Paris, St. Sulpice, with the financial backing of the government and the
full support of the Archbishop of Paris and the enterprising curate, Faydit de
Tersac.[19] It was consciously founded as a model hospice, a therapeutic and
administrative alternative to the Hôtel-Dieu. Each of its 138 patients slept in
single beds. Although conditions of ventilation and space were far from ideal,
each patient was assured medical and nursing attention by a competent staff.
Each received balanced meals and proper medication in quiet surroundings at
a cost one-third less than at the Hôtel-Dieu and with nearly one-half less
mortality. Its administration was subject to public scrutiny by the annual
publication of financial and clinical records. During the next five years three
parish curates established similar hospices: the abbé Jean-Denis de Cochin at
St. Jacques du Haut-Pas, Desbois de Rochefort at St. André des Arts, and
Viennet at St. Merry. In 1784 the parish hospice of St. Philippe du Roule,
founded by the financier Beaujon, was placed under the direction of the local
curate. These four hospices, taken together with the teaching clinic of the
College of Surgery (1775), the venereal hospital of Vaugirard (1780), and the
Maison Royale de Santé (1781), representing more hospitals than were built in
the capital during the previous 130 years,[20] prompted the publicist Bachaumont
to remark that a veritable fever of hospital-building had overtaken Paris.[21]

Condorcet's memoir was, in the main, a response to the large monolith
hospital plan of Poyet-Coquéau. It supplemented Du Pont de Nemours' *Idées sur
la nature, la forme et l'étendue des secours à donner aux pauvres malades dans
une grande ville*,[22] solicited by the Academy hospital committee and published
through the good offices of one of its leading members, the chemist Lavoisier,
and available to Condorcet in manuscript.[23] Like Du Pont, he would abandon

the large hospital with all its ills in favor of forty parish hospices. And like the distinguished physiocrat, whose economic views he shared, Condorcet saw medical assistance as the obligation of neighborhood constituencies.

Condorcet's ideas must be judged in the context of hospital reformers who, after the 1772 fire, would refashion the hospital from scratch.[24] The therapeutic needs of the sick man and the commanding requirements of health-delivery along rational and technical lines would dictate the hospital's architecture, size, policy, staffing, and management. In evidence throughout his plan is the analytical, statistical, quantifiable rigor of Condorcet's justly famous "social mathematics."[25] The plan followed closely on the publication of his classic *Essai sur l'application de l'analyse à la probabilité des décisions rendues à la pluralité des voix* (1785). Initially Condorcet addressed himself to two questions raised by Poyet and deliberated by the Academy committee: hospital size and mortality. Hospitals of the seventeenth and eighteenth centuries like the Hôtel-Dieu, the Invalides, Bicêtre, and Salpêtrière were vast structures whose administrators admitted maximum numbers of sick and homeless. They had not been planned in any modern sense in regard to medicine or the role of the physician. Their organization and services were not regulated by diagnostic or therapeutic principles, and there was no controlled ratio of medical, technical, and support personnel to the sick. A decisive change began to emerge in the second half of the eighteenth century, due in large measure to improvements in French surgery. Clinical methods being taught by eminent physicians like Desbois de Rochefort and Corvisart and surgeons like Desault produced greater agreement that the hospital was the only acceptable teaching center for physicians and surgeons. The "medicine of observation" and the Hippocratic revival led by Vicq d'Azyr, Cabanis, and Pinel contributed to reform of the hospital in accord with clinical and pathological innovations.

Condorcet's first proposal must be taken in this context. How determine the size of a hospital, he asked, between the extremes of the enormous Hôtel-Dieu and the private room of the rich man, that would be best suited to the care of the largest number of sick at least cost? The size of wards and ultimately of the hospital itself should be computed by the number of patients whose needs can be met effectively by a single doctor, nurse, pharmacist, and kitchen and service staff in accord with measurable standards of health-care, hygiene, and comfort exclusive of administration or the assignment of additional physicians and surgeons as needed. This idea bears a striking resemblance to the administrative procedures of military hospitals, which assigned a given ratio of physicians and support staff to patients.[26] The precedents of military medicine were widely hailed by contemporary reformers like Chamousset, Cabanis, Tenon, Chambon de Montaux, and others as models for civil hospital reform.[27] In July 1787 Jean Colombier, general inspector of civil hospitals and prisons, would institute these innovations at the Hôtel-Dieu.[28]

With a determinable number of beds in such a hospital, at a given capital investment and annual maintenance expense, the cost of increasing beds without sacrifice of quality can then be computed. The reduction of health-care to monetary cost per patient or per bed Condorcet judged the least fallible way to make decisions, to measure the extent of defects of large hospitals, and to judge the effectiveness of their management.

The second question involved mortality. One of the decisive arguments against the Hôtel-Dieu, as has already been observed, was its mortality rate. Insofar as a significant number of patients admitted to the Hôtel-Dieu were in advanced stages of illness, Condorcet observed, this would alter the validity of the statistics upon which mortality had been computed. The only statistically valid basis of measuring death is by morbidity tables.[29] The net effect of such a method might yield different results and diminish the gravity of charges leveled against the Hôtel-Dieu,[30] since its excessive mortality may be the function of the kinds of disease admitted to the hospital[31] or the effect of hospital contagion on diverse ailments.

The remainder of the memoir is a strong defense of the parish hospice. Many of the familiar arguments and contemporary prejudices against large health establishments are imaginatively reformulated by Condorcet or given a quantitative foundation. The errors of big hospitals are always serious and hard to overcome. Reform is difficult because abuses find powerful protectors. Poyet's assertion—in support of a single Hôtel-Dieu under one chief—that it would be nearly impossible to find fifty men of sufficient ability to administer parish hospices is false, since the same talent is required of one head and fifty assistants. The administration of a large health institution is as difficult to evaluate as it is to run. Since there is no real way to judge administrators, and since public opinion alternately praises and blames, they become insensitive to popular scrutiny. But with many administrations instead of a single one, useful "competition and emulation" would result. Because they were small, hospices would be easier to evaluate and would serve as vehicles of comparison. Public opinion could more effectively serve as judge and check. The same competition and emulation between the administration of each hospice would be reinforced by a similar competition between inhabitants of each parish. Enlightened one by the other, where each would stand to profit from the experience of all, errors are more quickly detected and corrected, improvements more prompt. No prevailing large hospital, Condorcet asserted, could boast of these advantages.

If the hospice was easier to run and less prone to abuse, it was also easier to get built. On the means to establish the parish hospice Condorcet reveals at once the most interesting and idealistic part of his plan. Giving another form to Du Pont's thesis of self-help and state non-intervention,[32] he restated Turgot's policy of making hospital relief and assistance the responsibility of local jurisdiction.[33] There is not a single parish of Paris which does not contain rich men, architects, mathematicians capable of judging architectural plans, physicians, surgeons, physicists, lawyers, businessmen, bureaucrats, men who have studied "the theory of political science." The parish curate should be the intermediary of these men and the initiating force of the hospice. He would call together men of the neighborhood from whom the most expertise and aid could be expected. A committee would draw up a plan of a hospice most suited to the needs of the parish. The plan would then be submitted to the local populace for evaluation and discussion and revised in accord with their observations. Supposing men to be animated by a very pure beneficence, by the satisfaction of participating in a common effort, and by mobilizing skills "in one of the cities where there has never been more," the hospice would be assured prompt and more considerable aid. Local participation and responsibility for medical assistance were hardly new with Condorcet, yet the grass-roots, democratic collaboration of multidisciplinary specialists for the realization of a hospice suitable to the needs of a local constituency and subject to its ratification through the mechanism of community participation is highly original. The hospice, the fruit of harmonious interaction of planners and populace, is an instance of Condorcet's faith in representative institutions.

Alluding to Du Pont's proposed forty parish hospices, Condorcet considered it very likely that they would cost no more than Poyet's single building, but that they could be more easily built and more quickly completed. The raising of cash from pledges payable on the death of donors, personal estate, life or term annuities would be easy for sums of 100,000–300,000 francs (the cost of building the hospice), but very difficult to raise 12 or 18 million livres (the cost of Poyet's Hôtel-Dieu). Finally the hospices could be established without cost to the government and without unjustly taxing the provinces for the exclusive aid of the Paris poor.

A logical development of Condorcet's hospice plan may be seen in his *Essai sur la constitution et les fonctions des assemblées provinciales* (1788).[34] Here he favored home care as appropriate to the rural population, most of whom had a dwelling place. In cities "where most poor live in severely crowded dwellings, often separated from their family," hospitals were necessary to assure the provision of medical care, medicine, proper food, and rest. As in 1786, Condorcet dismissed large establishments (which "almost always produce great abuses, and great abuses always find powerful protectors") in favor of hospices. Their size would be determined by the number of sick that a single physician could treat and whose administration and inspection a single official could assure. The hospice would retain the advantages of the hospital in separating accident, surgical, or obstetrical cases from cases of contagious disease without the "inevitable drawbacks of every large institution." Condorcet called on the representatives of the Provincial Assemblies to reform the abuses of the hospital, which he enumerated: an uncritical respect for the wishes of founders (recalling

Turgot's argument in the *Encyclopédie* against endowments), monastic ideals, the corporate spirit, long-perpetuated prejudices, and senseless routine.

How did the Academy committee respond to Condorcet?[35] It reviewed each of the three possible health systems: home, hospice, and hospital. Home-care was impracticable for the many indigent sick without homes or for those packed into attics unsuited to medical treatment for whom adequate attention, food, and medication could not be assured.

Parish hospices newly constructed in Paris and modelled on the exemplary "order, cleanliness and economy" of Mme Necker's Charité, served a useful function to the health needs of Paris neighborhoods. With nothing but praise for these hospices, their founders and supporters, and the superior treatment accorded the sick (making "the small hospital resemble a family whose children are treated by their parents"), the committee rejected it as the sole means of health delivery. Since existing parish hospices were housed for the most part in old ecclesiastical buildings, poorly arranged and lacking adequate space, they threatened to degenerate into miniature Hôtels-Dieu, incorporating all their vices, "a source of misfortune and a spectacle of misery" in each quarter of the city. Since there was no practical means of correcting these shortcomings, the Academy favored building anew. But there was no way to secure enough land in each parish to construct buildings large enough to assure minimum health standards and to separate patients with contagious disease from the sick and convalescing, contrary to Condorcet's assertion that they were large enough to accommodate the full spectrum of ailments including the isolation of contagion.

The hospices had other serious drawbacks. During years of epidemics, nothing short of large establishments could accommodate the vast numbers from Paris and its environs seeking relief. Since the hospice by definition was closed to all outside the parish, only a municipal hospital could continue to admit patients from outside the metropolitan area where vast numbers of workers lived. Many patients, ashamed of their poverty and wishing to escape the humiliation of being recognized by their neighbors in the local hospice, preferred the anonymity of the hospital. Only the large hospital could provide a maternity ward to accommodate unwed mothers deserving rehabilitation, without betraying their identity. Nor could the hospice provide either the facilities or the staff of skilled surgeons and physicians necessary for the treatment of the insane, or for surgical operations like lithotomy and trepan, caesarian section, removal of cataract, and amputation of limbs. Only in a general hospital were the poor assured of all the advantages of the rich. Because the hospices did not usually admit contagious diseases, only large institutions could accommodate contagion wards. In fine, only the hospital held the advantage of being able to plan for and meet the health needs of the entire community.

The hospice, for all its drawbacks in the eyes of the Academy scientists, proved a crucial element in their formulation of a distinctly original architectural hospital form—the pavilion building—intended as a "separate and isolated" ward, to be adopted all over France, Europe, and America in the nineteenth and twentieth centuries.[36] Consisting of ten pavilion units of 120 patients, their projected 1,200-bed hospital would lie half way between the large Hôtel-Dieu of Poyet and the single hospice advocated by Condorcet. Each of the pavilions would be in fact, an improved hospice. Functional in design, it was to be built according to medical, physical, and engineering principles on spacious grounds, assuring abundant air, light, water, and waste removal. Patients would enjoy their own beds in large wards, clinically organized and rationally administered, surrounded by pleasant arrangements of covered walks, gardens, and trees.

The early Revolution endorsed the propositions of local aid advanced by Condorcet and Du Pont. The Committee on Mendicity of the Constituent Assembly under its chairman, the noted philanthropist and humanitarian, the Duc de la Rochefoucauld-Liancourt, endorsed home-care in preference to hospitalization through a system of *maisons communales de malades.* These were to replace the hospital and be financed after November 1789 from the proceeds of sequestered ecclesiastical property, including a portion of the hospital domain, that was now proclaimed the patrimony of the nation.[37] Recourse to the hospital proved inevitable. With the aggravated economic, political, and religious crises of the Revolution, with its properties systematically sold off, and with drastically reduced revenues and personnel, the hospital, operating under local and regional jurisdiction, became nationalized and secularized by the Convention.[38] The policy of national administration of hospitals and government protection of health had already been advocated by the hospital committee of the Academy of Sciences, and in part legislated in 1787. The main lines of French national health policy, adumbrated in the *ancien régime* and reinforced by collaborative efforts of the state and communal authorities in the support and direction of hospitals after the Directorate and Consulate, would survive into the modern period.[39]

Notes

*A broader study by the present writer, "Health-Care and Hospital-Building in Eighteenth-Century France: Reform Proposals of Du Pont de Nemours and Condorcet," *Studies on Voltaire and the Eighteenth Century* 152 (1976): 895–930 develops the impact of physiocratic theory in the matter of hospitals and welfare and its influence on Condorcet.

1. The *Mémoire sur les hôpitaux* appears neither in Condorcet's collected works nor among his manuscripts deposited in the library of the Institut de France. A copy was found in the papers of Jacques Tenon in 1970, quite likely the one, or a copy of the one used by the hospital committee of the Paris Academy of Sciences (J. Tenon, *Mémoires sur les hôpitaux de Paris* [Paris, 1788], p. xii), Bibliothèque Nationale de France (Paris), Manuscrits, nouvelles acquisitions françaises, 22136, fols. 144–48. The present translation is taken from this manuscript rather than from the first printed version of A. Tzonis, "Un

'Mémoire sur les hôpitaux' de Condorcet," (*Dix-Huitième Siècle* [1977], 109–14) whose provenance is erroneously cited as B.N., n.a.f., 22116.

2. L. S. Greenbaum, "Scientists and Politicians: Hospital Reform in Paris on the Eve of the French Revolution," *The Consortium on Revolutionary Europe, 1750–1850, Proceedings 1973* (Gainesville, 1975), 168–91.

3. *Mémoire sur la nécessité de transférer et reconstruire l'Hôtel-Dieu de Paris suivi d'un projet de translation de cet hôpital, proposé par le Sieur Poyet* (Paris, 1785), 44 pp.

4. L. S. Greenbaum, "Jean-Sylvain Bailly, the Baron de Breteuil and the 'Four New Hospitals' of Paris," *Clio Medica* 8 (1973): 261–84.

5. L. S. Greenbaum, "'The Commercial Treaty of Humanity.' La tournée des hôpitaux anglais par Jacques Tenon en 1787," *Revue d'Histoire des Sciences* 24 (1971): 319–20.

6. Others are cited in Greenbaum, "Bailly, the Baron de Breteuil," 268.

7. L. Cahen, *Condorcet et la Révolution française* (Paris, 1904); H. Delsaux, *Condorcet journaliste* (Paris, 1931); Janine Bouissounouse, *Condorcet. Le philosophe dans la Révolution* (Paris, 1962); R. Reichardt, *Reform und Révolution bei Condorcet* (Bonn, 1973).

8. J. Tenon, *Mémoires sur les hôpitaux de Paris* (Paris, 1788), 196–98, 284.

9. Ibid., 260, 269.

10. Ibid., 303–4. For the enormous power exercised by religious nurses within the hospital cf. L. S. Greenbaum, "Nurses and Doctors in Conflict: Piety and Medicine in the Paris Hôtel-Dieu on the Eve of the French Revolution," *Clio Medica* 13 (1979): 247–67.

11. A. Soboul, *La France à la veille de la Révolution. Economie et Société* (Paris, 1974), 65.

12. J.-F. Marmontel, *La voix des pauvres. Epitre au roi sur l'incendie de l'Hôtel-Dieu* (Paris, 1773).

13. Tenon, *Mémoires sur les hôpitaux de Paris*, 278.

14. Mallet du Pan, *Mercure de France*, 11 février 1786, 63; F. M. von Grimm, *Correspondance littéraire, philosophique et critique* (Paris, 1882), 14:297–300; S. P. Hardy, "Mes loisirs ou journal d'événemens, tels qu'ils parviennent à ma connaissance," Bibliothèque Nationale, Manuscrits, Vol. 6, fol. 501.

15. *Extrait des registres de l'Académie royale des Sciences du 22 novembre 1786. Rapport des commissaires chargés. par l'Académie, de l'examen du projet d'un nouvel Hôtel-Dieu* (Paris, 1786), 40.

16. C. H. Piarron de Chamousset, "Exposition d'un plan proposé pour les malades de l'Hôtel-Dieu" (1754), *Oeuvres* (Paris, 1783), 1:135–52; [Régnier], *Projet d'un hopital de malades ou hôtel-Dieu* (Paris, 1776), 12–14; [Abbé de Malvaux], *Résumé des mémoires qui ont concouru pour le prix accordé en l'année 1777 par l'Académie de Chaalons-sur-Marne et dont le sujet étoit les moyens de détruire la mendicité en France, en rendant les mendiants utiles à l'Etat sans les rendre malheureux* (Châlons, 1779), 75–94; Abbé de Recalde, *Traité sur les abus out subsistent dans les hôpitaux du royaume et les moyens propres à les réformer* (Paris, 1786), 4–21; Rondonneau de La Motte, *Essai historique sur l'hôtel-Dieu de Paris* (Paris, 1787), 131–225.

17. "Analyses et critiques raisonnées: *Encyclopédie économique*," *Ephémérides du Citoyen* 11 (1771): 167; Cf. G. Schelle, *Du Pont de Nemours et l'école physiocratique* (Paris, 1888), 118.

18. Among these were the physiocrat abbé Baudeau, founder of the *Ephémérides du Citoyen*; the commission of mendicity named by minister Turgot in 1774 and placed under the direction of his friend, Loménie de Brienne, Archbishop of Toulouse; various authors competing for the prize of the Academy of Châlons in 1777 on the best ways to reduce mendicity; minister Necker; the populationist Montyon; the novelist and follower of Rousseau, Bernardin de Saint Pierre. (Greenbaum, "Health-Care and Hospital-Building...Du Pont de Nemours and Condorcet," 902–3.

19. Necker, *Administration des Finances* (Paris, 1784), 3:186–90; R. Gervais, *Histoire de l'hôpital Necker, 1778–1885* (Paris, 1885); V. Bindel, "Les origines de l'hôpital Necker. L'hospice de Charité de Saint Sulpice, 1778–1792," *Bull. de la Soc. d'hist. et d'Archéol. des*

VIIe et VIIIe Arrond. de Paris 37 (1938): 184-96.

20. Tenon, *Mémoires sur les hôpitaux de Paris*, 3-25.

21. L. P. Bachaumont, *Mémoires secrets pour servir à l'histoire de la république des lettres en France depuis 1762 jusqu'à nos jours* (1973), cited by D. Mornet, *Les origines intellectuelles de la Révolution française* (Paris, 1954), 266

22. Paris, 1786, 64 pp.

23. Greenbaum, "Health-Care and Hospital-Building...Du Pont de Nemours and Condorcet," 906, 921.

24. This paragraph is based on L. S. Greenbaum, "Tempest in the Academy: Jean-Baptiste Le Roy, the Paris Academy of Sciences and the Project of a new Hôtel-Dieu," *Archives Internationales d'Histoire des Sciences* 24 (1974): 122-40; L. S. Greenbaum, "'Measure of Civilization': The Hospital Thought of Jacques Tenon on the Eve of the French Revolution," *Bulletin of the History of Medicine* 49 (1975): 43-56. The pre-Revolutionary hospital question has recently been taken up by Michel Foucault and a group of co-workers, *Les machines à guérir: aux origines de l'hôpital moderne* (Paris, 1976). On the background of eighteenth-century French surgery cf. T. Gelfand, *Professionalizing Modern Medicine: Paris Surgeons and Medical Science and Institutions in the 18th Century*, forthcoming from Greenwood Press.

25. G.-G. Granger, *La mathématique sociale du marquis de Condorcet* (Paris, 1956); Keith Michael Baker, *Condorcet. From Natural Philosophy to Social Mathematics* (Chicago, 1975), 186-94 and passim.

26. *Ordonnance du roi portant règlement général concernant les hôpitaux militaires du 2 mai 1781* (Paris, 1781), 192 pp.

27. "Mémoire sur les hôpitaux militaires," *Oeuvres complettes de M. de Chamousset*, Abbé Cotton des Houssayes, ed. (Paris, 1773), 2: 1-24; Cabanis, *Observations sur les hôpitaux* (Paris, 1790), 20-29; Tenon, *Mémoires sur les hôpitaux de Paris*, 324-27; Chambon de Montaux, *Moyens de rendre les hôpitaux plus utiles à la nation* (Paris, 1787), 97-100; Dulaurens, *Essai sur les établissements nécessaires et les moins dispendieux pour rendre le service des malades dans les hôpitaux vraiment utile à l'humanité* (Paris, 1787), 37-51. Cf. M. Foucault, *The Birth of the Clinic. An Archaeology of Medical Perception*, A. Smith, trans. (New York, 1973), 28-30.

28. L. S. Greenbaum, "Science, Medicine, Religion: Three Views of Health-Care in France on the Eve of the French Revolution," forthcoming in *Studies in Eighteenth-Century Culture*, Volume 10.

29. For the modernity of this view and impact of statistical studies on medicine and public health, cf. R. H. Shryock, "The History of Quantification in Medical Science," *Isis* 52 (1961): 215-37 and *Development of Modern Medicine* (New York, 1969), 135-44; G. Rosen, *A History of Public Health* (New York, 1958), 111-14.

30. This argument was advanced by defenders of the hospital: [Chaumont de La Millière], *Rélevè des principales erreurs contenues dans le mémoire relatif à la translation de l'Hôtel-Dieu, et l'examen du projet du sieur Poyet cui est à la suite* (1785), 6.

31. The Academy committee denied this as being typical of all hospitals, attributing the unprecedented mortality of the Hôtel-Dieu to the effects of unparalleled overcrowding, vitiated air, and lack of space (*Rapport des commissaires...* pp. 77-78).

32. Greenbaum, "Health-Care and Hospital-Building...Du Pont de Nemours and Condorcet," 912.

33. The "Mémoire sur les municipalités" (1775) was written at the behest of Turgot (*Oeuvres de Turgot*, G. Schelle, ed. (Paris, 1922), 4: 568-621, (Paris, 1919), 3: 205-19); Condorcet, *Vie de Turgot* (1786) in *Oeuvres de Condorcet*, ed. Arthur C. O'Connor and Marie F. Arago, 12 vols. (Paris, 1847-1849), 5:140. Du Pont developed these same ideas under the patronage of Calonne for presentation to the Assembly of Notables. (*Procès-verbal de l'assemblée des notables tenue à Versailles en l'année 1787* (Paris, 1788), 104-7. Cf. Greenbaum, "Health-Care and Hospital-Building...Du Pont de Nemours and Condorcet," p. 912).

34. *Oeuvres de Condorcet* 8:115-622, esp. 460-68 and "Sur les caisses d'accumulation" (1790), 11:389-403.

35. *Rapport des commissaires...du 22 novembre 1786*, 99-105.

36. A. Chassagne, *Hygiène hospitalière. Les hôpitaux sans étages et à pavillions isolés* (Paris, 1878), 19–30; C. Tollet, *Les édifices hospitaliers depuis leur origine jusqu'à nos jours* (Paris, 1892), 222; P. Vallery-Radot, *Deux siècles d'histoire hospitalière* (Paris, 1947), 51–53; E. Wickersheimer, *Les édifices hospitaliers à travers les ages* (Paris, 1953), 23.

37. *Procès-verbaux et rapports du comité de mendicité de la constituante, 1790–1791*, C. Bloch and A. Tuetey, eds. (Paris, 1911), 395–96.

38. J. Imbert, *Le droit hospitalier de la Révolution et l'Empire* (Paris, 1954), 67–102.

39. J. Imbert, *Les hôpitaux en France* (Paris, 1958), 36–39.

7

Condorcet and Progressive Taxation: Theory and Practice

Jean A. Perkins

In the very first issue of the short-lived *Journal d'instruction sociale*, June 1, 1793, there appeared a short article by Condorcet entitled "Sur l'impôt progressif" in which he outlined what was meant by such a term, delineated his version of the Physiocrats' single tax on the net income from land, and then proceeded to investigate the justification for and utility of a progessive tax on personal wealth. The concluding section treats the actual situation in France during 1793, arguing in favor of a sharply rising rate on a forced loan, a fiscal measure often used during the French Revolution whereby all income or property above a certain level was confiscated by the government with a promise to repay with interest at a later date. That Condorcet should have written such an article is not surprising. From 1776 until 1790 he served as *Inspecteur général de la Monnaie*, advising the various finance ministers on the subject of public finance. When fiscal matters became most confused in 1790, Louis XVI named Condorcet as one of six members of the influential Treasury Committee, which reported its findings to the Constituent Assembly. He continued to be one of the most respected figures in the National Convention until he, along with most of the Girondin deputies, was eliminated by Robespierre and his supporters.[1]

Condorcet's conclusion in 1793, which advocated both a ceiling below which no taxes should be levied and a sharply rising rate as income increased, is most surprising in view of his open attack on the principle of progression in his *Essai sur les assemblées provinciales* (1788). A great deal had happened in that five-year interval; the surging force of events during the French Revolution compelled Condorcet to consider certain practical considerations of his theory of taxation; his shift in economic terms is parallel to a similar development in his political ideas.

We can do no better than follow the pattern that Condorcet established in his article, beginning with definitions and theoretical considerations and moving step by step toward the actual practices and reforms that were suggested and sometimes put into effect during the tumultuous years of the French Revolution. However, a quote fron Gunnar Myrdal's perceptive work, *The Political Element in the Development of Economic Theory*, is in order before we start:

> All normative economic doctrines are largely rationalizations of political attitudes and in the theory of public finance probably even more than elsewhere because stronger political pressures are at work here....It is characteristic of the theory that concrete conclusions of all types can be and have in fact been derived from any set of principles.[2]

In this field, theory and practice are inextricably intertwined and we delude ourselves if we assume that theory is basic and practice logically derived from it.

Starting with a definition of the term *progressive taxation*, we find that even here there is some confusion. Most people, both today and two hundred years ago, assume that a progressive tax is one in which the rate increases as taxable income increases. However this is not necessarily the only form of progressive taxation. In mathematical terms the distinction between a *proportional* and a *progressive* tax is based on the ratio between the amount of the tax and the amount taxed. If the ratio remains the same, you have a proportional tax; if the ratio increases as the taxable base increases, that is, if the tax represents a larger proportion of taxable income, you have a progressive tax.[3] One way to raise the ratio, of course, is to increase the rate as the amount taxed increases, but the same effect can be obtained by holding the rate steady and changing the amount assessed, imposing the same rate on a smaller amount. This is Condorcet's first argument in "Sur l'impôt progressif." He starts with the assumption that all forms of personal income are to be taxed and that a subsistence level will be exempted from everyone's tax base:

> Let's assume this necessary part to be £400 and that there is a proportional tax of 1/20th on the remaining part; the person with £800 will pay 1/20th of £400 or £20; that is to say 1/40th of the total; the person with £2400 will pay £100 or 1/24th of the total and so on. This gives us a proportional tax on the portion of the income over £400 but progressive on the whole.[4]

Technically this is a progressive tax based on a higher *average rate*, whereas increasing the rate would give you a higher *marginal rate*.

In terms of the justification of taxes, two theories dominate the field and reflect different ways of looking at the problem. If you start from the expenditure side of the tax system, the major justification relies on the benefits the individual taxpayer receives from the state in return for his financial contribution. Over the years this has been called the *benefit theory*, the *interest principle*, and the *quid pro quo system*, and it dominated eighteenth-century discussions of taxation. Under the influence of the natural law school and the social contract theory, it was natural to assume that payment of taxes was justified as the price for services rendered by the state, the primary one being the protection of the citizen and his property.[5] If you start from the income side, the major justification for taxes relies on the *ability-to-pay principle*, also often referred to as the *faculty theory*. Acccording to this view, the most important factor is the individual's ability to contribute toward the common costs; taxes are viewed as a necessary contribution to the good of the whole society.[6] In France the ability-to-pay doctrine became more important as the eighteenth century progressed, and it was openly invoked during the French Revolution.

Either the benefit or the ability-to-pay theory can, and often has, led to the principle of progressive taxation. Starting from the benefit principle, it can be argued that certain wants, technically known as *merit wants*, are more pertinent to particular groups within the society, most especially to the rich.[7] Starting from the ability-to-pay principle, it seems obvious that the rich can afford more taxes than the poor, but the justification of a progressive rate from this principle remained rather unsophisticated until the principle of equality of sacrifice entered the discussion.[8] Economic historians credit John Stuart Mill with inventing the principle of equal sacrifice. As we shall see, eighteenth-century French writers made use of a primitive form of this argument. Modern versions of the ability-to-pay theory draw their justification from the principle of income redistribution, a justification that became popular during the French Revolution. Many eighteenth-century theorists confused the progressive tax rate with sumptuary laws designed to discourage luxury, and they applied the progressive principle to the many indirect taxes on consumer goods that had been levied under the *ancien régime*.

Even today the issue of *indirect* versus *direct* taxes remains of interest; some theorists argue that indirect taxes are less painful and less noticed than direct ones and that this offsets the so-called *shifting effect* whereby the tax burden is eventually transferred through various price adjustments to someone else.[9] Shifting is one of the major objections leveled by the Physiocrats against the horde of indirect taxes of the *ancien régime*.

No one can ignore the central position of fiscal problems in eighteenth-century France, and failure to resolve this question was one of the major causes of the French Revolution.[10] Underlying all the tensions was the assumption that taxes should only be imposed in extraordinary situations, such as times of war.[11] At no time during the eighteenth century was a tax imposed on the basis of the regular on-going expenses of the state; indeed, in 1749, when Machault d'Arnouville, Minister of Finance, attempted to impose the *vingtième* on everybody, the privileged groups objected to being included, but a more general objection was raised to the imposition of a tax in peacetime. Until 1788, the King and his ministers were able to contain the opposition from various privileged groups and to impose new taxes, but they were forced to rely more and more heavily on loans to finance the affairs of state. By the time of the Revolution, the debt service came to almost one-half of the total expenses of the state.

During the period from mid-century to the French Revolution, interest in fiscal matters increased immensely and the number of books and pamphlets on the topic are legion. Right in the middle of this debate are the Physiocrats.[12] Quesnay wrote an article on taxes for the *Encyclopédie* but withdrew it during the 1759 troubles. In 1760 Mirabeau père published his *Théorie de l'impôt*, and his sharp attack on the General Farm led to his imprisonment and subsequent exile from Paris. By the time he published *La Philosophie rurale* in 1763, he and Quesnay had worked out the general theory of Physiocracy, including a stand on taxes. It is easy enough to state their goal in taxation: a single tax to be levied on the net profit of the land and to be paid in its entirety by the land-owners.[13] Their belief that agriculture is the only really productive enterprise justified this tax policy. According to them, no other source of revenue has a clear-cut annual rate of reproduction and no other segment of the economy can produce a clear-cut profit. Industry and commerce merely recirculate the wealth generated by agriculture, and so any tax on revenue from industry, financial speculation, commercial activity or on consumer goods would eventually be shifted back to the real source of wealth, agriculture. The limitation of the assessed base to the so-called *produit net*, or clear profit, made it possible for all costs, including capital investment, to be excluded from the tax base. In addition the farmer who actually works the land is protected since only landowners would pay the tax. The Physiocrats worked out a political as well as an economic justification of taxation: ever since the establishment of the state, the sovereign has been a co-proprietor of the nation with the landowners. The state was established to ensure the safety of property and thus, according to the benefit theory, landowners give up part of their net revenue in order to be able to continue producing wealth for themselves and the nation. From the point of view of a developing interest in progressive taxation, these theories are not very promising since both Quesnay and Mirabeau insisted that taxes should be levied proportionally to the landowner's net revenue. A fixed rate of no more than 30 percent of the *produit net* over a long period of time would enable taxes to be reflected in long-term leases of land. Many Physiocrats elaborated a theory to prove that no one would actually be paying this tax since the sales price of land would reflect the new owner's tax obligation. However it is clear that switching over to this tax system would not be easy, since current landowners would suddenly find themselves having to pay taxes on their farmers' rent payments. It is no wonder that the Physiocrats made so little headway on this particular item in their list of practical reforms.

Condorcet's political mentor, Turgot, was a follower of the Physiocrats when it came to fiscal policy. Responding to a request from Bertin, Minister of Finance from 1759 to 1763, Turgot as Intendant of the Limousin stated his belief in the Physiocrats' tax policy:

> Who owes taxes? It has been proved that they are only owed by land-owners, because they are the only ones who earn a net revenue which it is possible to assess.[14]

But Turgot acknowledges that he is talking about the best of all possible worlds and concludes that it would not be feasible to introduce such a policy, especially since this would leave the government isolated against everyone else.[15] Obviously Turgot did not subscribe to the political theory of the co-proprietorship of the nation between the king and the landowners. As a government administrator he took a much more practical view of political realities. During his ministry Turgot made no attempt to introduce any sweeping tax changes, but his edict abolishing the *corvée* and replacing it by a tax on land to be paid by all land-owners was sufficiently radical to contribute to his downfall.

In his *La Vie de M. Turgot* (1786) Condorcet repeated Turgot's arguments in favor of a proportional tax on agricultural profits to be paid by the landowner, and then went on to note that the main obstacle in the way of such a tax was the lack of an accurate land-survey and that, in any case, it is better to do things slowly.[16] But as far as theory is concerned, Condorcet was completely in accord with the Physiocrats as can be clearly seen in his *Essai sur les assemblées provinciales* (1788). He notes that there are only three sources of revenue: from land, from salaries, and from interest on capital. He first destroys the assumption that a tax on salaries would be desirable by arguing that salaries are fixed by the needs of those paying and those paid; therefore the imposition of a tax on salaries would automatically raise salaries and vice versa. Approximately the same argument is used about a tax on unearned income: what would really happen is a reduction in the interest rate. This leaves only the revenue from land as a true source of taxable wealth and in connection with this tax Condorcet makes an open attack on the principle of progression:

> It is not just for richer citizens to contribute according to a higher ratio, or for those with larger properties to pay according to a higher proportion, because property is an advantage independent of work, and in order to conserve it, it is just to contribute only proportionally to what it is worth.[17]

By 1788, Condorcet evidently felt it was necessary to argue against progressive taxes, something that never occurred to either Quesnay or Mirabeau. Many of the theories in favor of progressive taxation had been developed by writers arguing against the Physiocrats' single tax on land.

Three different approaches to progressive taxation can be distinguished. In the first place, some writers insisted on the necessity of exempting a certain subsistence level; secondly, a smaller group advocated the imposition of a progressive rate above that subsistence level; and finally there were the holdouts for indirect taxes who thought that different commodities should be taxed at varying rates according to their utility or superfluity. The concept of a basic exemption was fairly widespread. Indeed, the Physiocrats subsumed such an idea within their theory since the *produit net*, the base on which a land tax would rest, already excluded the subsistence of all farm workers, and of course no one else but landowners was to pay taxes. Montesquieu analyzed the earliest known example of a progressive tax, the Athenian tax on the net produce of land which was imposed on the Athenian population divded into four different classes, each paying a different rate. Montesquieu justified the principle of progression on the basis of differing needs of different groups:

> This tax was just even though it was not proportional; even if it did not follow the proportion of wealth, it followed the proportion of needs. It was decided that everyone has the same physical necessities that should not be taxed; that the useful comes next which should be taxed but less than the superfluous; that the size of the tax on the superfluous level would be enough to prevent it.[18]

His argument is based on the ability-to-pay principle, the fact that there is less sacrifice involved in giving up luxuries than in giving up necessities. But Montesquieu was not really in favor of taxes on individuals or their income; he explicitly stated that a tax on items consumed is more in keeping with the principle of liberty and is preferable because it is less noticeable.[19] Rousseau also came out bluntly in favor of a subsistence-level exemption in his *Encyclopédie* article "Economie politique" (1755): "The person who has only the basic necessities should not pay anything at all."[20]

Much less frequent was the justification for a progressive rate. Rousseau is almost always cited as an advocate of progressive rates, but this is true only if the *Considérations sur le gouvernement de Pologne* are ignored. In this work he cites a contemporary example of a progressive tax, the Genevan tax known as *payer les gardes*, imposed as a permanent fixture in 1709 with rates of .5 percent for the first 10,000 *écus* and 1 percent beyond that.[21] When he came to make suggestions about actual taxes for Poland, Rousseau advocated a return to taxes in kind, for instance the *corvée*, and clearly favored a proportional tax on land to be paid by all landowners.[22] In the more theoretical "Economie politique," he outlined most of the arguments in favor of a progressive rate without ever actually coming out in favor of it.[23] A much clearer defense of progressive rates occurs in Jaucourt's *Encyclopédie* article "Impôts," which follows Montesquieu's arguments on the distinctions between the amount of sacrifice involved in giving up necessities rather than luxuries and actually advocates a graduated personal tax which he outlines as following "a geometric progression, two, four, eight, sixteen on the well-to-do."[24] Jaucourt also follows Montesquieu in preferring indirect to direct taxes.

One of the more sophisticated exponents of progressive taxation was Graslin. In his *Essai analytique sur la richesse et sur l'impôt* (1767) he argued most strenuously against the Physiocrats' conception of land being the only real source of wealth and supported taxing all revenue on a progressive basis. Starting from the benefit principle, Graslin notes that taxes are paid in order to obtain protection and that the rich man has more to be protected than a man in comfortable circumstances. Switching to the ability-to-pay principle, he argues from a psychological point of view that the sacrifice made by a rich man has less value than that of a poorer man. What a rich man gives up is worth progressively less the richer he gets; hence the tax rate must grow progressively faster than the comfort of the taxpayer.[25]

As an example of the many theorists who argued that indirect taxes on consumer goods should be taxed at varying rates according to the level of need for the individual item, let us cite Forbonnais, who claimed in his *Principes et observations économiques* (1767) that no single tax base would produce sufficient revenue for the state, necessitating a combination of a land-tax with a series of consumption taxes varying in rate according to the product taxed. Indirect taxes were just about the first to disappear during the French Revolution, and Condorcet never once advocated them, so we need not return to this particular subject.

By June 1793 Condorcet had moved a long way from his outright condemnation of the progressive principle that he had enunciated so firmly five years earlier. "Sur l'impôt progressif" is tightly constructed in four distinct sections. In the first section [pp. 625-627] Condorcet defines his terms, noting that a proportional tax can be imposed on material goods but that a progressive tax is always personal since it makes a difference who owns the goods. His first example of a personal tax is the Physiocratic tax on the net revenue from land; along with most of the Physiocrats, Condorcet argues that this tax is not paid by anyone since it would be included in the value of the land at the time of inheritance or purchase. He implies that this is the very best type of tax as long as it is in effect over a long period of time and on a regular basis.

In the second section [pp. 627-628] he turns abruptly to a personal tax on all forms of revenue. First he excludes that part of the income necessary to the subsistence of the family, and then, as we have seen, proves mathematically that a proportional tax on the remainder is really a progressive tax on the whole. He concludes by stating that "this would be a useful reform in our personal tax," referring to the *contribution mobilière* in effect in 1793.

In the third and longest section [pp. 628-633], he asks a series of questions about the justification for a rising rate of taxation above a certain level of income. Following Graslin's argument, he first notes that some public expenses are not absolutely necessary and that there exist some taxpayers who are exchanging "the superfluous" for "the useful." Secondly these same taxpayers receive more benefits than do poorer people because there are certain expenses that are more useful to the rich than to the poor. His first example of what modern economists term a merit want is the creation and maintenance of a good road system, which has value for all, but a particular value for the rich who use roads for their personal enjoyment in traveling long distances. His second example is a government subsidy for the arts, in which the commercial support of the arts is beneficial to the economy in general but only the rich enjoy the products. His conclusion is that a progressive rate is therefore both just and useful, but it is obvious that Condorcet was not too comfortable with such a sweeping justification because he immediately goes on to suggest certain limits on the rate of progression. It must not be so high as to encourage fraud, or to limit the kinds of expenses that support certain trades, or to deflect fortunes into avaricious hoarding. At this point, Condorcet makes a concession to the principle of equality:

> I know that the existence of large fortunes is pernicious by itself, that it is useful for them to come closer to equality; I know that without that, equality of rights cannot be full and complete.[26]

But Condorcet is not willing to rely on fiscal measures to insure a proper distribution of income. He is worried that a sudden change in the tax laws will seriously disrupt the economy, and he argues in favor of a rather slowly rising progressive rate that would still encourage the acquisition of land and the proper use of capital while discouraging speculation and hoarding. He concludes this section with an appeal to the laissez-faire principle, based on his belief in a natural order which is favorable to equality:

> In the case of a large country, wealth and work are distributed according to a natural order that political institutions almost never alter except at the expense of the general good. This order favors equality; in order to enhance it, we must therefore uphold and not oppose nature's wishes. Therefore let wealth be divided and spent and don't let's force them to pile it up by hiding it.[27]

The fourth and concluding section [pp. 633–636] is devoted to extraordinary taxes that are not expected to be imposed more than once. Here he makes open reference to the dire straits of France in 1793 with a mass of useless paper money in the form of *assignats*. In a case like this, a forced loan, even one which is confiscatory above a certain level of income, is both useful and justified as a measure to stabilize the economy. He compares the situation to that of a flood that forces landowners to unite in making sacrifices for the common good. A forced loan does exactly the same thing for the nation as a whole and has the additional advantage of stimulating the sale of nationalized land.

Condorcet's shift from an outright attack on the principle of progression in 1788 to advocacy of a confiscatory forced loan in 1793 can only be understood in conjunction with the pressures of the Revolution. Keith Michael Baker has noted the same phenomenon in connection with Condorcet's attempt to reconcile scientific elitism and democratic liberalism.[28] Baker has traced Condorcet's movement in political terms from support of a property requirement for active citizenship to advocacy of universal male suffrage. Condorcet's theories of taxation followed the same path; property became less important as other values, in this case economic equality, came to the fore. But progressive taxation never assumed the status of an ideal in Condorcet's mind, as did universal suffrage.

During 1789 the fiscal situation in France deteriorated rapidly. The very day the National Assembly came into being, June 17, 1789, it issued a decree declaring all current taxes null and void but providing for the continued collection of already existing taxes until new ones were formulated. The fact of the matter is that no taxes were being collected during this hectic period, and by August Necker was forced into trying to float two new loans, neither of which was successful. On August 18 the King appointed a Treasury Committee, including Condorcet, which was charged with making recommendations about new taxes. In the interim the National Constituent Assembly voted the *contribution patriotique*, which relied on voluntary declarations and payments and which resulted in very few declarations and a paltry two million *livres* a month. This fiscal dilemma led to the confiscation of Church property and the creation of the notorious *assignats* that later became legal tender, an action that relieved the pressure on the Treasury for a while, although in the long run the *assignats* almost ruined the country. Condorcet supported the nationalization of church land, but he was aghast at the Constituent Assembly's hasty decisions.[29]

The Treasury Committee reported to the Assembly in August 1790, with La Rochefoucauld acting as spokesman.[30] The committee recommended a combination of different taxes to take the place of all the old ones: a land tax (*contribution foncière*), a personal and moveables tax (*contribution personnelle et mobilière*), and various duties to be paid on legal documents, stamps, imports, etc. The first to be accepted was the *contribution foncière*, promulaged on November 23. This tax remained basically without change as the primary source of public revenue until 1798. Unfortunately it was never very effective since the municipalities were slow in making up their land-surveys. On January 13, 1791 the Constituent Assembly voted the *contribution personnelle et mobilière* which proved to be even more difficult to collect and which was finally suspended in 1794.

Condorcet's pamphlet "Sur l'impôt personnel" (1790) gives his arguments in favor of a personal as well as a land tax at this particular moment. Such a tax would reduce the state's dependence upon a single source, it would serve as a substitute for the indirect taxes no longer in effect, and it would give some relief to the poorer classes:

> for the poorer people [it would] lighten the burden of a mass of taxes which have a very high ratio to revenue by making the rich support part of these taxes more than proportionally. This would be unjust and even useless as relief for the poor if the tax were moderate or even if there were a good general land-survey; but when taxes are very high and when nothing guarantees a proper distribution, when taxes are in large part used to pay off obligations from which the rich benefit the most, this higher proportion cannot be claimed to be really unjust.[31]

The many conditional clauses clearly show that Condorcet's adherence to the progressive principle was subject to a series of particular happenstances.

The early months of 1791 revealed that revenues from the *contribution foncière* and *mobilière* were not coming in fast enough to defray the expenses of the state. When the Constituent Assembly voted to abolish the guilds in May 1791, they took the opportunity to institute a licensing fee on all business activity, called *la patente*. It was no more successful as a money raiser than the others and reliance on the *assignats* became ever more necessary. Three months before going out of existence, the Constituent Assembly made an impassioned plea to the French people to pay their taxes, calling on their patriotic fervor.[32] But, as Marion wryly points out, "this patriotism never took on a fiscal form."[33] The Legislative Assembly was left with an inheritance of debt and growing fiscal needs due to the war. They met this crisis by nationalizing the land of the émigrés and by issuing additional *assignats*.

Condorcet served as a member of the Legislative Assembly, concentrating his efforts on the issue of public education and serving as president of the Committee of 21, which made numerous attempts to persuade Louis XVI to act as a constitutional monarch. The insurrection of August 10, 1792 led to the convocation of the National Convention in which Condorcet served as an exceptionally influential member of the Constitutional Committee. His pronouncements about progressive taxation must be considered in conjunction with the events surrounding the defeat of the Girondin party in the National Convention. By 1793 the King had been executed, the war had been extended, military reversals had been experienced, and civil war had broken out in the Vendée. The Jacobins accused the Girondins of seditious activities, and in late May they were successful in eliminating the Girondins from the Convention. Condorcet presented the proposed "Girondin" constitution to the Convention on February 15 and discussion of it was delayed by the Jacobins until April 17. It is in the context of this discussion that the most acrimonious debate over the principle of progressive taxation took place.

However, as frequently happened during the Revolution, events did not wait upon discussion. Early in the year, the Paris Commune had instituted a supplementary tax with a sharply progressive rate to subsidize the price of bread; similar measures went into effect in other cities either to subsidize the price of bread or to raise the funds needed to redeem the various municipal issues known as *billets de confiance*. The principle of progression was now presented as *the* patriotic measure which would insure the success of the Revolution. Riots broke out again in Paris in February, giving unusual weight to requests made by the Paris Commune. On March 9 this group petitioned the Convention for a war tax to be levied on the rich, a suggestion that occasioned much enthusiasm and was referred to the Committee on Taxes. On March 18, Barère, a moderate deputy, came out boldly in favor of progressive taxes, and, when he suggested that this should be referred to committee, Jacques Ramel de Nogaret, the future Minister of Finance under the Directory, intervened with a call for a vote on the following decree:

> In order to reach a more accurate proportion in the burden which each citizen must assume according to his abilities, a graduated and progressive tax will be established on all luxuries and wealth both landed and moveable.[34]

This decree passed easily, as did another making the death penalty the punishment for anyone who suggested an agrarian law in favor of nationalization of private property. The Convention was treading a very narrow path betweeen a desire to finance the Revolution through heavy "contributions" from the wealthy and a need to reassure property owners so that more nationalized land could be sold enabling the retirement of *assignats*. In its first report on March 21, the Committee on Taxes noted the projected deficit of some 28 million *livres* and suggested covering it by a progressive tax on the rich with a graduated rate going from about 2.5 to 9 percent. This report was not even discussed by the Convention, so the committee came back with a plan to reform the *contribution mobilière* in such a way as to impose a graduated tax ranging from 2 to 50 percent. Again the Convention found other items more pressing and did not discuss the report.

When the Convention formally discussed the Girondin constitution in April, the quarrel between the Girondins and the Jacobins had reached the point of no return. Numerous Jacobin representatives used the issue of taxes as an additional way of attacking the Girondin constitution. The constitution itself was preceded by a Declaration of Rights, amongst which the right of property figured prominently; within the constitution itself the articles on taxes assured an even distribution of the tax load with an exemption at the subsistence level but failed to delineate the method by which taxes would be imposed. On April 22, Danton objected that the omission of the word *progression* could limit the legislature from imposing such a tax which he deemed to be "eternally reasonable."[35] Two days later Robespierre was even more vehement, and he openly attacked Condorcet:

> You also speak of taxes and establish the incontestable principle that they are determined by the will of the people or its representatives, but you have forgotten to sanction the basis of progressive taxes....I suggest that you do this in an article conceived in these terms: "Citizens whose incomes do not exceed whatever is necessary for their subsistence are exempted from contributing to public expenditures; the others must support them progressively according to the extent of their wealth."[36]

This issue became another link in the chain of accusations being formed by the Jacobins to discredit the Girondin party.

But declarations and constitutions were not going to make much of a dent on the real deficit facing the Treasury, and during the months of April and May innumerable suggestions on special taxes on the rich were proposed and a great many went into effect on the local level. There were so many that even such a careful historian as Marion acknowledged defeat: "the historian, overwhelmed, has to give up the idea of enumerating them all."[37] In the Convention itself on May 20 Ramel introduced a tax bill based on a steeply rising progressive rate, but when it was noted that a tax always took a long time to collect, the proposal of a forced loan made by Joseph Cambon, who was later to convert the floating debt into a funded debt through the *Grand livre de la dette publique*, was accepted in principle. As enacted this "loan" instituted progressive rates from 10 percent to 100 percent and again failed to raise the necessary funds.

Condorcet's article "Sur l'impôt progressif," published on June 1, was written with these objections and conditions in mind. His calm, reasoned approach was a far cry from the tumultuous discussions taking place on the floor of the Convention. By the time the Jacobin constitution was substituted for the Girondin plan on June 10 even the Jacobins had seen the necessity for restraint on this issue. The Constitution of 1793, adopted in record time on June 24, does not even mention the principle of progressive taxation; indeed Article 101 expressly states that each citizen must pay some form of taxes: "No citizen is exempt from the honorable obligation to contribute to public expenses."[38] Robespierre had done a complete about-face on this issue, having become convinced in the interim that exempting the poor from taxation would not be a benefit but rather an insult to them and that it would lead to "the aristocracy of wealth;"

it was his support that was responsible for the adoption of Article 101.[39] By this time Condorcet was no longer engaging in public debate in the Convention, and he went into hiding shortly after the publication of his inflammatory pamphlet *Aux citoyens français, sur la nouvelle constitution* which precipitated the July 8 order for his arrest.

In the first three months of his period of hiding, Condorcet completed his best known work, the *Esquisse d'un tableau historique des progrès de l'esprit humain*, a summary of all his hopes and beliefs about human beings and their institutions. It is fitting to conclude this study of his theories on taxation by a quote from the *Esquisse*. Condorcet reiterates his adherence to the Physiocrats' idea of a single tax on the net revenue from the land, specifically noting that his theory allows for a subsistence level exemption. He justifies this kind of tax on the principle that it is the only form of revenue that is not the result of an individual's labor and that, therefore, it is the only proper revenue for the state to tax. Thus he reconciles his desire for economic equality with his belief in property; property owners are privileged but pay for this privilege through taxes. Workers may be poor, but they enjoy the benefits of state expenses without contributing toward them:

> Each year's reproduction provides an available portion, since it is not required to pay for either the work of which this reproduction is the result or the work which will assure an equally good or more abundant reproduction. The person who owns this available portion does not get it from his own work; he possesses it quite apart from the use to which he puts his means in order to meet his needs. Hence it is on this available portion of annual wealth that, without contravening any rights, the public authority can establish the funds required for those expenses which are needed to insure the security of the state, its internal peace, the guarantee of individual rights, the working of those bodies instituted to make or execute the laws, and, finally, the maintenance of public prosperity.[40]

After Condorcet's death, fiscal problems went from bad to worse during the Revolution. As finally enacted in September 1793, Cambon's forced loan exempted from taxation 1000 *livres*, placed a 10 percent rate on the first additional 1000 *livres* and confiscated all income above 9000 *livres*. Despite these draconian measures, or perhaps because of them, the final collection after a period of two years amounted to only one-fifth of the sum anticipated. It was obvious that the main result had been the horrors anticipated by Condorcet, that is, fraud, speculation, and hoarding. By 1799 the Directory had turned completely against progressive taxation, especially in the form of a forced loan; indeed it was this coupling of progressive taxation with the concept of a forced loan, that is, the confiscation of all income above a certain level, which was responsibile for France's rather belated acceptance of the principle of progression. During the Directory, the First Empire, the Restoration, and the monarchy of Louis Philippe, the principal source of public funds was indirect taxes. The 1848 Revolution raised the possibility of a progressive tax on income, but it was never accepted. In the late nineteenth century a rental or occupancy tax was finally imposed as an additional source of public funds; the conversion of this indirect tax into a direct income tax did not occur until 1917 and even today France relies far more heavily on indirect taxes than do most other Western nations. The legacy of the Revolution lingers on in the form of a determined effort by each French citizen to hide his true income from *le fisc*. Condorcet's prophecies about the consequences of a strongly progressive rate of income tax are clearly very perceptive and to the point, and his article "Sur l'impôt progressif" is still a useful guide to both the meaning and the consequences of progressive taxation.

Notes

1. I am not aware of any publication solely devoted to Condorcet's views on taxation and fiscal policy but have found the following works most pertinent: Franck Alengry, *Condorcet, guide de la Révolution française* (Paris, 1904; Genève, 1971) esp. 642-52, 717-21; Léon Cahen, *Condorcet et la Révolution française* (Paris, 1904: Genève, 1970) esp. 53-55, 205-13, 510-21; Eugène Caillaud, *Les Idées économiques de Condorcet* (Paris, 1908: New York, 1970) esp. 60-61, 163-82.

2. Gunnar Myrdal, *The Political Element in the Development of Economic Theory* (Cambridge, Mass., 1954), 156-57.

3. The standard modern reference on theories of taxation is Richard A. Musgrove, *The Theory of Public Finance* (New York, 1959). A very useful survey of progressive taxation is Edwin R. Seligman, *Progressive Taxation in Theory and Practice*, 2d ed., *American Economic Association Publications*, new series 3, vol. 9 (1908). I have used Musgrove primarily for definitions and Seligman for examples.

4. Condorcet, "Sur l'impôt progressif" in *Oeuvres de Condorcet*, ed. Arthur C. O'Connor and Marie F. Arago, 12 vols. (Paris, 1847-1849), 12:628. This, like subsequent translations, is my own. All references will be to this edition.

5. Musgrove, 64. See also Myrdal, 160 and Seligman, 150-53.

6. Musgrove, 90-91; Myrdal, 163-65; Seligman, 205-7.

7. Myrdal, 160-61.

8. Myrdal, 166-67.

9. Musgrove, 230-31.

10. Herbert Lüthy calls it "le problème clé de l'Ancien Régime" in *La Banque protestante en France*, 2 vols. (Paris, 1959-61), 2:466.

11. François Hincker, *Les Français devant l'impôt* (Paris, 1971), 79-81.

12. For a general discussion of the Physiocrats' tax theories see Georges Weulersse, *Le Mouvement physiocratique en France*, 2 vols. (Paris, 1910), 2:336-75. It is also necessary to consult Weulersse's two other books on later periods: *La Physiocratie sous les ministères de Turgot et de Necker* (Paris, 1950) and *La Physiocratie à la fin du règne de Louis XV* (Paris, 1959).

13. A clear statement of this policy is contained in Quesnay's *Maximes générales*, first published in 1767: "Taxes must be based directly on the clear profit of landed property." See Eugène Daire, ed., *Physiocrates*, (Slatkine reprint of Paris 1846 edition, 1971), 85.

14. Turgot, *Plan d'un mémoire sur les impositions en général* in *Oeuvres*, ed. Eugène Daire, 2 vols. (Paris, 1844), 1:395.

15. Ibid., 1:407-8.

16. Condorcet, *La Vie de M. Turgot*, 5:124-28, 137.

17. Condorcet, *Essai sur les assemblées provinciales*, 8:292.

18. Montesquieu, *De l'esprit des lois*, book 13, chap. 7 in *Oeuvres complètes*, ed. R. Caillous (Paris, 1951), 2:462.

19. Ibid., 467, (book 13, chap. 14) and 462, (book 13, chap. 7).

20. Rousseau, "Economie politique," *Oeuvres complètes*, ed. B. Gagnebin and M. Raymond (Paris, 1959-69), 3:273.

21. Rousseau, *Considérations sur le gouvernement de Pologne*, 3:1001.

22. Ibid., 3:1006, 1011. The *Considérations* were written in 1771 and circulated in manuscript before their publication in 1782.

23. Rousseau, "Economie politique," 3:273.

24. Jaucourt, "Impôts," in *Encyclopedie* (Paris, 1751-65), 8:601.

25. Jean J. L. Graslin, *Essai analytique sur la richesse et sur l'impôt* (Paris, 1767), 284.

26. Condorcet, "Sur l'impôt progressif," 12:631.

27. Ibid., 12:633.

28. Keith Michael Baker, *Condorcet. From Natural Philosophy to Social Mathematics* (Chicago and London, 1975), 363.

29. His support for confiscating church property occurs in the *Plan d'un emprunt public avec des hypothèques spéciales* (May 1788, *Oeuvres*, 11:351-61) and his dismay is expressed in *Réflexions sur les écrits publiés contre l'Assemblée nationale* (1790, *Oeuvres*, 9:487-541).

30. The most thorough investigation of fiscal measures during the Revolution occurs in Marcel Marion, *Histoire financière de la France depuis 1715*, 6 vols. (Paris, 1927), Vol. 1 covers 1715-1789; 2, 1789-1792; and 3, 1793-1797.

31. Condorcet, "Sur l'impôt personnel," 11:473-74.

32. Quoted at length in Marion, *Histoire*, 2:249-50.

33. Ibid., 2:71.

34. As quoted in Seligman, 33.

35. As quoted in Marion, *Histoire*, 3:43.

36. As quoted in Franck Alengry, *Condorcet, Guide de la Révolution française* (Paris, 1904), 417 and Marion, *Histoire*, 3:43.

37. Marion, *Histoire*, 3:62.

38. John H. Stewart, *A Documentary Survey of the French Revolution* (New York, 1951), 466.

39. Marion, *Histoire*, 66-67 and Seligman, 184-85.

40. Condorcet, *Esquisse*, 6:180-81.

REVOLUTION IN EDUCATION

8
Condorcet: The Problematic
Nature of Progress

Renée Waldinger

Condorcet's speech of reception of 1782 upon his election to the French Academy rings with his conviction that he was living in a outstanding epoch, one that testified to the progress made by mankind through the centuries, and that was sure to contribute to the acceleration of that progress through the achievements due to enlightenment. He claimed that the demonstrable progress of the natural sciences justified this assertion and that equal progress in the social sciences would occur if they would only use the same methods as the pure sciences, base their conclusions on the observation of facts, and acquire an equally precise vocabulary. He admitted that the social sciences were at a distinct disadvantage in reaching the same degree of exactitude as expected in the natural sciences, for the observer himself could not ever be entirely impartial since he belonged to the very group he studied; yet enlightenment had made such advances that leaders of genius would surely come forward and create for generations to come a system of laws and a method of education for the prosperity and happiness of all.[1]

This faith in progress, so eloquently asserted in this discourse, is at the core of Condorcet's *Sketch of a Historical Tableau on the Progress of the Human Mind* which has become so attached to his name. Its admirers often refer to it as the lofty expression of the goals and great hopes of the Age of Enlightenment; its detractors denounce it as the summary of the delusions of the period. For years critical opinion has emphasized this messianic aspect of Condorcet's thought, paying no, or little, attention to the numerous specific reforms he sponsored, and disregarding his reflections on the obstacles he saw in the path of the progress he so desired. Critics have repeatedly mocked what they have referred to as Condorcet's simple-minded optimism and guileless faith in progress. It is only recently that a few scholars have begun to probe deeper and revise that superficial judgment. Yet the name of Condorcet is traditionally so attached to the paean for progress sketched in the Tenth Epoch of his *Esquisse* that even a critic as balanced and well-disposed toward Condorcet as J. H. Brumfitt refers pejoratively to the *philosophe's* "naively confident optimism."[2] Peter Gay in *The Party of Humanity* is closer to the truth, when, having shown in the body of his text the thoughtfulness and lack of naiveté exhibited by the

117

eighteenth-century writer, calls Condorcet's optimism "a form of therapy: he hopes that he may not despair" (p. 273). In volume 2 of *The Enlightenment: The Science of Freedom*, Gay states: "Condorcet's optimism was not the facile cheerfulness of the man who ignores realities, but the stern, almost Roman determination of the man who has looked suffering in the face and take it into his philosophy" (p. 121). As early as 1958, Henry Vyverberg, in his study of the *Historical Pessimism of the French Enlightenment*, had noted that "Condorcet's doctrine of progress is in a sense a doctrine of regeneration" (p. 69). He traced briefly how it differed from the ideas of his precursors, Turgot in particular, and how "Condorcet the theorist became the inspired prophet" (p. 70). Roland Mortier in *Clartés et Ombres du Siècle des Lumières* also insists on the complexity of Condorcet's thought. He points out that Enlightenment represents to the *philosophe*, not only language and intellectual givens; from it derive sensitivity, action, life; it inspires the heart as much as the mind (p. 48). Mortier calls the Esquisse "une *Légende des siècles* en prose" filled with the same vision of history, which is an unending battle between the spirit of enlightenment and the spirit of darkness, with the latter eventually absorbed in the former (p. 48).

All the writers just cited note the slow maturation of Condorcet's thought and all agree that he is far more complex a thinker than literary history has admitted. Their concern with him is only peripheral, however. Their main thrust is of a much broader nature and they only indicate, as an aside, a need for a different reading of his work. Such an examination shows clearly that Condorcet did indeed know the torments and the contradictions that so many critics have denied him, that he was assailed by doubt and uncertainty, and that his optimism on the future possibilities of mankind expressed in the Tenth Epoch of the *Esquisse* rests on his unshaken belief in the value and impact of education on the future direction of society. The crucial role of education in the shaping of man's destiny, boldly voiced in this discourse to the French Academy and then developed under the pressure of revolutionary events into a full-fledged philosophy of education, lies at the core of Condorcet's conception of progress. It represents the pillar on which the *philosophe's* vision of the future is elaborated: the right education produces enlightened behavior, more egalitarian beliefs, and less prejudiced values. Concomitantly, material progress, in and of itself, yields a more educated and knowledgeable populace.

Yet Condorcet would be happy to know that his last work has represented for so long and for so many the basic credo of the Enlightenment, even if its readers disregarded the perspective from which it was written. Were we to reject this oft-repeated judgment and accept Brumfitt's contention that "if the philosophy *of* progress was the prerogative of a minority, a philosophy *for* progress was probably the most important thing which emerged from the collective thought of the *philosophes*,"[3] Condorcet would still feel vindicated. He always believed that political work directed to the welfare of society as a whole was the most valid occupation and deserved the highest recognition. That explains his admiration for Descartes, which stemmed from the importance he attached to any individual who caused man to think and consequently to question. He claimed that Descartes' contribution to human progress was paramount even if in the physical sciences he was weaker than Galileo, even if his philosophy was less wise than Bacon's, for he aroused the men of thought who had not been moved by the complacency of his two predecessors. He told men to shake off the yoke of authority and to recognize only the rule of reason. Descartes deserves to be glorified not for his scientific discoveries, but for his daring in asking questions and in so doing propelling mankind forward. Critics have often expressed surprise that Condorcet, a mathematician of note, who was elected at age 26 to the Academy of Science, turned away from active involvement in scientific research and embraced political action. The answer can be found in the *philosophe's* correspondence. To him only contributions to society deserved fame; all else was spurious. In a letter to Voltaire, written shortly after the fall of Turgot in 1776, a despondent Condorcet referred to Turgot's disgrace as "the fatal event that has dashed the courage and hope of all good people" (1:113) and announced that he was through with politics. "I am going back to geometry and philosophy. It is sad to be working only for vanity after laboring with pride for the public good" (1:115). For a man who believed all his life that scientific discoveries were at the root of all progress, the reduction of all possible scientific fame to "vanity" sounds strange indeed; but we must remember that Condorcet considered the incorporation and use of scientific discovery in the fabric of society as the point at which science became a propulsion for progress.[4] Thus true fame belonged not to the inventor, but to the one who integrated the invention into the social context.

He was well aware of the difficulties this process faced. He realized that progress was slow, and often repeated that man was easily turned away from the straight path. Moreover, wishing to return to the right path, man had the tendency to go too far to the other extreme and indeed "one could compare his gait to that of a wall clock which reaches the hour only after numerous oscillations from one side to the other" (7:3). His letters, speeches, pamphlets, and occasional publications are filled with doubts on the possibilities for change. His distress at the time of the fall of Turgot was so acute that he wondered whether the possibility for leadership by enlightened men was forever doomed and "the universe will remain condemned to darkness and evil" (1:112). He conceded that in all things man is subject to error and will be driven from truth by his personal passions (6:595). Even more depressing was his realization that error is as likely an outcome of man's activity as truth and that errors and prejudices acquired in childhood remain even after reason has unmasked them (6:21–22). In his *La Vie de M. Turgot* Condorcet emphasized how rarely man has cultivated his reason throughout the ages, and remarked that most men, whether because of poor education or failure to acquire the habit of reflection, do not arrive at their own conclusions but take their opinions from others (5:201-2). He had no illusions on man's nature and acknowledged that it is impossible to ever promulgate rigorously fair and just laws; the legislator is therefore limited to laws that tend to result in less injustice (5:213). Discouragement was a recurring theme: writing about a pamphlet he had just published anonymously, he noted: "all these brochures are nothing but pinpricks which the colossus of superstition hardly feels" (1:243), and elsewhere referred to "this hydra of prejudices which hasn't stopped devouring men since earliest times" (1:490). "Don't accuse me of being insensitive to the pain of humanity" he exclaimed; "I know that its wounds are still bleeding, that everywhere the yoke of ignorance still weighs heavily; that wherever a man of good will glances unhappiness and crime strike his eyes and break his heart" (1:394).

Vested interests constituted even more powerful and important impediments to progress. In defense of Voltaire's poem *La Pucelle d'Orléans*, he remarked that wherever one looks one sees the rights of man attacked and violated with impunity, his spirit brutalized by error, fanaticism and greed filling the minds of those in power (1:216). Changes leading to social improvement always need time. After a long and difficult fight enlightenment may triumph over the always-reborn obstacles that ignorance and self-interest oppose to it; but only an instant is needed to institutionalize abuses that never fail to find powerful and faithful allies in these very same prejudices and self-interests (8:119). He pointed out that even the best reform leading to general welfare would be harmful to some members of society. The destruction of one privilege necessarily took away advantages from those who had enjoyed them; they would be directly affected by its loss and feel it sharply whereas matters affecting the general welfare are felt by the general public only as time goes on. What makes reform even harder, Condorcet was forced to conclude, is that it is in the nature of man to feel evil more sharply than good (8:259). Moreover, in all countries, at all times, classs prejudice derived from lack of education, or professional prejudice, will always have an impact; those of philosophers harm the progress of truth, those of less enlightened groups retard the propagation of truths already accepted, those of certain powerful or accredited professions place obstacles in its path (6:22).

The most critical obstacle to enlightenment and progress was the clergy. Condorcet accused priests of trying to monopolize all knowledge in order to control society. He blamed them for fostering class divisions, in fact of separating humanity into two classes: "one destined to teach, the other to believe. One hiding proudly what it proclaims to know, the other accepting with respect what one deigns to reveal. One wishing to rise above human reason, the other giving up humbly and accepting in other men prerogatives higher than legitimate, given their own common nature" (6:30). Condorcet asserted that since the beginnings of society one class of men had always sought to separate itself from the rest, trying to hold on exclusively to science and art in order to subjugate all minds, and preventing anyone from unmasking its tyranny (6:35). He argued that progress had made great strides in Greek civilization, for the function of its priests was limited to the cult of the gods. Thus Greek genius could surge forward without being restrained by pedantic regulations. This made truth accessible to all men and it was this happy circumstance, even more than political liberty, which gave the Greeks their independence of thought, that guaranteed the speed and extent of their progress (6:61-62). The triumph of Christianity, however, signaled the complete decadence of science and philosophy, for Christianity feared man's belief in his own reason and his right to examine and doubt. It was suspicious of all the natural sciences, for they might reveal the absurdities of religious miracles (6:103). Condorcet's anti-clericalism has often been noted, but what has always been overlooked is that even in this matter he was besieged by doubt and he wondered whether the power exerted by priests throughout the ages was not really a consequence of man's very nature and therefore impossible to eliminate (6:30).

Such doubts on man's capacity to embrace and contribute to progress never disappeared from Condorcet's writings and even recurred while he was charting the constant progress of civilization in the *Sketch of a Historical Tableau on the Progress of the Human Mind* where he stopped repeatedly to wonder whether even an enlightened society could control the manner in which men carried out its policies. He asked himself again and again whether differences in enlightenment, in standards of living observed among civilized peoples, class differences keeping them apart, inequalities that social progress seemed to have increased, were derived from civilization itself or were due to the imperfections of social science (6:237). Questions were never entirely stilled, but the political events he witnessed in the France of his day, the revolutionary activities he participated in and the social turmoil he observed, brought him to the realization that education was the key to change and progress, and that it offered the means whereby mankind would be moved forward and find its full potential. He had alluded to the importance of education many times in his writings and had referred to its value in the molding of the citizen, but it was the crisis due to the fall of the church at the time of the French Revolution, bringing down in its wake the entire educational system, that led to a conclusion that became the core of his entire philosophic outlook. In 1791 Condorcet published in the *Bibliothèque de l'homme public* a series of five articles, each entitled *Memoir on Public Instruction*, which made the argument that education is a right, not a privilege, and that it is even *the* crucial right, for without it, all other rights remain unknown. To speak of freedom and equality, he asserted, is a sham so long as part of the population is not given the opportunity to participate fully in society because it lacks the basic tools needed to function in it. Without education a person is doomed to dependency on others, cannot be free, and is surely not equal. A society that proclaims freedom and equality must see to it that these rights are not merely abstractions, but become reality. The fundamental requirement to achieve that goal is the opportunity for education. It is "the means of realizing equality of rights" (7:169).

"It is the duty of society," he argued, "to offer to all the means of acquiring the knowledge which their level of intelligence and the time they can devote to study allows them to attain" (7:174). Condorcet never claimed that intellectual equality existed, or that education should be the same for all. Inequality of intellect and talent are a reality that must be accepted. The state's obligation is to make available to every citizen the level of instruction that he can attain. A basic education, on the other hand, must be provided for everyone, for all children are able to absorb the rudiments of reading and writing; in addition, this elementary education will provide a setting for nurturing and supporting all those who show talent and originality and who should be encouraged to go on. Opportunity for continued instruction must be secured for those who can profit from it. Condorcet did not coin the phrase of "open access" to higher education, but that is surely what he meant when he stressed the potential for growth inherent in all individuals and called on the state to facilitate and multiply the means for its development (7:175). He conceded that some people acquired knowledge and greatness even without this open access to further instruction, but however great their achievement, its personal cost was such that even these exceptional individuals remained "below their potential." It is in the self-interest of society to develop the talents of its citizens and to give them the means to push their capacities to their limits. A world that is constantly changing requires new inventions, new ways of dealing with problems, new ideas. Only a fully educated citizenry will know how to respond to new situations (8:184). A modern nation needs *all* its citizens and will grow by making it possible for all men born with genius to develop their capacities" (7:178). Condorcet realized that the ideals of the Revolution necessitated a participatory citizenry and that the future of the nation depended on the involvement of each citizen. "The responsibility of society is to make available to every person the education needed to exercise the common functions of man, head of family and citizen so that all will feel and know their responsibilities" (7:173). Informed citizenship requires education and the nation must be willing to defray its cost to reap its benefits. Condorcet's appeal was made on utilitarian grounds, not on abstract principles. He stressed the importance and usefulness of universal education for the general welfare and remarked that certain aspects of government may be suitable for one epoch, but not for another, and that political structures must bend with the times; that is why the citizenry must be prepared, through education, to adapt to new situations. He foresaw the demands attendant upon industrialization and explained that the future imposed a de-emphasis of classical learning and a stress on science. Rote-learning doomed the student to a repetition of the past; progress required a critical education. He tied the necessity for increased education to new agricultural methods, to discoveries in the arts, to the impact of population shifts. All these fields demanded educational training not only for the upper classes, but also for the masses. Individuals with higher intellectual endowments must be trained to deal with these matters on a more sophisticated level, but they affect all segments of the social body.

Condorcet did not limit himself to a description of the material benefits society would derive from an educated and therefore enlightened citizenry. He underlined constantly the long-range improvement in the quality of life that would be its inevitable consequence. He argued that even a minimal education would give an individual a spur to improve himself; increased educational opportunities would inspire him to raise his sights. A decent standard of living would become available to more people and would bring in its wake a heightened level of taste and a greater appreciation of beauty and art (7:176). Increased education narrows social differences and results in "gentler mores, greater integrity, more scrupulous honesty" (7:173). All aspects of man's life would be affected by enlarged educational opportunities. A fundamental result would be the awakening of his curiosity and, asserted the writer, "as more people are trained to search for truth, there is a greater chance of finding it" (7:180). Understanding something about the mechanisms of the body, man would take better care of his health and would be willing to take certain precautions that would prevent many illnesses. Having come into contact with beauty, he would want to recreate it, and having some notions of science, he is bound to acquire others and make useful discoveries (7:193). It is evident that for Condorcet education for all, limited only by individual capabilities, was a concept that included not only instruction, but that represented the source of the nation's strength. It was the surest guarantee of happiness, prosperity, and progress.

In writing these five *Memoirs on Public Instruction*, focusing on the nature and goals of public education, on universal education of children, on professional education, and on scientific education, Condorcet was quite aware that he was addressing one of the urgent issues facing the Revolutionary government. Indeed his philosophy of education evolved in a dialectic with Revolutionary activities. The abolition of taxes that had subsidized the schools and colleges controlled by the ecclesiastical authorities, the withdrawal of all sources of revenue coupled with the imposition of the constitutional oath on religious as well as lay teachers, resulted in the complete disorganization of the educational structure. Immediate steps had to be taken to establish public education. Unfortunately the political instability of the governing bodies prevented rational consideration of the proposals that were submitted. Mirabeau drew up a "Travail sur l'instruction publique," which was never laid before the Constituent Assembly. In 1791, during the last days of the Constituent Assembly, Talleyrand introduced a bill for the structure of national education in France. It was discussed, by never acted upon, for the Assembly was dissolved. Since Condorcet's writings on the subject of education were well-known and since he was a member of the Legislative Assembly where he sat as a representative of the City of Paris, the Revolutionary government turned to him and entrusted him with the difficult task of drawing up an educational system suitable for the nation. Condorcet accepted the challenge, for he was convinced that education was indeed one of the prime concerns of the political establishment, that in fact education is politics. He argued convincingly that different political outlooks demanded differing types of education, which in turn strengthened the political faction in power.

Working with great speed, Condorcet drew up a proposal which he submitted to the Legislative Assembly in 1792. This *Report and Project for a Decree on the General Organization of Public Instruction* was a detailed organizational plan for a system of public education to be sponsored by the new nation created by the Revolution. It provided the structure that would allow the development of the goals for education discussed in the *Memoirs*. It recommended the creation of a four-tier educational system with an independent administrative superstructure. The first two levels, the primary and secondary schools, would be compulsory, although Condorcet noted that farmers' children might be needed on the farm and would be able to study only during the winter. Opportunity for more advanced work would be available in "Institutes" of which there would be one in each Department. Professional training would be the province of 9 Lycées distributed all over France so that advanced work could be done not only in Paris, but also in the provinces. At the top there would be a National Society of Sciences and Arts. The order is significant and reflects Condorcet's concerns.[5] This society would monitor and direct the entire educational structure and would encourage and protect intellectual growth. Education on all levels would be free, for: "Public prosperity requires that children of the poorer classes who are most numerous have the opportunity to develop their talents; it is a means of assuring not only that the fatherland will have more citizens ready to serve it, that science will have more adherents capable of contributing to its progress, but also of bringing together all classes that differences in education tend to separate" (8:491).

Political and social imperatives were visibly the motivating force for Condorcet's recommendations. Education for citizenship was the original reason and long-range goal for his interest in the whole question. The subject itself, however, became a matter of such engrossing concern to him and received so much reflection that his contribution to pedagogical matters deserves our attention and should be noted for its modernity.

He insisted on the autonomy of the school system. Although subsidized by the state, schools must be independent from political authority. They should lead public opinion, correct it and form it, not be controlled by it (7:493).

Teachers must be free to choose their own books and to teach ideas contrary to those of the nation (7:493-501). The development of the critical intelligence of the student must be one of the basic goals of all education. Since nothing remains static in the social organism, students must be informed about the options they have so that they will know how to lead the nation in the future. On the other hand schools should also reflect the dominant values of the society and act as instruments of political socialization. Thus discussion of basic principles of moral and social conduct should begin at the lowest levels, where they should be presented "at the child's level" (7:454). The teacher should not impart information which will be regurgitated by the students, but rather, through probing questions, should make the students think...and then elicit answers. Political attitudes should be developed early by making children hold assemblies and elections. Condorcet pleaded for books written especially for children, so that reading will become a pleasure. What is called language arts today should be the main focus of the first two levels of education, for it is most important that: "language stop separating men into two classes" (7:461). Latin should be de-emphasized, for according to Condorcet, everything that counts has been translated into French (7:473). Science and mathematics should occupy the preponderant place in the curriculum. A library should be at the center of each educational institution and by library, he meant not only a collection of books, but a laboratory, which on the secondary level includes a few meterological instruments, a few models of machinery or tools, and a few items of natural history (8:462). This library becomes progressively more extensive and sophisticated as one ascends the educational ladder.

Education should be the same for women as for men. Women are as capable as men and should have the same access to all levels of education. Condorcet's reasons for urging that women share in the instruction given to men could be voiced today: they need it so that they can watch over the education of their children (7:217); because its lack introduces into the family an inequality that is contrary to happiness (7:218-19); so that they can talk with their men (7:220); and simply because, as human beings, they have the same rights to public instruction as men (7:220). For women as well as men education is not a privilege, but a right.

Condorcet's *Report and Project for a Decree on the General Organization of Public Education* was presented to the Legislative Assembly on April 20, 1792. He had high hopes for his proposals, but he was to be bitterly disappointed. On the very day that his report was due, war with Austria was declared, and the Assembly was dissolved without acting on it.

Condorcet was firmly convinced that he was living at an extraordinary time, that the events he witnessed would shape the future, but he was repeatedly distressed about the reality confronting him. He was quite aware that the progress that would result from the educational model he had proposed was problematic in several respects: scientific and industrial advancement does not necessarily increase man's well-being, and even more worrisome, there is often a gulf between political and economic change and the level of education and understanding. Condorcet foresaw the negative aspects of industrialization and warned that it might be stupefying rather than enlightening. He noted that economic development depends on the division of labor and that mechanical work, which does not require thinking, was becoming more prevalent. He was concerned that "the improvement of machinery would become, for one part of humanity, a cause of stupidity (7:463). Education is important, he argued, precisely because it will compensate for the deprivations involved in intrinsically boring and unsatisfying work. The same concern motivated his emphasis on education as a life-long process; it must not stop with the end of school, but be available for all ages. An early proponent of continuing education, Condorcet urged that periodic lectures on different levels and special events in the schools be offered to those who are no longer in school; these activities would make learning interesting and attractive.

The lag between reality and consciousness was the other matter that concerned him deeply. The "perfectionnement général" that he hailed so often and by which he meant, not perfectibility, but capacity for growth in the Rousseauan sense, was an extremely distant goal. "An immense distance separates us from it" wrote Condorcet, "genius has shown us the way and is propelling society forward but our descendants will find out that this goal is far more distant than they may think. Is it possible to avoid seeing how much remains to be destroyed? (7:184). Even if we are convinced that the capacity for growth inherent in humanity will lead us to reason and happiness, what will be the price? How many misfortunes will it cost?" he added (7:186). He stressed the immensity of the task that lay ahead. "What individual" he cried "who is in the habit of reflecting upon those matters would not be frightened at seeing on one hand a mountain of customs which would make happiness and prosperity impossible for generations to come by placing obstacles greater than those we deplore presently in the path of all growth, and on the other hand such a limited number of means whereby one could, without sacrificing whatever happiness is possible now, prepare greater prosperity for the future, and not contravene it" (7:657). He was particularly distressed by the speed with which the nation was being hurled forward and which allowed no time to prepare the population for the responsibilities liberty entailed. Events had moved faster than anticipated. Both leaders and the general public needed time to become legislators. How can one expect enlightenment, asked Condorcet, when censorship of the press had never permitted discussion of the most basic political questions. Writing shortly before the meeting of the Estates General, he bemoaned that only a few months remained to dissipate this "cloud of errors that ignorance and prejudice of several centuries had amassed, to destroy the sophisms used by those in power to reinforce error" (7:656). He rejected violently the theory that unfairness to a small minority could be justified in the name of welfare for the majority. In his pamphlet of 1781 on the "Status of Protestants in France" he affirmed that legislative power is the power to regulate how men joined in society will enjoy their rights and not to violate those very rights under the pretext of utility for the greatest number. No legislative corps can ever claim to speak for the majority as long as women and children are not represented, and in any case no human being can ever abrogate his rights (5:463-64). He feared the dangers of representative assemblies where personal or group interests could so easily defeat the general will of the citizens, but he saw just as clearly that a gullible and uninformed public was at the mercy of demagogy. He concluded that public opinion could be trusted only after it had enjoyed freedom of the press for many years (5:521-22). That is why he pleaded for a declaration of the rights of man. He argued that natural rights, which he defined as security and liberty of one's person and of one's property, as well as equality, may indeed be recognized by all those who knew how to think, but few people understood what these rights included, what were the consequences of such natural rights. Thus a declaration of rights would be a most useful work for humanity as a whole. Yet he doubted that a single people, even among those who hated tyranny the most, would be willing to adopt such a declaration in its entirety "for habit has made man so accustomed to his chains" (9:167). It is worth noting that when the Constituent Assembly promulgated a Declaration of the Rights of Man and of the Citizen, Condorcet attacked it for being too vague and incomplete. In 1790, while constantly embroiled in defending or attacking measures taken by the Constituent Assembly, he confessed that he had to face the truth that enlightenment, talent, and the superiority derived from reason, existed in France side by side with much corruption and vice. (9:524).

This confession is symptomatic of Condorcet's reaction to the political struggles between the Girondins and Jacobins which continued during the Legislative Assembly and came to a head during the National Convention. Caught between these two camps, he criticized both and was in turn attacked by both. In 1792, having become Chairman of the Commission appointed by the Convention to draft a constitution, he threw himself into the task with enthusiasm. The constitution he devised, sponsored by the Girondins and thus rejected out-of-hand by the Jacobins, is beyond the scope of this paper. What interests us, however, is the campaign Condorcet waged to prepare public opinion. He argued that a constitution was needed even if the changes that had already occurred were accepted as remarkable, for no human institution is exempt from underlying defects and abuses that only time reveals. Moreover one of the characteristics of a free nation is that it allows differences of opinion. Since men are human, reason will not always resolve these differences and they will degenerate into quarrels (12:548). The nation cannot survive without a firmly established body of laws. It is to the self-interests of men and not to their virtues that we must appeal, wrote Condorcet (12:556), and they will rally around the new constitution for all classes have the same interests. Tyranny exploits the apparent opposition of class-interests; it is to the advantage of all to work together. As much as he believed in the benefits derived from a constitution, Condorcet had no illusions that it would be a panacea. He noted that the strength of law may indeed stop injustices created by private interests or personal passions, but that it is much harder to regulate the desires of large groups of people set in motion by the Revolution and claiming redress (12:644–50).

Wishing to publicize his political ideas and to convince a wider public, Condorcet planned the publication of a *Journal of Social Instruction* in 1793. Only its "Prospectus" was ever published, but it provides some important insights on the obstacles to progress Condorcet saw. As set forth in the "Prospectus," the goal of the Journal was to clarify for the general public notions of political rights and public economy (12:606). Condorcet realized at once that he was faced with a basic difficulty in his attempt to reach a large audience and thus make participatory government possible: the language of political and social affairs was unknown to this readers. He announced, therefore, that political language, the analysis of the ideas that the words of the discipline expressed, would be one of the first tasks of the *Journal.* It would deal with all questions currently under discussion and all opinions would be welcome. Such open discussion, even if it only delays precipitous action by introducing salutary doubt will be very effective, he wrote. (12:607). It is particularly important to awaken the minds of uneducated people, for they may very well have "l'esprit juste," but their prejudices may be that much harder to uproot because their ideas are more circumscribed (12:610). Condorcet, who had fought so hard for free universal education, emphasized again the danger to good government inherent in an ignorant citizenry and the negative impact it could have. The *Journal* would help alleviate it, and he insisted that its ultimate goal was not to dictate opinion, but to bring its readers up to a level where they could formulate one (12:613).

At all times, Condorcet defended his right, even his duty, to speak out. He felt that it was his responsibility as a spokesman for the Revolution, who had urged other nations to follow its example, "to bring the crimes that have tarnished it to their attention so that they would avoid them" (12:527). He was ready to admit that the French nation might have paid too dearly for liberty and equality, but he was convinced that in the long run reason and the corollary impact of enlightenment would "triumph over the treachery of rulers and the errors and weaknesses of the masses" (12:165–66).

Notes

1. Condorcet, *Oeuvres de Condorcet*, ed. Arthur C. O'Connor and Marie F. Arago, 12 vols. (Paris, 1847-1849), 1:392-403. References to this edition will henceforth appear in the text.

2. J. H. Brumfitt, *The French Enlightenment* (London, 1972), 87.

3. Ibid.

4. Frank Manuel, *The Prophets of Paris* (Cambridge, Massachusetts, 1962), 63-90.

5. Sciences include both natural and social sciences. See Keith Michael Baker, "The Early History of the term 'Social Science'," in *Annals of Science* vol. 20, no. 3, 211-26.

9
Enlightenment and Revolution: The Evolution of Condorcet's Ideas on Education

Manuela Albertone

Condorcet's proposals on education lie at the very heart of the political and intellectual process from which the modern French school originates. When the educational heritage of the Revolution produced the first free, public, compulsory, and secular primary schools, Jules Ferry and his associates looked above all to the political teachings of Condorcet, generating the first real historiographical reflections on his revolutionary activity and educational philosophy.[1] The concept of progress as a constant reference point and total confidence in the validity of scientific knowledge, translated by Condorcet into an exaltation of public education, were the basic ingredients of the positivist Weltanschauung of the men of the Third Republic. The relationship between scientific knowledge and democratic reform, a fundamental component of the creed of the Third Republic, had already been implicitly present in the priority Condorcet accorded to the diffusion of education. Rather than presenting a systematic treatment of Condorcet's educational ideas, which would risk oversimplification, these pages will try to highlight the precise evolution of his thought using a number of key concepts.

Condorcet, according to his own words the last of the *philosophes*,[2] embodies the most vivid example of the encounter between *Lumières* and Revolution and of the resulting creative synthesis. Shaped by his contact with the most prominent members and with the *milieux* of the *philosophique* culture,[3] Condorcet gradually placed increasing emphasis in his works on problems related to education.[4] In his enthusiastic support for the first revolutionary outbursts, he gave the problems of education a synthetic and global status for the first time. In five *Mémoires* published in 1791 in the pages of the *Bibliothèque de l'homme public*, a paper he founded as an educational tool to mold public opinion,[5] Condorcet detailed his fundamental principles of public education and also outlined a new educational system for revolutionary France to establish.

Education as a basic individual right for everybody constitutes the heart of Condorcet's reflections. Drawing on the most original and fundamental aspects of the philosophical heritage of the Enlightenment, from the doctrine of natural rights to the work of Locke, elaborated in the light of the intellectual guides who influenced him, from d'Alembert and Turgot to Voltaire and the physiocrats, Condorcet was able to link his own revolutionary action to the political program of the most liberal elements of the *philosophique* movement. Such a program amounted to the transformation of the corporate society of the *ancien régime*, hierarchically divided into different orders and separate bodies, and its replacement by a political, social, and economic structure based on the body politic as the sum of free and unhampered energies.

Starting with the premise that individuals are unequal by nature and in social reality, while nonetheless equal before the law, guaranteed by the social contract,[6] Condorcet synthesized his ideas into the principles of universality, secularity, and the non-compulsory nature of free and graded education. From this definitely liberal standpoint, in which education would be offered freely to all those wanting it—"la société ne voue à l'ignorance que celui qui préfère volontairement d'y rester"[7]—through a school organization divided into several levels and severed from the religious education of the *ancien régime*, Condorcet placed the whole of culture in a position of complete independence from political power.[8] The state's role was not planning or welfare but guaranteeing the existence of those structures that make possible the free development of the educational system.[9]

Condorcet's general notion of the individual did not prevent him from turning his attention to both sexes and giving a general argument for the inclusion of women in his project. Both his firm belief in feminism and his battle, even prior to the Revolution, to extend to women voting rights in the name of total equality, are well known. Equally so was his emblematic marriage to a woman of high intellectual quality, Sophie de Grouchy. In his first *Mémoire* which, in order to avoid the numerous anticipated objections, wisely presented a feminine image associated with the traditional notions of family and household, Condorcet not only suggested coeducational schools, but also favored women teaching at the highest university levels.[10]

In light of this principled claim to a universal right of education, regardless of birth and sex, religion or color, the liberating role of learning inevitably gained weight. Condorcet rejected a utilitarian view of teaching and early educational specialization, arguing for the separation of technical knowledge from apprenticeship. He thus hoped to assure a thorough development of the individual critical sensibility while simultaneously viewing education as a remedy to the alienation consequent to the division of labor.[11] Hence he assigned to education a formative role, guaranteeing intellectual autonomy to each individual, to each citizen, to culture in relation to established power. This idea had also been particularly dear to Rousseau, the pedagogue, and remained a basic element in Condorcet's writings: "l'homme qui sait les quatre régles de l'arithmétique nécessaires dans l'usage de la vie, n'est pas dans la dépendance du savant qui possède au plus haut degré le génie des sciences mathématiques, et dont le talent lui sera d'une utilité très-réelle, sans jamais pouvoir le gêner dans la jouissance de ses droits."[12]

Consequently, although Condorcet accorded priority to a scientific method of teaching, he did not do so out of a belief in the dominant role of scientific subjects as such, as was common in the trend of educational theory in his century. Rather, he firmly felt that rigorousness, clearness, and precision in thought were directly related to and derived from the methodological and epistemological significance of the sciences, and particularly of mathematics.[13] In other words, the value of the sciences and mathematics lay fundamentally with the way of thinking they assured to the student.

The revolutionary explosion gave Condorcet a sudden opportunity to realize his deepest desires: "Longtemps j'ai considéré ces vues comme des rêves qui ne devaient se réaliser que dans un avenir indéterminé, et pour un monde où je n'existerais plus. Un heureaux événement a tout à coup ouvert une carrière immense aux espérances du genre humain; un seul instant a mis un siècle de distance entre l'homme du jour et celuî du lendemain."[14] Self-confident after ten years of experience and popular esteem acquired through his *Mémoires* among other works, Condorcet was elected to the first Committee of Public Instruction created by the Revolution, which a few months later produced his *Projet* submitted by him to the Legislative Assembly on April 20 and 21, 1792. The beginning of his political activity in the educational field coincided, of course, with one of the most delicate moments in the history of the French educational organization. The educational system of the *ancien régime*, mainly in the hands of the Church,[15] had already collapsed under the blows of the Revolution,[16] while the Constituent Assembly had not yet given birth to new institutions, issuing only incomplete and partial new measures to shield the existing system from complete disintegration.

Given this legislative vacuum, Condorcet consequently had a good chance of using the proposals published in the *Bibliothèque de l'homme public* as a framework for the *Projet* presented in the name of the whole Committee of Public Instruction.

Compared with his *Mémoires*, which represented the complete albeit journalistic presentation of his ideas, the *Projet* was more concise and less free in its exposition; this mainly resulted from its being formulated as a draft of law. There are, however, aside from these structural contrasts, differences in accent and content between the *Projet* and *Mémoires*. It is essential to understand these differences if one is to understand Condorcet's educational concepts. Although nearly contemporaneous, and fundamentally inspired by the same spirit, the two works denote two particular and distinct moments of his reflection and give substantial evidence to the evolution undergone by his thought. Propped up by revolutionary enthusiasm, the *Mémoires* were based on the struggle to demolish the structures of the *ancien régime*. Although drawn from a new, exalted reality, they continued to echo the battle cries of *Lumières* against the old world, in which Condorcet had been molded and with which he had struggled. In the *Projet*, on the other hand, the consciousness of dealing with a revolutionary reality was already present, although not without a prescient intuition of its possible future excesses.[17] The formulation of the *Projet* as presented to the Legislative Assembly reveals Condorcet's need to confront his ideas with those of others and to enrich his own proposals through contact with new problems and needs. However, there was not much substantial opposition to Condorcet's theses from with the Legislative Assembly's Committee of Public Instruction; hence we must conclude that differences between the *Projet* and the *Mémoires* derive from Condorcet's own intellectual evolution, in the circumstances as they developed.

Compared to the *Mémoires*, the *Projet* shows a more compact political formulation and a wider sensitivity toward the collectivity. Although an individualistic perspective was still present, even in its opening sentences Condorcet's report envisaged the citizens as a whole body, and referred to social needs, general welfare, and human advancement. As a member of the Committee of Public Instruction, itself born of a revolutionary process, he was more aware of national political responsibility: "l'instruction publique" as a "devoir de la société à l'égard des citoyens" thus became in the *Projet* "l'instruction nationale" which the "puissance publique" had to ensure as a "devoir de justice." Out of this new perspective, the need to guarantee educational autonomy from political power led Condorcet to recognize the unique and final authority of the Legislative body as an expression of popular sovereignty. According to the same constitutional principles, popular sovereignty was the basis of politically independent public education: "la constitution française...a reconnu que la nation a le droit inaliénable et imprescriptible de réformer toutes les lois: elle a donc voulu que, dans l'instruction nationale, tout fût soumis á un examen rigoureux."[18]

His profound cultural sensitivity, tolerance, and deep respect for pluralism, which had driven him, in his *Mémoires*, to claim an inalienable right for all kinds of intellectual, scientific, literary, and artistic expression, regardless of political considerations, are also clearly present in the *Projet*. In the latter, however, the need to assure a correspondence between culture and social needs is more intense. While in his *Mémoires* Condorcet proposed: "l'instruction nationale relative aux professions...aussi [à] celles que les hommes exercent pour leur utilité propre, sans songer à l'influence qu'elles peuvent avoir sur la prosperité générale,"[19] in the *Projet*, restating the same concept, he assumes a less individualistic perspective: "Si par des vues étroites, on voulait exclure les sciences qui paraissaient de pure curiosité, ou séparer dans chacune ce qui est utile de ce qui ne l'est pas, on nuirait à cette utilité même, pour laquelle on aurait voulu tout sacrifier; et on verrait bientôt qu'au lieu d'avoir écarté des spéculations on n'a fait que consacrer des erreurs et des routines imparfaites."[20]

Consequently, the educational and organizational proposals dealing with primary schools were meant to assure teachings of practical and immediate use to the student, while guaranteeing a complete intellectual development for every individual and even genetic enrichment for the whole human species.[21] Although the proposals in the *Mémoires* concerning primary schools in no way distinguished between city and countryside, the report presented in the name of the Committee of Public Instruction indicated a certain preference for more emphasis on agricultural learning in country schools and commercial and mechanical instruction in the city, while maintaining the need for general educational national uniformity. On the whole, the general scheme of school organization, as detailed in the *Projet*, was more articulated (school levels were raised from three to five), more uniform, and less discriminatory; vocational training, which in the *Mémoires* was left to special schools, was now assigned to the third level of instruction, the *instituts*, compulsory for those wishing to go on for a higher degree.

As far as university teaching was concerned, Condorcet had such resolution in his own ideas that he succeeded in challenging and winning the only skirmish that occurred in the Committee of Public Instruction, some of whose members still clung to positions expounded in the *Mémoires*, but discarded by Condorcet in the *Projet*. This report proposed a fourth educational level composed of nine *lycées*, in which both professional and scholarly training would take place. While he continued to emphasize the autonomy of scholarship, Condorcet put a new and stronger emphasis on learning's social function. He set knowledge at the service of equality, recognizing the existence of a close link between the pure and applied sciences in their role of accelerating the material progress of the nation.

It is precisely this great sensitivity toward problems of equality that pushed Condorcet, who had reconfirmed in the *Projet* the notion of the right to a free education at all levels, to reflect at greater length on the role of the state in the field of education: "La gratuité de l'instruction doit être considérée surtout dans son rapport avec l'égalité."[22] In his report he points out that a free educational system would constitute one means of acquiring national homogeneity. Although invoking independence of education, Condorcet did not think that the state should abstain from supplying the bases of scholastic organization. Education left to itself, he states, would become a prerogative of the wealthier part of the population, would spread unevenly through the nation, and would turn into a privilege of the most affluent areas.[23]

Aside from these fundamental differences, the plan presented to the Legislative Assembly followed in its general outlines the tendencies already expressed in the *Mémoires*: the same scientific formulation and the same role allocated to schools in the development of both critical intellectual abilities and the entire personality. In the *Projet's* notes, however, Condorcet felt, in the light of the developments in revolutionary events, a new urgency to place greater emphasis on rationality, conceived as both absence of the passions and as cold analysis of reality. Rationality as a product of education was considered as a weapon against all sort of demagogy available to the citizenry: "former d'abord la raison, instruire à n'écouter qu'elle, à se défendre de l'enthousiasme qui pourrait l'égarer ou l'obscurcir, et se laisser entraîner ensuite à celui qu'elle approuve; telle est la marche que prescrit l'intérêt de l'humanité, et le principe sur lequel l'instruction publique doit être combinée."[24] This quasi-desperate appeal to reason may be regarded as a final cry in the face of the reality of 1793, whose meaning Condorcet was slow to digest. These appeals represent, however, the evolution of his deepest beliefs. Education as a rational individual and collective choice stands at the very heart of Condorcet's reflections on the validity of democracy. According to Condorcet, only a skilled and specialized group, only an élite of brains, was competent to make fundamental national choices, because only this restricted group was capable of applying intellectual principles with scientific and mathematical rigor to the problems of politics.[25] Consenting to a ruling minority, however, Condorcet did not modify his opinions on the authority of popular sovereignty. The majority should be able to evaluate, through widened general educational diffusion, the validity and rationality of élite decisions, though without disputing the élite's authority. Thus élite meant to Condorcet the elimination of ignorance and a complete reshaping of the entire body politic through the national organization of education.

The autonomy of culture, reasserted in the concept of a ruling élite of merit, implied a hierarchy in the educational system that had not emerged in the *Mémoires.* On the contrary, in the *Projet*, the corporatist consolidation was almost accomplished, by means of an institution located in Paris. This fifth educational level was called *Société nationale des sciences et des arts.* In addition to being a center of advanced research, the *Société nationale* was in charge of supervising the whole school system, a solid, centralized pyramid in which every level was strictly dependent on the one immediately above. The whole body gravitated toward the *Société nationale*, an entirely new body that would ensure academic freedom and independence against possible political control and the cultural centralization of the *ancien régime.*

The role assigned by Condorcet to science and scientists within the structure of society was not aimed at creating a closed, technocratic society. Instead, its goal was the development of individual participation by selection based on a merit system, for which public education was one of the more appropriate vehicles. In this framework, Condorcet's evolution had been not only cultural but also political. He had changed his positions, proclaimed on the eve of the Revolution in his *Essai sur la constitution et les fonctions des Assemblées provinciales*, and accepted universal suffrage, and later drafted the constitutional project of February 1793.[26] Despite his efforts and the evidence we have of the evolution of his thought, his liberalism remains confined to objective limits. Condorcet was never able to develop a clear-cut position on the social question, not even when confronted by the harshest critiques. While on the one hand he thought that educational institutions at all levels should be open to all without discrimination, on the other hand he acquiesced to the objective economic and social obstacles that prevented his ideas from becoming a reality.

Enriched by these developments and restricted by these contradictions, Condorcet's proposals on education encountered their first obstacles with the advent of the revolutionary crisis in mid-1792.[27] The financing of such a complex and articulated plan could not fail to meet opposition in a country undergoing revolutionary crisis. The same day Condorcet mounted the tribune to expound his proposals, war, with its obvious financial implications, was declared. At the same time, in the face of such a critical state of emergency, the political necessity for the rallying of prompt popular support for the menaced government prevented the men of the Revolution from waiting for the gradual enlightening effects of a cathartic education and a cultural policy founded on the autonomy of the intellectual class. Thus the primary function of education, especially after the proclamation of the Republic, became pure and simple propaganda in the service of the Revolution. In short, something occurred that was very far from the critical reshaping of society envisaged by Condorcet.[28]

Aside from this objective discordance between the spirit of the project presented to the Legislative Assembly and the contingent needs of the Revolution, the educational concepts of the former secretary of the *Académie des Sciences* also met increasingly harsh criticisms in the Convention. One of the weakest and more disputed points of Condorcet's concepts was clearly represented in his belief that education could actually serve to overcome social differences. The origin of such a belief can be traced back to the influence exercised upon him by the social analysis of the physiocrats, to whom Condorcet was intellectually akin. Condorcet had borrowed the theory of the structure of society from Quesnay and his circle. The proclamation of a harmony of interests between classes, which would exist when all previous obstacles were removed, and the consequent need to guarantee a general diffusion of knowledge in order to render self-evident this harmonic principle, were the centerpieces of physiocratic doctrine. The physiocrats' campaign on behalf of primary education is one of their most original and novel insights. Condorcet writes, with respect to this: "Ceux qui ont dit les premiers que les principes de l'administration des états étaient dictés par la raison et par la nature...ont été utiles aux hommes, en leur apprenant que le bonheur était plus près d'eux qu'ils ne pensaient; et que ce n'est point en bouleversant le monde, mais en l'éclairant qu'ils peuvent éspérer de trouver le bien-être et la liberté."[29] Hence educational differences, themselves products of social inequalities, would not evolve into conflicts, since differences were needed in order to guarantee the harmony that could result from setting learning at the disposal of the whole of society: "Je vais donc essayer de prouver"—wrote Condorcet in 1793 when the contrast of interest had developed in France into a cruel fight—"que ces prétendues oppositions d'intérêts n'existent pas...que l'homme ne peut devenir ennemi de l'homme que par l'effet des lois injustes, ou des institutions corruptrices."[30]

Within the limits of his own liberalism, Condorcet demonstrates the belief that not only natural inequalities but also social, economic, and professional differences could be overcome with a system of public education in which every citizen would have the chance of thoroughly developing his own personality. "Le plan de votre comité est presque tout à l'avantage du riche:"[31] with these words, filled with tragic veracity, and obscure and fierce antimontagnard deputy, Joseph Serre, launched one of the most bitter attacks against Condorcet's *Projet*.

The unresolved contradictions in Condorcet's thought could not be denied by the few partisans of his plan. Jean-François Ducos, "orateur de la Gironde," and Marie-Joseph Lequinio, for example, emphasized the ineffectiveness of a non-compulsory school system, which was, as we have seen, one of the corner-stones of Condorcet's thought. Their position was aimed at ensuring a real diffusion of education on the one hand, and Revolutionary supremacy of the primary school on the other.[32] Gilbert Romme was the staunch upholder of the plan submitted by Condorcet to the Legislative Assembly. His point of view,[33] during the struggle for an Encyclopedic concept of learning and his recognition of the universal value of scientific research over narrow, utilitarian preoccupations, was close to Condorcet's. This is the most significant example of how Condorcet's heritage evolved and changed beyond its own limits through contact with the requirements of a revolutionary situation. The strong Jacobin sense of national unity distinguished Romme's vision from Condorcet's individualism and implied the recognition of public education as a vehicle for assuring a national moral and intellectual unity. Condorcet, too, believed in the socially unifying force of culture, but his political and collective vision was always tempered by the interest of the single individual. The force of national unity and the social value of education brought Romme to underline, in a fashion far stronger than Condorcet, a respect for labor and a sense of duty that education should communicate. His "n'être pas un être inutile à la société"[34] emerged as a fundamental lesson of the republican school which, starting from Condorcet's premises, had gradually assumed a somewhat different intonation than the plan submitted by Condorcet to the Legislative Assembly.

The demand for greater equality and social justice was not a major cause of the hostility encountered by Condorcet's proposals in an assembly pervaded by that century's individualism. Condorcet's deeply-rooted secularism caused only sporadic criticism, even though the current deism, which soon materialized into the cult of the Supreme Being, was far from the clear church-state separation suggested by Condorcet. For him, consequently, the sacred individual right of conscience demanded the division between religion and educational instruction.[35]

For the men of the Revolution, the major fault of the *Projet*, which eventually led to a complete rejection of Condorcet's proposal, was its alleged corporatism. They were convinced that it would have produced a complex and articulated educational hierarchy which would eventually come to monopolize the country's culture. "Le privilège des lumières est de tous le plus dangereux."[36] This harsh condemnation concealed threads of Rousseau's thought which, used by each in his own fashion, pitted science against "republican virtue." Thus, the heart of Condorcet's educational theories was attacked in the name of limited, utilitarian, and politically controlled instruction. With reference to Rousseau's influence on Revolutionary ideologies, his cultural and educational ideas were variously elaborated by those who, in the name of his theories, wanted to reject Condorcet's proposals (themselves strongly influenced by Rousseau). From the two *Discours* to the pedagogic theory found in *Emile*, from the eduational and legislative proposals in *Economie politique* to the *Contrat Social*, from the draft of Corsica's constitution to *Considérations sur le gouvernement de la Pologne*, the revolutionary period found a whole web of proposals in Rousseau. There was the community school of Michel Lepeletier de Saint Fargeau, the civic *fêtes* system of the Protestant pastor, the Girondin Jean-Paul Rabaut Saint-Etienne (an alternative to the hierarchical school system), and the rejection of public education by Antoine-Claire Thibaudeau as a "belle production de quelques philosophes" in the name of education left to the family. Rousseau's thought was interpreted in various ways, but always with the aim of opposing an organic and Encyclopedic view of learning.[37]

These various references to Rousseau's impact concealed, through personal attacks against Condorcet's association with the older and more prestigious cultural institutions of the *ancien régime*, the basic irreconciliability of contrasting cultural ideas that were gradually taking shape in the course of the revolutionary debate. In contrast with the classic distinctions between political groups, three distinct positions can be synthetically determined.

Condorcet's proposals can be located as a position that we may clearly define as liberal. He viewed education as an instrument of collective and individual improvement, aimed at guaranteeing full liberty and the autonomy of the school system.

This position was quickly confronted by a second, which featured total indifference toward any education beyond the elementary level and aimed solely at political indoctrination. Such a view is best represented by the two projects that provoked the demise of Condorcet's proposals: the Sieyès-Daunou-Lakanal plan and the Gabriel Bouquier project.[38] Their partisans referred to "freedom of learning," rejecting a complete and graduated school system. In contradistinction to Condorcet's liberalism, this position is inspired by pre-revolutionary concepts, which held that the state should not interfere with education except in respect to technical and military schools. The educational function would be delegated to the clergy and to private tutors, with the justification that education should not represent a financial burden to the state. This implied the teaching of a submissive mentality consistent with either the spirit of absolute monarchy or, in the new political reality, a kind of revolutionary ideology.

Finally, there was a third position, embodied by Michel Lepeletier de Saint Fargeau and by Robespierre, marked by notions of *dirigisme* of the state. The state, recognizing the political and scientific value of a uniform school organization, was ready to promote such a system while retaining decisive control. "Il ne s'agit plus de former des messieurs, mais des citoyens; la patrie seule a le droit d'élever ses enfants; elle ne peut conférer ce dépôt à l'orgueil des familles, ni aux préjugés des particuliers."[39] Starting with these convictions, Robespierre outspokenly opposed not only freedom of learning but also any kind of cultural autonomy. This doctrinaire interpretation of culture, added to a violent anti-*philosophique* spirit,[40] led Robespierre to reject any form of university organization, although he recognized the value of science.

In the most radical phase of the Revolution, Robespierre, while never departing from a fundamentally utilitarian cultural position, was nonetheless quick to realize the support that scientific research could bring to the republican cause. In this he was joined by the Committee on Public Safety, which gradually undermined the authority of the Committee on Instruction. Immediately after the presentation of Lepeletier's plan, Robespierre had, in fact, exhibited his sure political intuition concerning the actual advantages of national supervision over all cultural activities. He thus expressed his sensitivity toward scientific research, but also confirmed his adhesion to a managerial vision of the state that denied free and autonomous development to the nation's intellectual life. His philosophy therefore violently clashed with Condorcet's liberalism. Faced with the political necessity of suffocating the dechristianization movement, Robespierre nevertheless did not hesitate to support the freedom of teaching sought by Gabriel Bouquier and his refusal to organize a complete and graduated national system of education that would go beyond primary schools. In fact, against the strong anticlerical movement, Bouquier's plan offered Robespierre an effective political instrument which, in the name of freedom of teaching, allowed him both to break the anti-religious movement by giving clerical representatives the possibility of teaching, and also to redeem himself in the eyes of more moderate political elements. In addition, Bouquier's well-known anti-intellectualism could be reconciled both with Robespierre's own sharp anti-encyclopedism, which had been strengthened during the bloody climate of the Reign of Terror, and also with the *sans culottes'* cultural insensitivity, thus heightening the political prestige of Robespierre. But when faced with the urgencies of revolutionary crisis and the burden of war, Robespierre and his collaborators did not hesitate to remove their support from Bouquier and become actively interested in coordinating the country's scientific activities.

In effect, Robespierre and the Committee on Public Safety initiated the creation of the institutions of higher learning that remained a major result of the Revolution. In the deepening military and economic crisis, the first courses were taught on how to prepare saltpetre. The *Ecole de Mars* was founded with the aim of ensuring the production of a military class. The *Ecole normale, Ecole centrale des travaux publics*, and the *Ecoles de santé*, which even today remain among the bases of France's system of higher education, were founded during the Thermidorean period, when Condorcet's views of learning received full recognition.

Those who had rejected the most valid and insightful of Condorcet's proposals, and who attempted to transform the school system into a tool of political propaganda, became the founders of a number of France's higher educational and research centers. Thus, paradoxically, they assured the triumph of some of Condorcet's ideas.

The Revolution hence sanctified his partial victory and testified to the importance of his educational ideas, annulling the attacks and persecutions of his political adversaries. The Revolution is testimony to the validity of Condorcet's educational thought and the revolutionary value of learning, research, and the free expression of intellectual activity.

Although Condorcet's *Projet* was controversial in the political events of the revolutionary period, the value of his basic educational ideas has survived intact, above and beyond the particular historical moment in which they were formulated. The principles of a national, multi-leveled educational system, free and available to everyone without distinction of class, sex, race, or religion and of an encyclopedic, scientific, and secular method of education were to remain down to the present the highest goals of an authentically democratic school.

Notes

1. Among the historiographical products of the Third Republic see: Jean-François-Eugène Robinet, *Condorcet, sa vie, son oeuvre (1743-1794)* (Paris, 1893); Francisque Vial, *Condorcet et l'éducation démocratique* (Paris, 1902) (Genève, 1970); Franck Alengry, *Condorcet, guide de la Révolution française* (Paris, 1904) (Genève, 1971); Léon Cahan, *Condorcet et la Révolution française*, (New York, 1904, repr. 1971); Henri Bigot, *Les idées de Condorcet sur l'instruction publique* (Poitiers, 1912); Ferdinand Buisson, *Condorcet* (Collection des "Reformateurs sociaux") (Paris, 1931); Jammy-Schmidt, *Les grandes thèses radicales, de Condorcet à Edouard Herriot* (Paris, 1931).

2. See L. Cahen, *Condorcet...*, 277.

3. See Keith Michael Baker, *Condorcet. From Natural Philosophy to Social Mathematics* (Chicago and London 1975).

4. In addition to his published works, clear evidence of the political and pedagogical importance of educational problems in Condorcet's thought during the period preceding the Revolution may be found in his handwritten, unpublished papers at the Bibliothèque de l'Institut de France in Paris (MS 884), the object of my present research.

5. See the five *Mémoires: Sur l'instruction publique par M. de Condorcet. Premier Mémoire. Nature et objet de l'instruction publique; Second Mémoire. De l'instruction commune pour les enfants; Troisième Mémoire. Sur l'instruction commune pour les hommes; Quatrième Mémoire. Sur l'instruction relative aux professions; Cinquième Mémoire. Sur l'instruction relative aux sciences*, published in volumes 1, 2, 3, and 11 of 1791 in *"Bibliothèque de l'homme public, ou Analyse raisonnée des principaux ouvrages françois et étrangers; Sur la Politique en général, la Législation, les Finances, la Police, l'Agriculture et le Commerce en particulier, et sur le Droit naturel et public*, Paris, 1790-1792. They have been published together with the *Projet* submitted to the Legislative Assembly in volume 7 of Condorcet's complete works, Jean Marie Antoine Caritat de Condorcet, *Oeuvres de Condorcet*, ed. Arthur C. O'Connor and Marie F. Arago, 12 vols., Paris, 1847-1849. In these pages we will always refer to the edition of *Mémoires* and *Projet* published in *Oeuvres, O.D.*

6. Jean Marie Antoine Caritat de Condorcet, *Sur l'instruction publique. Premier Mémoire. Nature et objet de l'instruction publique.* See *Oeuvres...*, 8:169-73. (From now on we will indicate only the term *Mémoire* preceded by *Premier, Second*, etc.)

7. *Cinquième Mémoire*, 413. With the exception of this short sentence, no systematic treatment of the issue of the compulsory nature of schools exists in the *Mémoires, Projet* and the other works by Condorcet. However the importance of the problem for Condorcet is evident throughout his work. Moreover, he was attacked during the Revolution for his ideas on this issue.

8. "En général tout pouvoir, de quelque nature qu'ils soit, en quelques mains qu'il ait été remis, de quelque manière qu'il ait été conferé, est naturellement ennemi des lumières ...plus les hommes sont éclairés, moins ceux qui ont l'autorité pourront en abuser, et moins aussi il sera nécessaire de donner aux pouvoirs sociaux d'étendue ou d'énergie. La vérité est donc à la fois l'ennemie du pouvoir comme de ceux qui l'exercent. (*Cinquième Mémoire*, 420-21).

9. For a liberal interpretation of Condorcet's thought, cf. J. Salwyn Schapiro, *Condorcet and the Rise of Liberalism* (New York, 1934).

10. On the role of women in the Enlightenment see Paul Hoffmann, *La femme dans la pensée des Lumières* (Paris, 1977); on Madame Condorcet see Antoine Guillois, *La marquise de Condorcet, sa famille, son salon, ses amis (1764-1822)* (Paris, 1897); on Condorcet's proposals on the voting rights for women see: *Lettres d'un bourgeois de New Haven à un citoyen de Virginie sur l'inutilité de partager le pouvoir législatif entre plusieurs corps, O.C.*, 9:1-93, *Sur l'admission des femmes au droit de cité, O.C.*, 10:119-30.

11. On the role of education as a remedy for alienation resulting from the division of labor, Condorcet wrote in the first *Mémoire:* "M. Smith a remarqué que, plus les professions mécaniques se divisaient, plus le peuple était exposé à contracter cette stupidité naturelle aux hommes bornés à un petit nombre d'idées d'un même genre. L'instruction est le seul remède de ce mal...[for] l'individu destiné à la branche la plus resserrée d'une profession mécanique, afin qu'il puisse échapper à la stupidité, non par l'étendue, mais par le choix et la justesse des notions qu'il recevra." (*Premier Mémoire*, 191-92).

12. *Premier Mémoire*, 171.

13. *Second Mémoire*, 243, 262-63. On the relations between science and knowledge in Condorcet see Keith Michael Baker, *Condorcet. From Natural Philosophy....*See also *Scientism, elitism and liberalism: the case of Condorcet, Studies on Voltaire and the XVIIIth Century* 55 (1967): 129-65.

14. *Cinquième Mémoire*, 433.

15. On this subject, see the history of two major religious schools in the *ancien Régime* in the works of: Robert R. Palmer, *The School of the French Revolution: A Documentary History of the College of Louis-le-Grand and its Director, Jean-François Champagne, 1762-1814* (Princeton, 1975), and: Jean De Viguerie, *Une Oeuvre d'éducation sous l'Ancien Régime. Les Pères de la Doctrine Chrétienne* en France et an Italie (1592-1792) (Paris, 1976).

16. The abolition on August 4, 1789, of the feudal system and the confiscation, on November 12, of Church property, had impoverished the main sources of educational revenues; the abolition of religious orders on February 15, 1790, the Civil Constitution of the Clergy on July 12, the dismissal of non-juring priests on April 15 and 17, 1791, decimated and split the teaching staff.

17. The distance between Condorcet's formulation and the evolution of the revolutionary process was more evident in the notes he added to the new edition of the *Projet*, decreed by the Convention at the beginning of 1793. This enlarged text was later published in volume 7 of Condorcet's complete works, 449-573.

18. *Rapport et projet de décret sur l'organisation générale de l'instruction publique, présentés à l'Assemblée nationale, au nom du comité d'instruction publique, les 20 et 21 avril 1792, O.C.*, 7:526-27.

19. *Premier Mémoire*, 175.

20. *Rapport...*, 569-70.

21. In his first *Mémoire* Condorcet wrote: "Il est...assez simple de penser que si plusieurs générations ont reçu une éducation dirigée vers un but constant...les générations suivantes naîtront avec une facilité plus grande à recevoir l'instruction et plus d'aptitude à en profiter... Ainsi, l'intensité de nos facultés est attachée, au moins en partie, à la perfection des organes intellectuels, et il est naturel de croire que cette perfection n'est pas indépendante de l'état où ils se trouvent dans les personnes qui nous transmettent l'existence." (*Premier Mémoire*, 182-83).

22. *Rapport...*, 494.

23. *Rapport...*, 491-92.

24. *Rapport...*, 475.

25. See Keith Michael Baker, *Scientism...*

26. For a complete exposition of the evolution of Condorcet's political ideas, which parallel the evolution of his ideas on education, cf. the books on Condorcet by Cahen, Baker, and Alengry, cited in notes 1 and 3.

27. Even today scholars of education in revolutionary France must rely on the works of Third Republic historians. See the clerical historians, Albert Duruy, *L'instruction publique et la Révolution* (Paris, 1882); Augustin Sicard, *L'éducation morale et civique avant et pendant la révolution (1700-1808)* (Paris, 1884); Ernest Allain, *L'oeuvre scolaire de la Révolution, 1789-1802. Etudes critiques et documents inédits* (Paris, 1891). Among the secular scholars see Louis Liard, *L'enseignement supérieur en France* (Paris, 1888-1894). Cf. also Gabriel Compayre, *Histoire critique des doctrines de l'education.* (Paris 1880) and Manuela Albertone, *Fisiocrati, istruzione e cultura*, (Torino, Fondazione Luigi Einaudi, 1979).

28. For an examination of this attitude, well exemplifed by the critiques of the Girondist Lanthenas to Condorcet's position, see Manuela Albertone, supra, note 27, 75-80.

29. Condorcet, *Notes sur Voltaire, O.C.*, 4:300.

30. Condorcet, *Que toutes les classes de la société n'ont qu'un même intétêt, Jounal d'instruction sociale*, 8 juin 1793, *O.C.*, 12:646-47. Condorcet had been strongly influenced by the Physiocrats' concepts in his thoughts on education. He went beyond them, while nonetheless bearing in mind the Physiocrats' teachings, graced with a greater cultural sensibility and strong faith in democratic principles. See Manuela Albertone, *Fisiocrati, istruzione e cultura* (Torino, 1979).

31. Joseph Serre, *Je vous prie de lire jusqu'au bout. Quelques réflexions sur l'instruction publique par Joseph Serre, Des Hautes Alpes*, s. l., De l'Imprimerie nationale, 1793, 4.

32. Cf. *Archives parlementaires. Recueil complet des débats législatifs et politiques des chambres françaises. Première Série (1787-1799)*, Paris, 1867, Mendeln Lichtenstein, 1969 (hereinafter called *A.P.*), Dec. 18, 1792.

33. On Gilbert Romme see the outstanding biography by Alessandro Galante Garrone, *Gilbert Romme, storia di un rivolizionario* (Torino, 1959), and *Gilbert Romme et son temps*, Actes du Colloque tenu à Riom et Clermont les 10 et 11 juin 1965 (Paris, 1966).

34. *A.P.*, 55, meeting of Dec. 20, 1792.

35. *Rapport...*, 483–84.

36. *A.P.*, 55, meeting of Dec. 24, 1792, speech by Bancal des Issarts. In his speech critical of Condorcet's plan, the *girondin* Bancal coined for the first time, referring to secondary education, the term *écoles centrales* which then later appeared in the law of 3 Brumaire year III (1795), which sanctioned the first revolutionary reorganization of the educational system.

37. On the complex and debated problem of Rousseau's influence on revolutionary thought, see Albert Soboul, *Jean-Jacques Rousseau et le jacobinisme.* In *Etudes sur le Contrat social de Jean-Jacques Rousseau* (Paris, 1964), 405–24; Joan Mc Donald, *Rousseau and French Revolution, 1762–1791* (London, 1965); Irving Fetscher, *Rousseaus Politische Philosophie. Zur Geschichte des demokratischen Freiheitsbegriffs* (Newiedam Rhein-Berlin, 1968).

38. On the contents of these two projects see Manuela Albertone, supra note 27, chap. III and IV.

39. *A.P.*, 90, meeting of May 7, 1794.

40. On the attacks against the Encyclopedist movement and against Condorcet, "grand géomètre...au jugement des littérateurs, et grand littérateur, au dire des géomètres," see the whole text of the speech by Robespierre on the cult of the Supreme Being (*A.P.*, 90, meeting of May 7, 1794).

THE QUEST FOR JUSTICE

10
Un Provincial Eclaire:
Thomas Riboud, Emule de Condorcet

Louis Trénard

Abstract

The historian is often attracted by the great thinkers, those who have left us imperishable works. But if he has in mind everyday life, if he wishes to follow the spread of fundamental ideas, he must examine the intermediary role affirmed by lesser writers. Riboud represents one of those relay stages.

Like many of his contemporaries, he was preoccupied by public *instruction*, meaning the acquisition of basic techniques and essential knowledge. *Education* is a product of family, church, and so-called educational societies.

As a member of the Committee on Public Instruction, Thomas Riboud, despite his admiration for Condorcet, differed on several points from his proposed Decree on Public Instruction and induced Condorcet to refurbish its concepts. Riboud is an example of those talented bourgeois whose careers allowed for the regeneration of France.

Le marquis de Condorcet, après une vie dévouée aux lumières, meurt victime de la Révolution montagnards. Son projet scolaire est abandonné en l'An II... Mais ce théoricien des progrès de l'esprit a marqué son âge. l'optimisme des lumières qu'il incarne a rayonné dans l'espace comme il rayonnera dans le temps. Le Bressan Thomas Riboud, lecteur de Voltaire, et de Rousseau, s'inspire volontiers des conceptions condorcétiennes.

I. Un Notable Bressan

Né à Bourg-en-Bresse en 1755, Thomas Philibert Riboud appartient à une famille ancienne de magistrats vraisemblablement originaire de Pont-d'Ain, à l'ombre du château des ducs de Savoie. Son grand-père fut châtelain royal de la ville de Bourg, conseiller de la province de Bresse puis syndic général du Tiers Etat, chargé de s'occuper des affaires pendant l'intervalle des sessions des Etats de Bourgogne. Son grand-oncle, Jean Bernard Riboud fut maire de Bourg et premier syndic du Tiers sous Louis XV; l'intendant de Dijon même tremblait devant ce puissant personnage. Le père de Thomas, Jean Bernard, dit Riboud des Avinières, assuma les fonctions d'Elu de Bresse, recouvrant les impositions.

Elève précoce, le jeune Thomas, à 4 ans, sait lire, écrire, faire des thèmes; à 9 ans, il entre au Collège de Bourg; à 12 ans, il étudie la logique. Il poursuit ses classes au Collège de Beaune tenu par les Oratoriens: deux ans de rhétorique puis logique et physique. A 16 ans, il termine sa carrière scolastique; à 19 ans, il reçoit ses grades à l'université de Dijon. De 1774 à 1778, il exerce en qualité d'avocat au barreau de Lyon. Il est nommé à 24 ans procureur du roi au bailliage de Bresse et siège présidial de Bourg, occupant ainsi un poste élévé de la justice.[1] En 1781, il épouse Marie-Catherine Rocoffort, fille d'un riche négociant de Lyon. Deux ans plus tard, l'intendant de Bourgogne, Feydeau de Brou; le choisit comme subdélégué. "Je ne sais pourquoi," note Riboud dans son journal, "j'ai été préféré; le public m'a jugé avec bonté et mes concitoyens m'ont donné une marque précieuse d'estime. Ils avaient paru désirer le choix de M. de Brou et ils y ont applaudi; cette circonstance a donné un prix véritable au nouvel emploi dont j'étais revêtu; elle m'a fait contracter intérieurement l'engagement sacré de continuer à me rendre digne de la Patrie et de faire tout de qui sera en mon pouvoir pour lui témoigner mon zèle et mon attachement."[2]

Cet avocat, né à peu près en même temps que l'*Encyclopédie*, se passionne pour les lumières. À Lyon, il crée, avec les abbés Royer et Tabard, les érudits Béraud et Geoffroy, son confrère Delandine, la *Société Littéraire*. Ce cénacle s'occupe d'économie politique et répand les idées nouvelles: on entend un discours contre le fanatisme, on dispute la question de savoir "jusqu'à quel point l'esprit philosophique peut influencer la législation," on reprend le débat sur le rôle des lettres, des sciences et des arts…Cette "petite académie" porte la marque du siècle: activité intense dans tous les domaines, optimisme à l'égard de l'homme, de ses facultés, de ses possibilités de développement, confiance, un peu naïve dans le progrès et, par dessus tout, une recherche d'esprit, un jeu de la pensée et du style.[3]

Comme beaucoup de membres de ces sociétés de pensée, Riboud tourne ses regards vers les Insurgents. Dès 1778, il lit à la *Société littéraire de Lyon* un *Quatrain pour le portrait du général Washington*:

Sous ce guerrier modeste et sage

Insurgent, tu seras vainqueur:

Car dans son bras est le courage,

Et la liberté dans son coeur.

Ses *Notes philosophiques et littéraires* contiennent un article intitulé "Administration intérieure de l'Amérique-unie." Sa première phrase affirme l'intérêt porté par les Français à cette libération des colonies. "Tout le monde connaît la forme de l'administration de la nouvelle république américaine…" Chaque citoyen y possède une parcelle du pouvoir. "Ce sont autant de petites républiques qui correspondent par divers échelons à la masse générale." En chaque district, vit une

communauté qui peut se réunir à la demande de sept habitants. "Il y a nécessairement, chaque année, plusieurs de ces assemblées et tout homme, de la première
comme de la dernière classe, paysan, marchand, journalier, gentilhomme,
magistrat a le droit de voter et de dire son opinion sur les affaires publiques."
Chaque citoyen peut donner des conseils à ses représentants et participe ainsi,
comme le souhaitait Rousseau, aux affaires publiques." La correspondance du
citoyen avec la tête de l'Etat est parfaite et le bien peut partir et être indiqué par
l'homme le plus inconnu." Cette démocratie directe garantit la liberté mais à
condition que chaque individu exerce réellement ses droits et prenne conscience
de ses responsabilités: "Tant que le peuple usera souvent de la faculté de
s'assembler, il sera vrainment libre;"[4] Dans l'itinéraire spirituel de Riboud,
l'influence des philosophes français se trouve confortée par la fascination
exemplaire de la jeune republique américaine.

Des propos analogues parsèment le discours que prononce Riboud en qualité
de procureur du roi du bailliage de Bresse à l'Assemblée générale du Tiers Etat,
tenue à Bourg en avril 1781, dans lequel il célèbre Necker. "J'ai payé, écrit-il dans
ses *Notes*, "à M. Necker, le tribut de reconnaissance que lui doit tout bon citoyen
dans le discours que j'ai prononcé aux Etats de cette année le 24 avril 1781. A
l'instant où je l'ai répandu, la démission de M. Necker dont on parlait depuis 15
jours a été confirmée. Le mémoire que M. Necker avait fait en 1778 concernant
les Parlements et les Intendants a transpiré, il a même été imprimé. Ce mémoire
renferme les vues les plus saines et les plus patriotiques. Son cime est d'avoir
développé des vérités humaines; d'avoir mis au jour de grands abus qu'on ne
soupçonnait pas pouvoir frapper les yeux d'un homme en place." Plus tard, il
confirme son attachment admiratif au ministre de Louis XVI: "Parmi la foule des
libelles que l'intérêt et la haine ont enfanté contre M. Necker, un des plus mauvais
et des plus injurieux est parti des mains de Beaumarchais, mauvais citoyen et
très mauvais sujet qui abuse d'une réputation littéraire acquise dans un temps de
fomentation."[5] Lors de la rentrée du présidial en 1779 et 1781, il encourage la
sensibilité et le patriotisme chez le magistrat.[6]

Cet amateur de littérature s'est d'abord passionné pour la poésie légère; lui-
même avoue, dans son journal: "Il est malheureux que ce que l'on dans le genre
libertin ne puisse pas être lu; nous n'avons pas de meilleur poème que la *Pucelle*
et Vénus a donné l'être aux plus jolies pièces de vers…J'ai commencé par faire des
pièces un peu libres, ce sont les meilleures que j'aie faites. L'imagination est
puissamment émue en parcourant ces matières. Je devins un peu plus sérieux
ensuite; je fis des contes, des moralités, des fables, des épithalames, des épîtres…,
et enfin, j'ai fini par abandonner les muses, je crois parce que les muses m'aban-
donnaient."

Admirant Delisle et Bernis, Riboud estime qu'un homme "qui est dans le cas
d'écrire, devrait toujours faire de temps en temps des vers, non pas pour acquérir
un nom en ce genre, mais parce que la poésie apprend à donner du nombre et de

l'harmonie au style.'' Rousseau est alors son modèle. Quand, en 1781, revenant du château de Châtenay, Riboud tombe de cheval et se blesse, il compare sa chute à celle que le promeneur solitaire raconte dans sa deuxième promenade. Notre Bressan avoue: "J'ai l'âme formée à peu près comme la sienne: même sensibilité, même amour du bien; il y a des ressemblances suivies entre lui et moi qui m'ont souvent frappé. Les différences sont celles du génie et de l'éloquence, il les avait apportées en naissant et je ne lui ressemble que par les malheurs et la sensibilité. Aussi, est-il peu d'ouvrages que je lise avec plus de plaisir que les siens, quoique je n'admette ni ses erreurs ni ses paradoxes.'' L'aveu est intéressant; la fascination n'entraîne pas l'adhésion.

Le journal intime se poursuit sur le ton de la confession: "Plus je lis cet écrivain, illustre et malheureux, plus je hais ses persécuteurs...Incapable de haïr fortement, je déteste tout ce qui est injustice. Ce sentiment remplit ma vie d'amertume; je ne puis voir sans une espèce de fureur la bassesse et l'intérêt triompher sans cesse de la vertu et de la probité; dans mon indignation, je regarderai l'homme comme l'être le plus méchant; une action inique me soulève et je désire alors l'autorité non pour dominer mais pour punir et pour ramener l'homme au bien, comme Rousseau. J'ai apporté en naissant cette fierté d'âme qui me rend insupportable toute espèce de servitude qui n'est pas fondée sur la raison ou sur l'utilité publique.''[7]

Au même moment, avec lucidité, il analyse l'organisation provinciale: "Cette administration a, comme toutes les autres, un appareil imposant et, dans le vrai, ce n'est que pure cérémonie. L'usage de continuer le Conseil et les Syndics par ordre de la Cour les rend inamovibles et fait cesser tout le bien qu'on pourrait attendre de citoyens qui y seraient successivement appelés et qui, animés par le patriotisme, tâcheraient d'emporter de la gloire et de l'estime à la fin de leur triennalité.''[8] Riboud souhaite une efficace gestion provinciale avec une participation des Bressans désireux de promouvoir leur région. Pour une telle mission, il faut du zèle et des lumières.

Membre de l'Académie des Sciences et Belles-Lettres de Dijon, membre associé de plusieurs compagnies savantes, Riboud réunit, chez lui, le 16 février 1783, douze personnes susceptibles de constituer une société utile à la Bresse, ayant pour objet la culture des sciences et des lettres. Trois ecclésiastiques sont là dont le Père Pacifique Rousselet, religieux augustin, prieur de Brou, quatre nobles dont M. de la Bevière, syndic de la noblesse; les autres appartiennent à l'élite burgienne. Selon les usages pratiqués à cette date, se forme la *Société d'Emulation* avec quatre classes d'associés; les véritables membres, au nombre de seize, doivent financer et gérer la société; ils s'engagent à présenter des communications aux séances qui se tiendront chaque quinzaine. Une amende sanctionnera les absences et même les retards.[9]

M. de la Bévière est élu directeur et Riboud secrétaire. C'est lui qui prononce le discours inaugural le 24 février. Il justifie l'utilité de la société nouvellement créée par un hymne à la raison, à la science, au progrès. Les sociétés littéraires permettent la diffusion de l'instruction et de la vérité. Elles répandent les bienfaits de la sociabilité, fournissent des occasions de travail, suscitent l'émulation. C'est l'absence d'un tel groupement qui a paralysé la Bresse; curieux reproche de la part de Riboud: l'astronome Jérôme Le François de Lalande avait fondé, en 1755, un Cercle littéraire que l'on a parfois présenté comme l'annonciateur de la *Société d'Emulation*; mais les assemblées de la "petite académie" de Lalande furent interdites en 1757. Alors que le Beaujolais profitait de son Académie, la Bresse souffrit de l'absence d'un foyer de réflexions. Elle était déjà handicapée par sa géographie, ses difficultés de communication, le peu d'entrain de ses habitants. Le Bressan ne s'est pas vu refuser les dons de l'esprit; sa mollesse peut être imputable aux effets du climat. Riboud reprend une thèse, fréquemment formulée au XVIIIe siècle, accordant à la météorologie une influence déterminante sur la psychologie collective.

L'orateur énumère enfin les améliorations à apporter dans les différents domaines: agriculture, commerce, éducation, moeurs...Il présage "une heureuse révolution" provoquée en Bresse par le *Société d'Emulation*."[10]

La nouvelle institution se dote d'un règlement, d'un emblème, d'un protecteur. Elle choisit la Ruche d'abeilles avec, pour devise, le vers de Virgile *Labor omnibus unus*; elle prie le duc de Bourbon d'agréer le titre de protecteur. Il s'agit de Louis Joseph de Bourbon (1736-1818), fils du prince de Condé, gouverneur de la Bourgogne; ce sera, plus tard, le général en chef de l'armée des émigrés à Coblentz. Désormais, Riboud partage son temps entre ses responsabilités politiques et son activité intellectuelle: il présente diverses communications sur l'histoire, l'archéologie, l'agriculture...Plusieurs sont insérées dans le *Journal des Savants* et dans *le Journal de physique* de Dijon, il publie, en 1785 un *Éloge d'Agnès Sorel*, il compose des *Etrennes littéraires* ou *Almanach offert aux amis de l'humanité.*[11]

Son journal intime consigne les difficultés rencontrées: "La formation de cette société m'a coûté des peines considérables, des soins, des démarches dont j'ai été pleinement récompensé par le succés; j'ai cherché à être utile à mon pays... Ainsi, pour arriver à mon but, j'ai été obligé de combattre, de persuader presque tous ceux qui ont été les premiers membres de la société. Il a fallu ensuite lui donner sa forme, ses statuts, établir sa correspondance...Il est facile de juger par ce coup d'oeil leger du courage qu'il a fallu employer et des travaux auxquels j'ai été obligé de me livrer."[12]

Fonder une académie ou une société littéraire au XVIIIe siècle, signifie vouloir échapper au rythme de la vie de tous les jours, s'organiser pour la stabilité, songer à la durée, à l'héritage culturel et même à l'immortalité. Au rythme du temps court de la vie, l'événement marquant que représente une création académique est riche d'un sens aussitôt chargé de permanence. C'est le passage de la rencontre amicale à l'institution, de l'irrégularité à la règle, ce qui dépasse la vanité de faire connaître son nom.

Fondateur de traditions, le discours inaugural déclenche une histoire ou même une hagiographie. Désormais, dans les registres manuscrits et dans les mémoires publiés, l'allocution est célébration et affirmation de l'existence de la société; un rituel s'instaure.[13] Les motivations qui poussent un homme comme Riboud à provoquer cette cristallisation, à animer désormais de façon rythmée, un cénacle, sont diverses et difficiles à pénétrer; confiance dans la force rayonnante des lumières, désir de sociabilité, sens des responsabilités, joie de l'esprit.

On peut aussi voir, dans la carrière académique, un moyen pour un bourgeois éclairé d'accéder à une certaine noblesse. A Dijon, Bernard de Ruffey exprime, en 1769, sa conception du rôle de la noblesse: "Ceux à qui des emplois importants soit dans l'épée, soit dans la robe, le ministère, ne permettent pas des études assidues, se plaisent à en faire le délassement de leurs travaux et à encourager les talents par leur protection. Les princes donnent eux-mêmes l'exemple et pensent avec raison que la culture de leur esprit est nécessaire pour élever leur âme au niveau de leur rang et soutenir avec honneur la gloire de leur naissance." La mission intellectuelle de la noblesse couronne le rôle social. Il appartient à tout noble d'aider à "affranchir les esprits des ténèbres de l'ignorance et du fanatisme de la superstition."

Or, le groupe dominant à l'Académie de Dijon est constituê par la bourgeoisie qui cherche, comme l'écrit Richard de Ruffey dans son *Histoire secrète de l'Académie de Dijon* (Paris 1909), à "racheter la bassesse de sa naissance par ses talents littéraires." Il est vrai qu'en cette docte compagnie, les robins étaient les plus nombreux, depuis les conseillers modestes jusqu'aux présidents du Parlement. Les sociétés de pensée favorisaient la promotion de cette élite.[14]

En même temps, cet enrichissement culturel conduit à une action politique. Les hommes éclairés doivent gouverner, à tout le moins administrer. Les philosophes ont transmis leur conviction: les valeurs scientifiques ont préparé le terrain de la Révolution, l'élite a voulu une démocratie politique. Le progrès intellectuel ne pouvait se parfaire dans une société d'Ancien Régime fondée sur des principes étrangers à ces données nouvelles. La méthode scientifique encourage la critique ouverte et directe des habitudes traditionnelles. Elle exige des explications fondées sur la raison et non pas sur la coutume ou le droit établi; elle détruit les principes d'autorité dérivés de tout autre source que la nature; elle permet par la diffusion du nouveau savoir, une égalité sans liaison avec l'origine sociale.

En réalité, ces liaisons ne se produisent pas toujours. La plupart du temps, le progrès scientifique implique l'acceptation momentanée des principes existants. Le savant tend, malgré les apparences, à conserver ses paradigmes. Mais ce qui compte dans l'histoire, ce sont les espérances et les illusions d'un Condorcet et d'un Riboud.[15]

II. L'engagement Politique

Riboud lit beaucoup et, dans ses *Notes philosophiques et littéraires*, il consigne ses jugements. Il se plaint de la quantité de mauvais écrits; en revanche, il déplore les entraves à la liberté d'écrire: *"L'histoire philosophique et politique du commerce des Européens dans les deux Indes* par l'abbé Raynal est un ouvrage qui a été accueilli soit en France, soit à l'étranger avec un enthousiasme bien fondé …Tout y est réussi…Je ne lus pas cet ouvrage, je le dévorai. Le temps et la réflexion n'ont pas diminué l'estime du public…Cet ouvrage pouvait-il manquer d'être persécuté? A la honte de notre temps, il l'a été et l'est encore." En 1781, en effet, le Parlement ordonna de brûler le réquisitoire de Guillaume Raynal contre la conduite des Européens dans le Nouveau Monde et dans les colonies.

Après Beccaria, qu'il a lu, Riboud se fait l'écho des critiques adressées à la justice; comme Voltaire, il condamne la torture et appelle une réforme de la jurisprudence criminelle. Il songe au sort des paysans victimes de la corvée, de la main-morte, de la fiscalité. "Simplifier les moyens de perception, diminuer le nombre de gens qui y sont nécessaires, réduite leurs profits et faire arriver les deniers au trésor public par les voies les plus directes et les plus simples sont les grandes sources de l'aisance publique." Comme Voltaire, il considère que le luxe a un effet stimulant sur l'économie. "La base essentielle de la population est l'agriculture. Dans un grand état, dans un pays formé, le luxe ne peut être qu'avantageux à la masse. Il propage l'industrie, multiplie les ressources de la classe indigente, il favorise par là l'agriculture, puisqu'elle attire plus de consommateurs. Il verse les trésors de l'opulence dans les familles des travailleurs

Ce disciple des philosophes observe les changements de mentalités sociales. "Les nobles ignoraient autrefois qu'ils ne devaient la différence qui les séparait du peuple qu'au hasard, que ce menu peuple les nourrissait et les enrichissait! Ils voudraient bien encore l'oublier de nos jours, mais malheureusement pour eux, les parchemins ne font plus le mérite. Tel gentilhomme qui se croit important est rencontré par un roturier qui ne le salue pas. On a perdu le respect de servitude et le plus simple citoyen s'estime beaucoup plus qu'un noble orgueilleux et inutile. Le temps de leurs vexations est passé comme celui de la puissance intéressée du clergé."

Riboud n'est pas un adversaire du principe nobiliaire. Il commente, en 1777, l'éloge de Louis Claude Bourdelin, médecin des filles de Louis XV, professeur au Jardin du Roi, membre de l'Académie des Sciences. "Cette noblesse académique, dit le marquis de Condorcet, a un avantage bien précieux sur les autres noblesses: l'illustration qu'elle donne finit dès qu'on a cessé de la mériter; elle est tout à la fois plus flatteuse pour ceux qui la possèdent et plus utile pour la société à qui jamais elle ne peut devenir onéreuse." C'est une élite éclairée qui est ainsi définie.

Riboud songe encore à cette élite quand il est consulté par son ami le comte de Montrevel sur l'inscription qu'il convient de placer sur l'obélisque dressé dans son parc de Challes: "Le but de M. le comte de Montrevel étant d'exprimer sa sensibilité envers les Bressans, il semblerait naturel de les nommer, car l'inscription devient trop générale: en désignant le clergé, la noblesse et les peuples *populorum*, on dit trop; on pourrait croire qu'il s'agit de regrets de toute la nation et des peuples en général. Si on substitue *populi*, du peuple, alors on ne désigne pas la classe nombreuse intermédiaire dans la société entre le peuple et al noblesse."[16]

Confiant, le subdélégué bressan passe d'un pôle à l'autre, de la diffusion culturelle á l'administration de sa province. Le geste symbolique de cette liaison des deux registres réside dans le fait qu'il prononce, en 1784, d'abord son *Discours à l'Assemblée générale du Tiers Etat de Bresse* et qu'il le répète à la *Société d'Emulation*. Il accorde une large place à la guerre d'Amérique qui s'achève, il se félicite de la modération de Louis XVI, du rétablissement de notre marine, de l'indépendance des Etats-Unis, de l'accroissement de notre commerce. Propos optimistes qui enregistrent le succès de la France au Traité de Versailles.[17]

En 1787, Calonne venant d'être congédié, les projets de réforme n'aboutissent pas, Riboud manifeste son inquiétude dans son allocution d'ouverture de l'Assemblée du Tiers Etat: "Ce n'est pas toujours le mot de liberté qui est la preuve de son existence réelle; et dans les pays qui s'en glorifient le plus, elle dégénère souvent en véritable anarchie...On doit en conclure que, dans une monarchie modérée, l'homme peut être plus facilement heureux que dans les républiques."[18] Ce discours s'insère dans le débat relatif à la rénovation de l'administration: après l'expérience des Assemblées provinciales dans le Berry puis à Montauban, les Notables, réunis à Versailles en février 1787, envisageaient l'établissement des Etats provinciaux.

Lors de la réunion des trois ordres du bailliage à Bourg, Riboud prêche la nécessité des réformes tout en mettant en garde contre les excès: "L'histoire de la monarchie française n'offre point d'époque plus remarquable que celle à laquelle nous sommes arrivés: elle fixera les regards de la postérité sur le XVIIIe siècle, déjà si célèbre par tant de révolutions morales et politiques...Sagesse et Modération doivent être la devise du Tiers Etat, comme Générosité et Désintéressement celle du Clergé et de la Noblesse."

En ce climat de liberté de la presse, établie par l'arrêt du 5 juillet 1788, une brochure anonyme intitulée *Observations sur la constitution politique de Bugey et sur la mission de ses députés aux Etats Généraux* parut dirigée contre le discours de Riboud. Ce dernier réplique dans une lettre adressée à un député du Tiers Etat du Bugey, soit Anthelme Brillat-Savarin, lieutenant-général au bailliage de Belley, soit Joseph Delilia de Croze, avocat au Parlement.

Riboud remarque, au préalable, que la Bresse, "nourrice et compagne fidèle du Bugey," a vécu la même histoire et connaît la même administration que le Bugey mais que son propre discours sur l'administration ancienne et moderne de

la Bresse ne s'applique pas aux deux provinces. En tout cas, il n'a point affirmé
que ces régions jouissaient de "la constitution la plus parfaite qui peut convenir
à une monarchie;" il a constaté seulement qu'elle permettait "des rapports entre
les peuples et le souverain." On ne peut...l'accuser d'être un agent du pouvoir
arbitraire alors qu'il écrit qu'un tel pouvoir "énerve les esprits, détruit l'amour de
la patrie et prépare la chute des empires par l'infortune des individus."

Ses propos ont incité les communautés de Bresse à solliciter le rétablissement
des anciens Etats provinciaux. Mais après avoir retracé l'histoire des impositions
en Bresse, Bugey et Gex, Riboud rappelle l'arrêt du Conseil de 1697 décidant
que le suffrage du Tiers Etat doit balancer celui des deux autres ordres en
matière d'impositions communes. Selon lui la présence de représentants du Tiers
Etat de Bresse auprès de l'intendant ressèrve les liens qui unissent les peuples au
Prince et "secondent les vues d'un Roi uniquement occupé du bonheur de ses
sujets." Son contradicteur lui reproche d'avoir décrit l'administration sous des
couleurs trop flatteuses mais Riboud rétorque qu'il a surtout voulu faire
connaître ces mécanismes administratifs, qu'il les a jugés convenables, sans
exclure la possibilité de les améliorer. Il reconnait que son optique est modifiée
par les événements survenus entre 1787 et 1789, notamment la création des
Etats du Dauphiné, la réclamation du Tiers Etat contre les privilèges des deux
autres ordres, la renonciation que leurs sentiments généreux permettent
d'espérer.

Il convient de replacer son exposé dans son contexte: en 1787, la Bresse
jouissait d'une administration supérieure à celle des grands pays d'Etats; en
1789, "une grande révolution nous a éclairés sur les abus qui s'y étaient
introduits...; la régénération de la France peut être l'ouvrage des Etats
généraux," les anciens Etats provinciaux doivent être rétablis avec la nécessaire
adaptation aux circonstances actuelles.[19] Réplique courtoise qui s'insère, en ce
printemps 1789, dans le débat sur la centralisation, sur le rôle des intendants, sur
les avantages des Etats provinciaux.

Subdélégué de l'intendant, appartenant à un rouage très critiqué de la
centralisation monarchique, Riboud ne brigua pas, comme bon nombre d'avocats
ou de robins, un siège de député aux Etats généraux. En revanche, il fut élu
procureur général syndic du nouveau département de l'Ain, en mai 1790. Son
rôle était de représenter l'intérêt public auprès des differents corps administratifs
et de veiller à l'application de la loi. Il demeure attentif aux questions administratives et écrit, au moment où l'Assemblée Nationale Constituante s'occupe de
la réorganisation des finances: "Je crois observer que le mot impôt doit
disparaître comme celui de despotisme, son étymologie indique un fardeau
placé ou imposé sur une tête qu'on force à se plier. Il semble qu'il peut être
remplacé par celui de subsides."[20]

Depuis l'automne 1789, la région lyonnaise souffrait de la disette. La Bresse,
malgré une abondante récolte, hésitait à livrer son blé, selon le réflexe psycholo-

gique en période difficile. Certains spéculaient en accaparant, d'autres en exportant en Savoie et en Suisse. Les ruraux des plaines de la Saône déléguèrent des députés à Lyon pour demander une organisation rationelle du ravitaillement: fixation du prix, facilités pour acheminer le grain à Lyon, interdiction d'exporter …Les représentants des principaux marchés de la région se réunirent à Bourg et envoyèrent des commissaires aux frontières: Riboud en fit partie. A l'automne 1790, il se préoccupe de la défense éventuelle de la frontière franco-savoyarde et transmet à l'Assemblée une description de la vallée du Rhône dominée de hautes montagnes, n'offrant que de rares passages étroits, comme le défilé de Pierre-Châtel, faciles à contrôler. Une activité intense, dans une obsédante psychose de peur, tournée vers les problèmes existentiels, succédait à la douceur de vivre.[22]

Le vente des biens ecclésiastiques décidée le 2 novembre 1789 allait s'effectuer. Le procureur général syndic proposa de distraire les livres des couvents et d'en former une bibliothèque publique. A cette intention, il adressa, le 25 juillet 1790, à l'Assemblée Nationale, une pétition caractéristique de la génération encyclopédiste. "Il manque, au département de l'Ain, un des objets les plus essentiels au progrès des lumières: il ne s'y trouve pas une seule bibliothèque publique." Pour en constituer une, une occasion se présente: "Il existe dans le département sept chartreuses et huit à dix maisons religieuses qui ont des bibliothèques, dans lesquelles outre les livres qui concernent l'état religieux, il s'en trouve un grand nombre d'autres, relatifs aux sciences, à l'histoire, aux arts, à la littérature." La vente publique serait de peu de profit, "les maisons qui les possèdent étant situées en des lieux déserts, loin des grandes villes." Argumentation habile, plus que fondée, qui associe culture et milieu urbain. Après avoir loué "la belle constitution, fille de la raison et de la philosophie," Riboud exhorte, au nom du Directoire de l'Ain, les députés à sauvegarder ces collections. "Personne ne sait mieux que ceux qui font les lois, combien les lumières contribuent à rendre les hommes dignes de la liberté." Il eut gain de cause: 40,000 volumes furent réunis à Bourg et permirent de fonder une bibliothèque publique,[23] une des premières en France.

C'est à la même époque et dans le même esprit qu'il sauva de la destruction l'église de Brou, une des merveilles de la Renaissance. Se référant au décret du 13 octobre 1790, il transmet à l'Assemblée Nationale un mémoire où il expose l'urgence de défendre le patrimoine architectural. "La beauté de cet édifice et les chefs-d'oeuvre qui y abondent le rendent précieux pour les arts…L'époque de notre régénération ne peut être celle de sa destruction…" Cette église est aussi "le dépôt des cendres de plusieurs des anciens souverains de la Bresse qui y reposent sous de superbes mausolées. Il semble que les égards que l'on doit à la Maison de Savoie et à la mémoire des morts ne permettraient pas de détruire leur asile…" Démarche audacieuse qui se réfère à la dynastie des ducs de Savoie, à une terre étrangère devenue un refuge pour les émigrés, à la valeur des traditions. Riboud joint à sa requête la description du monument publié en 1767 par le P. Rousselet, son confrère de la *Société d'Emulation.*[24] Soutenue par Gauthier des Orcières, député de la Bresse à l'Assemblée Constituante, la proposition aboutit au décret du 13 mars 1791, classant l'église de Brou au nombre des monuments nationaux à conserver par l'Etat.

Avec l'application de la Constitution civile du Clergé votée le 12 juillet 1790, les fonctions de procureur-général devenaient délicates. 'L'évêque de Belley étant décédé, les électeurs, définis par le système censitaire, se réunirent le 6 février 1791 en l'église Notre-Dame de Bourg pour choisir le nouvel évêque. Le Père Pacifique Rousselet, prieur des Augustins de Brou, était l'un des deux candidats; En ouvrant la séance; Riboud attira l'attention sur la gravité du choix d'un pasteur: il faut "un ecclésiastique pieux, eclairé, prudent, un citoyen dépouillé de toutes les préventions particulières, un Français persuadé de la sagesse d'une Constitution qui détruit les abus et prépare à la France des jours de grandeur et de prospérité."[25] Lorsque l'évêque de Genève qui administrait sous l'Ancien Régime, le Pays de Gex, le Val de Chézery, la Michaile et le Valromey, diffusa une lettre hostile à l'Assemblée Constituante, Riboud fit interdire, le 12 février 1791, l'impression et la vente de ce document dans l'Ain. La même mesure fut prise dans les diocèses voisins à l'égard de Mgr. de Marbeuf, à Lyon et de l'évêque de Saint-Claude.[26]

En août 1791, aux élections à l'Assemblée Législative, Riboud fut élu et, selon son biographe Philibert Le Duc, il n'accepta son mandat qu'avec répugnance. "Dès le premier moment," confesse-t-il dans son *Journal intime*, "un grand nombre (d'électeurs) m'ont manifesté le désir de me nommer député. Je les ai formellement priés de diriger leurs suffrages sur d'autres sujets et, comme les bruits à cet égard se soutenaient, j'ai engagé quelques amis à faire connaître plus particulièrement mon intention. La situation critique des affaires publiques, le danger de voir les troubles augmenter, mes affaires personnelles, ma famille, mes biens, étaient les motifs principaux de ma détermination. Malgré mes efforts, une nomination inattendue et rapide a eu lieu le 2 septembre à la presque unamimité des suffrages. J'ai voulu résister, mais les instances ont été si vives que toutes les considérations ont dû cesser; il m'a été impossible de refuser malgré ma répugnance."[27]

Ce sont les mêmes sentiments qu'il exprime à la fin du mois de septembre lorsqu'il quitte Bourg avec ses collègues Rubat et Jagot dans un cabriolet acheté à frais communs. Avec méthode, il note qu'il a laissé une procuration générale à son épouse, un pouvoir à un ami pour administrer les biens de campagne à Jasseron, qu'il a soldé les dettes de son père et réglé ses affaires avec sa famille, qu'il espère revenir bientôt quoiqu'il n'épargne pas ses sacrifices pour la chose publique. Trois jours plus tard, il arrivait à Paris, assistait à la dernière séance de l'Assemblée Nationale Constituante et, dès le 2 octobre, transmettait à ses compatriotes, ses premières impressions.[28]

Le 14 octobre, l'Assemblée Législative, s'occupant de l'établissement des Comités, décide que l'un d'eux se chargerait de l'Instruction publique. Les membres seront élus dans les bureaux, au scrutin de liste simple, à la pluralité relative. Nul ne pourra être membre de deux comités. Le Comité d'instruction publique comprit 24 membres élus le 28 octobre: Lacépède, Condorcet, Romme, Carnot aîné..., Riboud.[29]

Ce Comité compte douze officiers et administrateurs, six ecclésiastiques, trois professeurs, trois militaires...Attentifs aux questions scolaires, tous sont persuadés que l'école peut changer la société. Le marquis de Condorcet est la personnalité dominante. Il avait une attache avec la Dombes par son épouse, Sophie de Grouchy. Celle-ci avait vécu avec Mesdemoiselles de Fénelon, de Forbin, de Levis-Mirepoix au chapitre noble des chanoinesses de Neuville-les-Dames. C'était à la fois un centre de mondanités et de réflexion philosophique; elle y lut Voltaire, Rousseau, Condillac, y rencontra Melchior Florent de la Baume, comte de Montreval et le commandeur de Monspey qui se passionnaient pour le mesmérisme.[30]

Sophie, devenue l'épouse de Condorcet, exerça une profonde influence sur le philosophe. Député de Paris à l'Assemblée législative, Condorcet présida le Comité d'Instruction publique. Il avait abordé les questions scolaires à propos de la situation légale des réformés. En 1778, dans ses *Réflexions d'un citoyen catholique sur les lois de France relatives aux protestants*, il demande l'abrogation de la déclaration de 1724 obligeant les anciens membres de la Religion Prétendue Réformée à envoyer leurs enfants à l'école catholique. "Ainsi," dit-il, "la loi enlève aux réformés le droit qu'ont les pères de veiller à l'éducation de leurs enfants, ce droit de la nature, antérieur à toutes les lois."

Il réaffirme le principe de la liberté d'enseignement en 1781 dans un autre mémoire *Sur les moyens de traiter les protestants comme des hommes sans nuire à la religion catholique.* "Si c'est un devoir de justice de laisser au père le soin de ses enfants, c'en est un de politique de faciliter aux pères livrés à des fonctions publiques ou au soin de leur fortune, les moyens de procurer à leurs enfants une éducation propre à former des citoyens honnêtes, éclairés, courageux. Or, les pères protestants ne peuvent profiter des établissements formés par le gouvernement, s'ils sont obligés de confier leurs enfants à des maîtres d'école catholique, moins occupés de les instruire que de les convertir."[31] Condorcet distinguait ainsi les établissements publics dont les buts consistent à dispenser une culture profane, des écoles privées, dépendant de l'Eglise, dont les finalités demeuraient fondalementalement religieuses. Les pères devaient pouvoir choisirent ces deux orientations de la scolarisation.

Au Comité d'Instruction publique, Condorcet participa surtout aux travaux de la Commission s'occupant du plan général d'enseignement, Riboud de la Commission dépouillant les pétitions. C'est lui qui examina, avec Lacépède et Gilbert Romme, l'opportunité d'acquérir la collection d'oiseaux du voyageur et botaniste François Le Vaillant, en février 1792.[32]

III. Le Projet De Condorcet

Le Comité écarte, en novembre 1791, l'analyse du projet Talleyrand et entreprend l'élaboration d'un nouveau plan. *Le Rapport et projet de décret sur l'organisation générale de l'instruction publique*, présenté par Condorcet les 20 et 21 avril 1792 à l'Assemblée Législative, se situe dans une tradition idéologique qui compte Diderot et Turgot et dans un contexte ponctuel avec la confrontation des plans de Talleyrand et de Lepeletier de Saint-Fargeau. Les axes directeurs, laïcité, gratuité s'expliquent par les idées exprimées un peu plus tard dans l'*Esquisse d'un Tableau historique des Progrès de l'esprit humain*. Le projet de décret est l'application de ces principes et le moyen de leur plus grande réalisation. Un peuple instruit est apte à disposer de lui-même, à ne pas succomber aux tyrans, à mettre en oeuvre des expériences conduisant au bien-être culturel et social. Il faut rendre les citoyens capables d'exercer leur raison, suel moyen de progresser.[33]

Dans la *Chronique du mois ou les Cahiers patriotiques*, revue nouvelle mensuelle fondée par Nicolas de Bonneville, Condorcet justifie, en janvier 1793, par des raisons politiques, la généralisation de l'instruction publique: "Au commencement du XVe siècle, l'Europe entière, plongée dans l'ignorance, gémissait sous le joug de l'aristocratie nobiliaire et de la tyrannie sacerdotale; et depuis cette époque, les progrès vers la liberté ont, dans chaque nation, suivi ceux des lumières avec cette constance qui annonce, entre deux faits, une liaison nécessaire fondée sur les lois éternelles de la nature." Après avoir constaté cette loi d'économie politique: L'ignorance engendre la servitude, Condorcet l'explique: "Un peuple éclairé confie ses intérêts à des hommes instruits, mais un peuple ignorant devient nécessairement la dupe des fourbes qui, soit qu'ils le flattent, soit qu'ils l'oppriment, le rendent l'instrument de leurs projets et la victime de leurs intérêts personnels."[34]

Pour Condorcet, la liberté ne peut se maintenir sans l'instruction; les progrès des lumières doivent en assurer l'éternelle durée. Les tyrans savent prendre le masque de la popularité ou celui de la justice et ils parviennent à tromper le peuple. Cette instruction, garante de la liberté et de l'égalité, doit suivre l'évolution des lumières; elle doit transmettre en un petit nombre d'années un ensemble croissant de connaissances. Les ambitieux doivent toujours être menacés de la censure des hommes éclairés." Les préjugés qui, dans presque tous les pays, sont la seule instruction de la portion la plus nombreuse, ne sont pas l'ouvrage de la nature, mais celui de l'ambition qui, trompant l'ignorante simplicité des pères, s'empare du droit de livrer à l'abrutissement et à l'erreur les générations naissantes."

L'instruction doit être étendue, pour ainsi dire "horizontalement;" au plus grand nombre et "verticalement," aussi complète que possible. Elle permet ainsi, d'"embrasser le systeme entier des connaissances humaine," et de résister aux adversaires du peuple.[35]

Dans son *Esquisse d'un Tableau historique des progrès de l'esprit humain*, Condorcet pose en 1793, l'hypothèse d'un parallélisme entre l'histoire de l'espèce et la génèse des facultés individuelles. Il étend la théorie sensualiste de l'individu, élaborée par Condillac, à la réunion des individus qui forment l'humanité. Pour diffuser les connaissances de manière systématique et uniforme, il faudrait une langue universelle qui éviterait le double écueil de la communication ésotérique réservée aux savants et du langage métaphorique des religieux; elle éviterait aussi de diviser la société en deux groupes: les initiés et les ignorants. L'écriture, le discours permettent la diffusion du savoir et assurent la capacité des hommes à transformer leurs conditions d'existence. L'esprit s'associe au progrès matériel.

Si la science historique veut éclairer les jugements et les actions, elle doit aussi définir et énoncer des lois. Après avoir ordonné les faits sociaux, elle dégage, par la statistique, des probabilités qui permettent de maîtriser les composantes et les rythmes du progrès. Le progrès est continu mais avec des rémissions temporaires: "Le passage orageaux et pénible d'une société grossière à l'état de civilisation des peuples éclairés et libres, n'est point une dégénération de l'espèce humaine, mais une crise nécessaire dans sa marche graduelle vers son perfectionnement absolu."[36] Condorcet estime que le nombre des génies, à chaque âge, dépend du nombre des personnes instruites. En dispensant cette instruction, l'Etat bénéficiera d'une élite active. Condorcet rejette l'idée répandue parmi les philosophes qu'il existe des connaissances diluées pour la masse et un progrès scientifique intense pour l'élite. Réserver la culture à une minorité, ce serait refaire ce qu'a fait le clergé, constituer une caste avec un langage distinctif et à la longue provoquer un désséchement de la pensée. L'emploi du langage vernaculaire dans l'enseignement évite ce repli et rend la science accessible à tous, pour le profit de la plus grande masse des hommes. En réalité, Condorcet admet une différenciation dans la distribution du savoir: une sélection transparaît même si l'on tient compte que les instituteurs doivent assurer une sorte d'éducation permanente en donnant des conférences qui soient des sortes de messes dominicales.

Comme son ami Cabanis, Condorcet admet les inégalités sociales; elles lui paraissent même stimulantes; elles font progresser la science et n'entraînent aucune humiliation. Ces progrès bénéficient à tous, ils conditionnent l'évolution future de la société; ils réduisent la misère. Comme Leibniz, Condorcet réaffirme la relation entre la science, la technologie, le niveau de vie. La notion de l'utilité de la science se répand à l'age de l'*Encyclopédie*. Les sciences forment la raison tandis que la rhétorique peut séduire les foules et jouer un rôle néfaste.[37]

Sur tous ces principes fondamentaux, Riboud souscrit au rapport de Condorcet. La divergence survient à propos de la liberté d'enseignement. Condorcet veut rendre l'instruction publique "indépendante de tout autre pouvoir que celui de l'opinion et ne la soumettre qu'à l'autorité de la renommée." Il vaut mieux s'en remettre aux corporations savantes puisqu'on ne peut "plus compter pour les dépenses nécessaires aux progrès des lumières, sur les richesses individuelles." Dans une monarchie constitutionnelle comme au temps de l'Assemblée législative, le ministère peut chercher à s'unir avec les administrations départementales pour balancer le pouvoir législatif. Même après l'abolition de la royauté, Condorcet répète que le gouvernement ne doit jamais avoir d'influence sur les choses qui sont enseignées.[38]

"L'instruction est un devoir de la société à l'égard des citoyens" qui ont le droit d'exiger l'organisation d'un enseignement public, mais l'Etat ne doit pas sortir des limites posées à son autorité par la liberté de l'individu. "Les établissements d'instruction seront aussi indépendants qu'il est possible de toute autorité publique...Le devoir comme le droit de la puissance publique se borne à fixer l'objet de l'instruction et à s'assurer qu'il sera bien rempli." L'Etat ne doit pas porter "atteinte aux droit des parents;" il doit seulement "régler l'instruction, en abandonnant aux familles le reste de l'éducation." Contrairement à d'autres réformateurs du siècle des Lumières, Condorcet redoute l'emprise d'un corps sur la société: "Créez des corps enseignants et vous serez sûrs d'avoir créé ou des tyrans ou des instruments de la tyrannie."

Il reconnaît que l'éducation représentait chez les Grecs une partie importante de la politique. "Elle y formait les hommes pour la patrie bien plus que pour eux-mêmes ou pour leur famille," mais elle "se bornait presque aux exercices du corps, aux principes des moeurs, aux habitudes propres à exciter un patriotisme exclusif. Le reste s'apprenait librement dans les écoles de philosophie ou de rhéteurs, dans les ateliers des artistes. Et cette liberté est encore une des causes de la supériorité des Grecs." Condorcet redoute, en guise de civisme, un endoctrinement politique: Si l'on entend qu'il faut enseigner la Constitution comme une doctrine conforme aux principes de la raison universelle, ou exciter en sa faveur un aveugle enthousaisme qui rend les citoyens incapables de juger, si on leur dit: "Voilà ce que vous devez adorer et croire," alors c'est une espèce de religion politique que l'on veut créer, c'est une chaîne que l'on prépare aux esprits et on viole la liberté dans ses droits les plus sacrés, sous prétexte d'apprendre à les chérir."[39]

Sur ce principe exprimé par Condorcet, "L'instruction doit être entièrement indépendante de tous les pouvoirs publics," Riboud se sépare dès le 7 novembre 1791 de son président. Pour notre Bressan, ce principe ne tendait rien moins qu'à ôter à l'Etat la direction de l'enseignement. Or, tout le gouvernement a le devoir de l'encourager et de le contrôler. "Il importe grandement," dit Thomas Riboud, "de la surveiller pour que l'esprit de système et d'innovation ne prépare pas sans cesse des révolutions dont la fréquence serait infiniment funeste. Il est prudent de ne pas abandonner la jeunesse à l'influence d'un enseignement contraire à la Constitution. Si l'Etat s'effaçait complètement, on verrait surgir une nouvelle corporation aussi dangereuse que puissante. Les établissements d'instruction ou plutôt leurs directeurs et professeurs s'isoleraient bientôt du reste de la société, bientôt ils s'uniraient pour la mouvoir à leur gré. Rien ne pourrait résister à leurs efforts; peu à peu, ils concentreraient les lumières dans leur enceinte et exerceraient sur l'opinion un empire irrésistible."[40]

Riboud adopte ici le point de vue de Turgot qui, dans sa *Lettre au roi*, proposa que l'instruction morale et civique qu'on donnerait aux enfants "leur manifestât bien les obligations qu'ils ont à la société et au pouvoir qui les protège et les devoirs que ces obligations leur imposent;" il suit les parlementaires, de la Chalotais au président Rolland, que Condorcet utilise cependant souvent.[41]

Condorcet réplique que toute la force de l'éducation réside dans l'émancipation intellectuelle et morale de l'enfant, dans le développement libre de ses facultés. Que le pouvoir de l'Etat, s'écrie-t-il, expire au seuil de l'école et que chaque maître puisse enseigner les opinions qu'il croitvraies, non celles que l'Etat a jugées telles. Que les pouvoirs publics ne s'arrogent pas le droit de choisir les maximes philosophiques, morales et politiques qui doivent être inculquées aux citoyens. Ces règles "influent grandement sur le bonheur," nul ne saurait s'ériger en juge du bonheur des autres; ce sont les élèves seuls, ou s'ils en sont encore incapables, leurs parents qui ont qualité pour choisir. "L'indépendance de l'instruction fait en quelque sorte une partie des droits de l'espèce humaine… Le devoir de l'Etat est d'armer contre l'erreur qui est toujours un mal public, toute la force de la vérité, mais il n'a pas le droit de décider où réside la vérité, où se trouve l'erreur." Et encore: "L'Etat ne peut, sur aucun objet, avoir le droit de faire enseigner des opinions comme des vérités, il ne doit imposer aucune croyance. Si quelques opinions lui paraissent des erreurs dangereuses, ce n'est pas en faisant enseigner les opinions contraires qu'il doit les combattre ou les prévenir…C'est en assurant aux bons esprits les moyens de se soustraire à ces erreurs et d'en connaître tous les dangers."[42]

Riboud a-t-il infléchi la pensée de Condorcet? Quand, en décembre 1792, la Convention décida de réimprimer le rapport déjà diffusé par l'Assemblée Législative en avril 1792, l'auteur atténue ses propos. Il persiste à réclamer, pour le haut enseignement, une indépendance absolue; mais il admet que l'Etat établisse "sur l'opinion universelle des hommes éclairés, une instruction élémentaire conforme à la vérité et dirigée par une bonne méthode…Il serait dangereux d'abandonner la direction de l'instruction élémentaire parce que les lumières ne sont pas assez généralement répandues pour n'avoir pas à craindre qu'elle ne soit égarée, soit par les préjugés, soit par une haine de ces mêmes préjugés puérilement exagérée; qui répondra que la même superstition ne s'emparera pas des nouvelles écoles?"[43]

Sur ces principes admis par le Comité, Condorcet bâtit son édifice scolaire en cinq degrés. A l'école primaire, répartie sur l'ensemble du territoire, a raison de une pour 400 habitants, l'instituteur (ce mot remplace le terme de régent) enseignera la lecture, l'écriture, les règles de l'arithmétique, l'arpentage, des notions sur les productions du pays, les "premières idées morales," les principes de l'ordre social. Chaque dimanche, l'instituteur exposera, en une conférence publique, les données de la Constitution, les lois nouvelles, la théorie du droit naturel…"Mais ni la constitution française, ni même la déclaration des droits ne seront présentées à aucune des classes de citoyens comme des tables decendues du ciel et qu'il faut adorer et croire."

Les écoles secondaires, placées dans les districts et dans les villes de plus de 4000 habitants, se chargent d'enseigner les mathématiques, l'histoire naturelle et la chimie nécessaire aux arts, la morale, la science sociale, les notions de commerce.

Les instituts accordent une place considérable aux sciences physiques et mathématiques car elles constituent "contre les préjugés, contre la petitesse d'esprit, un remède sinon plus sûr, du moins plus universel que la philosophie elle-même. Elles sont utiles dans toutes les professions." Le latin est réduit, l'éloquence, "germe d'une corruption destructrice," s'efface. Il ne s'agit plus d'émouvoir mais d'éclairer. Condorcet justifie ce choix par les nouvelles conditions sociologiques et psychologiques. "Nous avons senti que, par une suite des progrès de l'espèce humaine, ces études qui offrent à son activité un aliment éternel, inépuisable, devenaient d'autant plus nécessaires que le perfectionnement de l'ordre social doit offrir moins d'objets à l'ambition ou à l'avidité…, qu'il était important de tourner vers des objets utiles ce besoin d'agir, cette soif de gloire et de substituer enfin l'ambition d'éclairer les hommes à celle de les dominer." Tandis que le savoir engendre la vertu, les mauvaises habitudes naissent de l'oisiveté.

Les neuf lycées forment les savants, les lettrés, les professeurs. Enfin, la Société Nationale des Sciences et des Arts couronne l'ensemble et coordonne les recherches. Au XVIIIe siècle, les recherches scientifiques s'effectuaient isolément, sans plan. Les hommes de sciences demeuraient des empiriques, se défiant de l'esprit de système condamné par Condillac. Entre Universités, entre Académies, l'idée d'une communauté européenne du culture n'écartait pas la rivalité. Condorcet souhaitait une coopération et non une concurrence; il souhaitait une liaison au moyen de corps interdisciplinaires, comme il l'expose dans les Eloges de Haller et de Linné. S'inspirant de François Bacon, il propose une planification de la recherche par des institutions spécifiques composées de savants. Ils s'efforceront de maintenir l'équilibre entre l'innovation et la conservation, entre la liberté et la contrainte.[44]

Les Académiciens se considéraient comme les protecteurs de la République des Sciences mais, avant la Révolution, des savants s'étaient dressés contre la tyrannie de l'Académie. La Révolution sembla fournir l'occasion de résister à cette corporation. Réorganisant l'enseignement, Condorcet, membre de cette élite, souhaitait garder la forme académique pour la recherche. Son projet de décret proposait d'établir, à la tête de son système hiérarchisé, une sorte

d'académie suprême; afin de garantir la liberté de cette bureaucratie intellectuelle et administrative, Condorcet insistait sur le fait que la République des
Lettres devait être organisée comme une entité aidée par l'Etat mais libre de tout
contrôle politique. En définitive, Condorcet proposait à l'Etat de sanctionner
une bureaucratie d'intellectuels gouvernés par des académiciens. Ce système
oligarchique lui paraissait le meilleur.

Il provoqua une explosion de réactions contre cette tutelle académique; des
déclarations vengeresses firent rejeter les clauses les plus importantes du projet
de loi et sont à l'origine de la suppression des Académies en août 1793.[45]

IV. Débats et Testament Final

La chute du roi, le 10 août 1792, entraîna la réunion d'une Convention
nationale qui proclama la République et mit en place, le 13 octobre 1792, un
nouveau Comité d'Instruction publique de vingt-quatre membres. Condorcet,
élu, n'accepta pas sa nomination. Il fut néanmoins adjoint, en même temps que
Sieyès, par décret spécial.[46]

Le Comité adopte, dans leur ensemble, les vues de Condorcet, décide qu'il
y aura cinq degrés d'instruction, puis examine, en décembre, le projet sur les
écoles primaires, fragment détaché du rapport de Condorcet. Marie-Joseph
Chénier, au nom du Comité, lit le titre I. On applaudit particulièrement l'article
6 où il est dit que "tout ce qui concerne les cultes religieux ne sera enseigné
que dans les temples."

Durand de Maillane s'élève alors contre ce plan que le Comité fait sien. Les
écoles primaires proposées "ne sont que le premier échelon de cette suite
d'enseignements qui, sous les noms d'instituts, de lycées et de Société Nationale,
va former dans la nation, et à ses dépens, une corporation formidable." Rien de
plus dangereux pour la République qu'une semblable organisation. "Après
avoir secoué le joug des tyrans, après avoir fait disparaître la domination
sacerdotale, il est bien étrange que, sous prétexte de sciences et de lumières, on
propose à la nation de faire, à ses propres frais, un état particulier et permanent
à une classe de citoyens: et quels citoyens? Les hommes les plus capables de
dominer l'opinoin publique en la dirigeant, car il y a une superstition pour ce qu'on
appelle savants, comme il y en avait une pour les rois et pour les prêtres; appelle
à nos tant célèbres académies."

Cet orateur de la Plaine reproche ainsi à Condorcet le caractère élitiste de son
projet. L'égalité serait blessée si la République rétribuait les professeurs. "On
ne doit pas nous proposer d'ajouter à trente, quarante mille places fixes et bien
salariées pour les premières écoles, un très grand nombre d'autres places
distinguées et mieux payées, pour des connaissances, la plupart de pur goût et
d'embellissement, que la nation ne peut être tenue de fournir à ceux-là mêmes

qui ont ou doivent avoir tous les moyens suffisants pour se les procurer." Athènes et Rome n'entretenaient pas d'écoles publiques et elles s'en sont bien trouvées. Il est préférable pour l'enseignement, sauf celui des degrés élémentaires, de s'en remittre à l'initiative des particuliers.

Contrairement à Condorcet, Durand-Maillane (qui supprime la particule en l'An II) estime qu'un développement excessif de la culture peut être dangereux. "Peut-être ne sommes-nous si corrompus que parce que nous sommes trop savants...Le peuple français, pour être heureux, n'a besoin des sciences que ce qu'il lui en faut pour arriver à la vertu...Il n'importe à la République, que de faire des citoyens vertueux...Jamais Rome ne fut plus florissante ni plus heureuse que lorsqu'elle ne fut qu'agricole."[47]

Claude Masuyer, député de Saône-et-Loire, reproche au projet son coût excessif et ses tendances centralisatrices. "Ce n'était point assez pour le Comité dont Condorcet était l'interprête, d'avoir anéanti tous les anciens Collèges pour leur substituer un collège par département; ce n'était point assez d'avoir institué neuf lycées dominateurs des instituts des départements; il fallait encore créer une Société Nationale dominatrice des lycées et, toujours fidèle au système destructeur des centralités, resserrer, concentrer les instituts dans les lycées, les lycées dans la Société nationale et la Société nationale dans Paris, c'est-à-dire toujours resserrer, concentrer la nation dans Paris seul...Sommes -nous donc revenus au XIVe siècle, où il n'était permis de penser que d'après les autorités?... Vous repousserez avec une juste indignation la conception monstrueuse de cette Société nationale qui ne serait bonne, tout au plus, qu'à introduire dans l'Etat une régie nationale, un gouvernement autocratique pour les sciences et les arts, un séminaire, un sacerdoce littéraire qui nous ramènerait le Collège des prêtres de Memphis, qui ne serait bientôt qu'un foyer d'intrigues et de corruption...."[48]

Le projet se trouvait ainsi attaqué principalement par des Girondins modérés; leurs discours provoquèrent des réactions d'ordre politique et philosophique mais sans que le plan de Condorcet fût défendu. A la mi-décembre, François Lanthenas, député de Rhône-et-Loire, propose de reprendre la discussion sur les bases de l'instruction publique; il était hostile aux conceptions de Condorcet et il ne voulait pas que les degrés supérieurs d'enseignement fussent établis par l'Etat; il fallait songer davantage à l'instruction des adultes, encourager la morale et les moeurs républicaines...Cette proposition de Lanthenas fit reprendre les débats, tantôt sur les écoles primaires dont la création paraissait urgente, tantôt sur l'ensemble du système éducatif. Se mêlaient les considérations sur les Lumières, indispensables à la survie de la Révolution, sur le rôle de l'Etat dans l'enseignement, sur les principes de la morale...

Au moment où Gilbert Romme, l'ancien précepteur du comte Strogonov, présente un nouveau rapport général, la Convention décide l'impression du projet que Condorcet avait présenté à l'Assemblée législative, le jour de la déclaration de guerre. Condorcet ne défendit pas à la barre son propre texte.

Jean-Paul Rabaut, Saint-Etienne, député girondin de l'Aube et Bancal des Issarts, député de Puy-de-Dôme, dirigent désormais la discussion critiquent les vues de leur prédécesseur, en retiennent parfois de éléments. Ainsi, Bancal ramène l'édifice universitaire à deux niveaux, les écoles élémentaires et les écoles centrales; celles-ci étant l'équivalent des lycées de Condorcet. Mais le député du Puy-de-Dôme redoute la constitution d'une corporation enseignante: "toutes les corporations tendent à l'aristocratie."[49]

C'est dans la *Chronique du mois*, en janvier 1793, que Condorcet réfuta ses contradicteurs. Il montra l'intérêt que la République aurait à organiser elle-même le haut enseignement, rappela les services rendus par les corporations savantes et justifia sa suggestion de créer la Société nationale par le contexte politique: "C'est qu'alors—en avril 1792—, le pouvoir exécutif général était aux mains d'hommes choisis par le roi...Il était donc important, nécessaire, d'ôter au gouvernement non seulement toute action directe sur l'instruction, mais même de ne lui laisser aucune influence directe. L'abolition de la royauté peut donc permettre de faire à cette partie du plan des changements utiles."[50]

C'était laisser entendre que son plan pouvait être amélioré et adapté aux nouvelles circonstances. En ce sens, Lepeletier de Saint-Fargeau, député montagnard de l'Yonne, tout en gardant les grandes lignes précisées par Condorcet, les complète en adjoignant tout ce qui concerne l'éducation. Mais le Comité de l'Instruction publique était, au printemps 1793, de plus en plus dominé par Sieyès, Daunou et Lakanal. L'oratorien Pierre Daunou expliqua très longuement que le plan de Condorcet avait l'inconvénient de placer l'enseignement public entre les mains d'une corporation de professeurs, d'une "vaste agrégation de lettrés" qui disposerait d'une influence dangereuse: "elle dicterait la pensée publique, elle administrerait l'opinion." Pour éviter ce danger, l'enseignement, dès qu'il ne s'agit plus du degré élémentaire, doit rester entre les mains de l'industrie privée. "Au lieu de ces brillantes et dangereuses institutions, je demanderai la liberté, l'égalité et l'abolition des privilèges...Alors, sous les auspices de la liberté et sous la commune protection des lois, vous verrez s'ouvrir des écoles secondaires, des instituts, des lycées, des académies et d'un seul mot vous aurez appelé à une grande concurrence, à l'activité la plus féconde, toutes les sciences, tous les arts, toutes les opinions, toutes les méthodes..."[51] Daunou se rendait-il compte qu'en laissant l'enseignement à la spéculation privée on permettrait aux anciennes congrégations, toujours en possession de leurs collèges, de reprendre leur activité, ainsi que Romme l'avait prévue en décembre 1792?

En ce printemps 1793, les amis de Condorcet disparaissaient de la Convention. Lui-même, député de l'Aisne, son pays natal, vota lors du procès du roi, contre l'appel au peuple et contre la mort de Louis XVI. Il s'abstint, après le 2 juin 1793, après la chute des Girondins, de paraître aux séances du Comité de l'Instruction publique et à celles de la Convention; il vit bientôt sa sécurité menacée à cause de la brochure qu'il avait publiée contre le nouveau projet de Constitution. Décrété d'arrestation le 8 juillet, il dût chercher refuge chez des amis sûrs. Décrété d'accusation le 3 octobre, il se donna la mort à moins qu'il ne mourut d'épuisement, à Bourg-la-Reine, devenue Bourg-Egalité, le 9 germinal An II (29 mars 1794).

Riboud faillit connaître le même sort. De retour en Bresse, le 21 septembre 1792, il se tint à l'écart de la vie publique mais son passé le rendait suspect. Inscrit sur la liste de proscription du 22 mars 1793, il fut arrêté en février 1794 et ne dut son salut qu'à la chute de Robespierre. Sous le Régime thermidorien, il posa sa candidature, en novembre 1794, au poste de professeur d'histoire naturelle à l'Ecole centrale de l'Ain. En fait, il devait enseigner l'histoire philoso-phique des peuples et l'économie. Atteint par la loi d'octobre 1795 interdisant toute fonction publique aux parents d'émigrés, il fut suspendu. Sous le Direc-toire, il retrouva ses responsabilités judiciaires au tribunal de l'Ain; en décembre 1796, membre du jury d'instruction publique, il prononca l'allocution d'ouver-ture de l'Ecole centrale de l'Ain.

Ce *Discours sur l'enseignement dans les Ecoles Centrales et les effets qu'on peut attendre de leur établissement* fait référence au projet de Condorcet. "Ces Ecoles occupent, dans la nouvelle organisation de l'instruction publique, la place des Instituts proposés par le projet qui fut présenté à l'Assemblée Législative… Ce projet contenait cinq degrés d'instructions, le plan adopté par la Convention ne renferme que trois degrés qui sont Ecoles primaires, Ecoles centrales, Institut nationale des sciences. Ainsi, le projet de l'Assemblée Législative avait des Ecoles secondaires et des Lycées qui offraient des degrés intermédiaires."

"Ce n'est point ici le cas de discuter s'il était plus convenable de graduer davantage l'instruction, de la distribuer à la généralité des citoyens et à tous les âges. Les législateurs ont pensé sans doute que le petit nombre de rouages faciliterait le jeu de la machine.., qu'au delà des Ecoles primaires, l'instruction publique cesse d'être une dette de la Patrie; qu'il suffisait d'offrir ensuite aux esprits un moyen de développement dans les Ecoles centrales, que si une instruction intermédiaire était indispensable, elle s'établirait nécessairement bientôt elle-même et qu'une concurrence avantageuse produirait de bons instituteurs secondaires."

Il était difficile pour un membre du jury d'instruction publique de critiquer la loi du 3 brumaire an IV établissant les Ecoles centrales. Il tient cependant à les situer et à prodiguer quelques conseils qui visent à rétablir ces degrés intermédiaires prévus par Condorcet. L'élève sortant de l'école primaire ne profitera de l'Ecole centrale que si on lui a donné des secours intermédiaires, si on l'a aidé à s'orienter. "En partageant son temps et ses études avec intelligence, il faut éviter de le surcharger, lui laisser les moyens de répéter chez lui et de méditer l'objet des leçons qu'il aura entendues, veiller à ce qu'il les suive avec exactitude, parce qu'en échappant quelques chaînons, il ne pourrait les ressaisir."

Riboud met en garde contre les ambitions excessives: "il vaut bien mieux le borner à un petit nombre d'objets que de lui faire trop embrasser et de charger son esprit d'une masse incohérente et confuse." L'élève qui sort de l'Ecole centrale ne peut être un mathématicien profond, un grand physicien, un jurisconsulte formé, un homme de lettres distingué. Il a acquis des connaissances utiles, mais il n'a pas atteint la vérité. "En un mot, il en saura assez pour s'avancer plus facilement dans des routes difficiles ou obscures; il sera dans le parvis du temple, mais le sanctuaire ne sera pas encore ouvert pour lui."

L'orateur justifie la présence des cours prévus en insistant sur leur utilité mais aussi en montrant qu'ils appellent des compléments. "Ainsi le cours d'histoire disposera à bien connaître et juger l'esprit des peuples les événements et les hommes," mais il apprend surtout à apprendre à étudier l'histoire. "Ce n'est ensuite qu'en lisant soi-même, c'est par la réflexion, les rapprochements et l'étude du coeur humain que l'on parviendra à bien connaître l'Histoire."

L'Ecole centrale prépare l'élève à l'entrée dans les Ecoles spécialisées. Elle est une étape et un stage d'orientation. "Le grand avantage des écoles centrales sera donc de fournir au génie des occasions de développement, de le dégager des masses sous lesquelles son feu est captif et de lui ouvrir une heureuse issue d'où il s'échappe pour éclairer et servir les hommes." L'école centrale a pour finalités de former le raisonnement, d'orner l'esprit d'enrichir la mémoire, de rendre capable de bien écouter, de savoir juger ou rectifier les idées, de faire sentir le prix des lumières. Elle a aussi l'avantage d'éloigner les jeunes de l'oisiveté, génératrice de vices. Pour Riboud, l'ignorance demeure la cause de la corruption, des désordres, des violences. "L'ignorance ternit d'abord la splendeur des états policés, elle rend les moeurs grossières, laisse tout se détruire, ne rétablit rien; elle abrutit les esprits, énerve l'âme et bientôt elle amène le plus honteux et le plus intolérable des esclavages."[52]

Cette confiance dans les Lumières fait songer à l'hymne aux progrès de l'esprit humain, le testament spirituel de Condorcet.

Notes

1. Louis Michaud, *Biographie universelle*, Paris, 1854-1865.

2. Marcel Passot, "Thomas Riboud, fils du XVIIIe siècle bourgeois" dans *Visages de l'Ain*, No 33, 1956, p. 24-36. Cité p. 25. Le mot Patrie est vraisemblablement employé dans le sens de province natale.

3. Louis Trenard, *Lyon, de l'Encyclopédie au préromantisme*, Paris, P.U.F., 1958, p. 73. –Philibert Le Duc, *Thomas Riboud et la Société littéraire de Lyon*, Lyon, 1852, 12 p.

4. Alain Gros, "L'engagement de la Bresse dans la Révolution américaine" dans *Visages de l'Ain*, No 163, mai-juin 1979, p. 9-20.

5. M. Passot, *ib.* dans *Visages de l'Ain*, 1956, p. 33.

6. Th. Riboud, *Discours prononcé à l'Assemblée générale du Tiers Etat de Bresse, tenue à Bourg*, les 23 et 24 avril 1781, s.1, 1781, 35 p.; *Discours prononcés à la rentrée du bailliage et siège présidial de Bourg-en-Bresse* en 1779 et en 1781, s.1, 1781, 80, 36 p.

7. M. Passot, *ib*, dans *Visages de l'Ain*, 1956, p. 32.

8. Les archives de Th. Riboud et de la *Société d'Emulation* sont déposées aux Archives départementales de l'Ain. Le Journal de Riboud, intitulé "Notes philosophiques et littéraires," a été utilisé par M. Passot et par A. Gros.

9. Arch. Dép. Ain: Registres de la *Société d'Emulation*, No 1, du 16 février 1783 au 17 mai 1785, p. 1-6.

10. Th. Riboud, *Discours lu à la première séance de la Société d'Emulation de Bourg*, Lyon, 1973, 80, 47 p.

11. Th. Riboud, *Eloge d'Agnés Sorel*, Lyon, Faucheux, 1785, 80, 39 p.; *Etrennes littéraires ou Almanach offert aux amis de l'humanité*, s.1., 1785, 22 p.

12. M. Passot, *ib.*, *Visages de l'Ain*, 1956, p. 34

13. Daniel Roche, *Le siècle des lumières en province. Académies et académiciens provinciaux 1680-1789*, Paris, 1978, t.1, p. 16-18.

14. D. Roche, "Milieux académiques provinciaux et société des lumières" dans *Livre et société dans la France du XVIIIe siècle*, Paris, 1965, p. 135-140.

15. Roger Hahn, "Elite scientifique et démocratie politique dans la France révolutionnaire," dans *XVIIIe siècle*, No 1, 1969, p. 229-232.

16. Toutes ces considérations sont empruntées aux *Notes philosophiques et littéraires* et sont citées d'après Marcel Passot (*Visages de l'Ain*, 1956 p. 35)

17. Th. Riboud, *Discours prononcé à l'Assemblée générale du Tiers Etat des provinces de Bresse et Dombes*, 27 avril 1784, Lyon, 1784, 18 p.

18. Th. Riboud, *Discours sur l'administration ancienne et moderne de la Bresse*, 10 avril 1787, 87 p.

19. *Lettre de M. Riboud, procureur du roi et subdélégué à Bourg, à un député du Tiers Etat du Bugey, à l'Assemblée générale des Trois ordres de cette province*, Bourg, 19 mars 1789, 12 p.

20. Th. Riboud, *Essai sur les moyens à employer pour subvenir aux besoins publics; Projet de décret relatif aux liquidations et à l'ordre des remboursements de la dette exigible*; 12 décembre 1791, Paris, s.d., 80, 12 p.

21. L. Trenard, *Lyon, de l'Encyclopédie...*, 1958, 1, p. 236.

22. Th. Riboud, *Rapport contenant les détails principaux de la gestion du Directoire du Département de l'Ain jusqu'au 1er nov. 1790*, Bourg, 1790, 40, 148 p., p. 131.

23. Philibert Le Duc, *Histoire de la Révolution dans l'Ain*, Bourg-en-Bresse Martin-Bottier, t. 11, 1880, p. 7-9.

24. *Réquisitoire de M. le procureur général syndic pour la conservation de l'église et maison de Brou*, ms. in fo, 8 p. (Arch. de Philibert le Duc, descendant de Th. Riboud).

25. *Discours prononcé par M. Riboud, procureur-général-syndic, à l'ouverture de l'assemblée des électeurs réunis le 6 février 1791...*, ms, 8 p. (Arch. Ph. Le Duc)

26. *Extrait des registres des délibérations du Directoire du Département de l'Ain*, 12 février 1791, Bourg, 1791, in-40; *ib.* du 10 juin 1791, Bourg 1791, 4 p.; *Arrêté du Directoire du Département de Rhône-et-Loire*, 10 mars 1791, Lyon, 1791, in-40, 8 p.

27. Ph. Le Duc, *Hist. de la Révolution...*, 1880, T. 11, p. 208.

28. Ph. Le Duc, *op. cit.*, 1, pp. 218-228.

29. M. James Guillaume, *Procès-verbal du Comité d'instruction publique de l'Assemblée Législative*, Paris, Impr. nat., 1889, p. XVIII.

30. Gabrielle et Louis Trenard, *Le diocèse de Belley*, Paris, Beauchesne, 1978, p. 128.

31. Félix Ponteil, *Histoire de l'enseignement*, Paris, 1966, p. 60.

32. M. J. Guillame, *op. cit.*, pp. 113, 143, 144.

33. Catherine Fricheau, "Tableau noir et révolution" dans *Condorcet Cahiers de Fontenay-aux-Roses*, No 5, 1976.

34. M. J. Guillaume, *Procès-verbaux du Comité de l'Instruction Publique de la Convention*, Paris, Imp. nat. 1891; t. 1, p. 609.

35. M. J. Guillaume, *op. cit*, p. 610.

36. Michèle Jalley, "Représentation tabulaire et statut de l'histoire" dans *Cahiers de Fontenay-aux-Roses*.

37. Frank Manuel, *Prophets of Paris*, pp. 75-76, 79.

38. M. J. Guillaume, *op. cit.*, 1, p. 6–12.

39. *Arch. parlementaires*, Ière série. t. XLII, pp. 227–245.

40. Th. Riboud, *Observations lues au Comité de l'Instruction Publique*, le 7 nov. 1791, ms de 8 p., Arch. Ph. Le Duc cité dans *Hist. de la Révolution*, II, p. 234.

41. L. Trenard, "Enseignement et instruction civique en France, de 1762 à 1799" dans *Modèles et moyens de la réflexion politique*, Lille, 1973, 1, pp. 397–424.

42. Francisque Vial, *Condorcet et l'éducation démocratique*, Paris, 1906, pp. 26–30.

43. Condorcet, "Sur l'instruction publique" dans *Oeuvres*, t. VII, pp. 166–573.

44. M. J. Guillaume, *Procès-verbal du Comité de l'Instruction publique de l'Assemblée Législative*, 1889, p. 226–246.–Sergio Moravia, *Il tramonto dell' illuminismo*, Bari, 1968, pp. 327–341.

45. Roger Hahn, "Elite scientifique et démocratie politique dans la France révolutionnaire" dans *XVIIIe siècle*, No 1, 1969, p. 229–235.

46. M. J. Guillaume, *op. cit.*, 1891, pp. IV-XI.

47. M. J. Guillaume, *op. cit.*, 1891, pp. XVI–XIX.

48. M. J. Guillaume, *op. cit.*, 1891, p. XX.

49. M. J. Guillaume, *op. cit.*, 1891, pp. XXVIII–XXX.

50. *La chronique du mois*, janv. 1793, p. 26.

51. P. Daunou, *Essai sur l'instruction publique*, Paris, Imp. nat. 1793.

52. Th. Riboud, *Discours sur l'Enseignement dans les Ecoles centrales et les effets qu'on peut attendre de leur établissement*...Bourg, 21 déc. 1796, in-80, 19 p.

11
Une Contribution de Condorcet a la Reforme de la Législation Pénale —

Pierre Antoine Perrod

Abstract

In 1785, the case of the "trois roués de Chaumont," three men condemned to torture on the rack, posed the whole problem of justice in the defense of the poor. The unfortunate suspects had languished in jail for thirty months. Their judges had scarcely heard them. Not a single lawyer had been appointed for their defense. Dupaty, writing his *Mémoire justificatif pour Trois Hommes Condamnés à la Roue*, saved them just in the nick of time, as they were on their way to be tortured.

Condorcet, on this occasion, not only issued a generous statement, but he put on trial the kind of Legislation which he deemed unworthy of an enlightened populace. Through his *Réflexions d'un Non-Gradué sur une Affaire Bien Connue* (1786), he launched an appeal to public opinion, for to Condorcet the question of the possible innocence of anybody is everybody's concern. He is desirous of sweeping away institutions that obliterate a man's rightful due, especially as concerns the poorest and the most disinherited.

In our entire literature on Justice, this first text to the glory of Condorcet occupies a place all by itself. First he argued for procedural reforms guaranteeing due process. The natural expansion of his position was his demand for the abolition of capital punishment....Inasmuch as the possible innocence of a defendant declared guilty can never be entirely eliminated, Condorcet hence will proclaim that any irreversible penalty is unjust.

After a lapse of nearly two centuries, will the world finally listen to his voice?

Maire Jean Antoine Nicolas de Caritat de Condorcet devait éspouser Sophie de Grouchy, la niece of Fréteau, conseiller au Parlement de Paris, En cette qualité, celui-ci avait été un des juges d'appel d'une décision provenant du Bailliage de Chaumont. Le 11 août 1785, aprês avoir entendu les sieurs Lardoise, Semare et Bradier, une condamnation aux galêres perpétuelles avait été prononcée contre eux. Sur appel "de droit" du Procureur du Roi, les accusés transférés à Paris, traduits le 20 octobre 1785 devant la Chambre de vacations du Parlement de Paris, avaient vu leur peine aggravée. Ils périraient sur la roue.

Le Conseiller Fréteau s'était refusé à condamner les accusés au supplice de la roue: il avait cependant retenu leur culpabilité, en opinant pour la confirmation. Mais à cette occasion il avait dû constater de nombreux vices de la procédure qui le laissaient inquiet.

Les faits étaient les suivants: dans la nuit du 29 au 30 janvier 1783, trois individus s'étaient introduits dans la maison des époux Thomassin, laboureurs à Vinet, petit bourg en Champagne, près de Troyes. Le lendemain, ces derniers avaient porté plainte à la maréchaussée pour violence et vols avec effraction. Il s'agissait d'effets et de bijoux de peu de valeur et les violences ne paraissaient pas avoir laissé de traces importantes. Les plaignants ne pouvaient donner qu'un signalement vague des "brigands."

La maréchaussée commeça par arrêter un nommé Lardoise, "mendiant, sans passeport ni certificat," puis un sieur Guyot, parce qu'il était vêtu d'un vêtement gris, mentioneé dans un des trois signalements par les plaignants. Le 4 février, le sieur Guillaume, assesseur du prévot de Toyes, aussi ignorant que manquant d'humanité, interrogeait Lardoise et Guyot, et arrêta Simare et Bradier, sur la seule présomption qu'ils avaient été vus avec Lardoise dans un cabaret à Salon.

Comment la procédure se déroulera-t-elle alors?

Le 7 avril, le Président de Troyes, jugeant l'affaire grave, se déclare incompétent et renvoie les accusés devant le Juge de Vinet sous la prévention de vol. Le jeu du renvoi alors continue: le Juge de Vinet, au bout d'un mois, retourne l'affaire à Chaumont, estimant qu'il s'agit de "cas royaux" relevant de l'exclusive compétence du Bailliage.

Pendant vingt-six mois, les quatre hommes seront ainsi détenus à Chaumont sans être interrogés. Guyot ne supporte pas la prison et meurt. En juin 1785, à l'occasion d'une autre procédure, le Procureur du Roi de Chaumont et son assesseur se transportent à Pincy, à quelques lieues de Vinet. En sept jours, l'information du procès à l'extraordinaire est bâclée. Après cela la procédure se précipite très vite. Le 11 août, les juges du Bailliage de Chaumont entendent les accusés et les condamnent aux galères perpétuelles.

Sur appel "de droit" du Procureur du Roi de Chaumont ("l'appel" de contrôle était automatique en raison de la nature de l'affaire et de la condamnation), les accusés transférés à Paris sont traduits le 20 octobre 1785 devant la Chambre de vacations du Parlement de Paris. Leur peine est aggravée et c'est la condamnation à mourir sur la roue. Tel avait été le procès et le jugement.

Fréteau, un des conseillers, s'entretînt incidemment de cette affaire avec son beau-frère Jean-Baptiste Mercier Dupaty qui, après des difficultés dues à son adhésion au courant philosophique, avait été nommé en 1778 Président à Mortier, au Parlement de Bordeaux.

La carrière de Dupaty n'était pas allée sans vicissitudes: elle avait été particulièrement mouvementée. Né à La Rochelle en 1746, il avait été installé comme avocat général au Parlement de Bordeaux. Reçu par l'Académie de cette ville, il marqua très rapidement sa place. En 1770, il prenait parti pour La Chalotais, ce qui lui valût d'être enfermé au Château de Pierre—Encise à Lyon. Libéré au bout de quelques mois, il s'était retiré à Roanne où, pendant plusieurs années, il s'était consacré à l'étude et à la traduction du *Traité des Délits et des peines* de Beccaria. Bourdeaux l'avait de nouveau réclamé: ne lui faisait-il pas honneur, et c'est ainsi que réintégré dans sa charge, il avait été nommé en 1778 Président à Mortier. Mais en lutte à des oppositions et tracasseries multiples, il venait de donner sa démission.

Quand Dupaty rencontra Fréteau à Paris, il rentrait d'un voyage avec un jeune avocat, Romain Desèze, au cours duquel il était allé saluer à Ferney Voltaire. Il avait pu ainsi avoir communication du dossier par Fréteau (bien que ce fût là une indiscrétion grave en contradiction avec les usages et les règles Parlementaires). Il s'était rapidement convaincu de l'innocence des accusés, relevant de plus dans la procédure des irrégularités multiples, qui avaient vicié toute l'instruction.

Dupaty était un homme de coeur, qui ne manquait pas de courage. Prenant feu pour les accusés, il obtenait un arrêt de sursis, faisant rattraper les malheureux condamnés sur la route de Chaumont, où ils allaient être exécutés. C'est alors qu'il rédigea et publia son *"Mémoire justificatif pour trois condemnés à la roue,"* qui eut un retentissement immense.

Condorcet, également proche de Fréteau, par les liens conjugaux qui devaient le rapprocher de lui, se lança dans ce combat pour la Justice, où se jouaient les têtes de trois malheureux. Il écrivit et publia, sans nom d'auteur, les *"Réflexions d'un citoyen non gradué sur un procès très connu."*[1] L'intervention de Condorcet constitue une date dans l'histoire de la Justice. Pour *la première fois*, il est rappelé que la Justice est l'affaire de tous, et qu'un procès jugé a une résonance générale. Il écrit: "Tel était l'état de l'affaire, lorsqu'il apparût un mémoire pour la défense des trois accusés, et dans un pays où la Justice criminelle agissant toujours dans les ténèbres, ensevelit dans la poussière d'un greffe les fautes et les prévarications, ce mémoire est non seulement un acte d'Humanité envers ces infortunés, mais un service rendu à la Nation qu'il a réveillée sur de grands intérêts trop longtemps oubliés." En cela Condorcet agissait déjà comme un homme du XXème sièle.

Pour bien comprendre la portée de l'intervention de Condorcet, qui dans ses réflexions éleva le débat jusqu'aux conceptions les plus hautes, il est indispensable de résumer rapidement ce qu'il advînt de l'affaire des "trois roués."

Le Mémoire de Dupaty, considéré comme attentatoire au Parlement de Paris, fut déféré devant lui. C'était là une des originalités de la procédure d'alors. Après un réquisitoire de l'avocat général Séguier, on voulut poursuivre Dupaty, qui ne fut sauvé que grâce à l'intervention du Roi.[2]

Avant d'en revenir à Dupaty, rappelons le sort en définitif des trois roués. Le Conseil d'Etat du Roi, sur rapport du maître des Requêtes Blondel (qui devînt plus tard un des rédacteurs du Code d'Instruction Criminelle), cassa à l'unanimité le 30 juillet 1787, l'arrêt qui avait condamné Lardoise, Simare et Bradier, et Dupaty obtînt du Bailliage de Rouen, le 5 novembre 1787, une décision d'acquittement, qui fût confirmé le 18 décembre 1787 par le Parlement de Rouen. Le condamnés furent remis en liberté aux applaudissements de 20.000 personnes.[3]

On imagine mal "la révolution" – le terme n'est pas excessif – que cette affaire provoqua parmi les gens de Robe (ce qui donnera plus de poids aux *"Réflexions"* de Condorcet et les expliquera) Fréteau avait manqué aux consignes les plus expresses du Parlement de Paris, d'autant plus que lors du délibéré il avait opiné pour les galères perpétuelles (des douze juges, huit avaient opiné pour la roue, trois pour les galères perpétuelles, et un seul pour un plus ample informé). Il sembait donc mal placé pour se faire le champion de l'innocence des accusés. Le Président réprimanda Fréteau, lui disant que "c'était une prévarication de ne pas céder à la preuve faite par deux témoins non reprochés."[4] Mais le Parlement de Paris avait des armes qui lui permettaient de défendre ses décisions: il les employa. Le 7 mars 1786, le Parlement de Paris, deux Chambres étant assemblées, arrêta qu'un imprimé intitulé *"Mémoire justificatif pour trois homme condamnés à la roue,"* serait remis au Parquet pour en rendre compte et y donna ses conclusions. Avec le *Mémoire* était également visée la consultation, qui le suivait et qui était signée par un jeune avocat Legrand de Laleu. Le 5 mai, la Cour délibérant toutes Chambres réunies, confirma la saisine du Parquet.

Le Barreau d'alors manqua de courage. Il se "coucha" devant la Cour et ajourna Me Legrand de Laleu au 9 mars pour explication. Ce dernier, bien que n'ayant que trois ans de Barreau, revendiqua pleinement sa responsabilité dans la publication du *Mémoire* devant la députation des avocats constituée à la requête du Bâtonnier d'alors. Les avocats hésitèrent à le frapper d'une peine définitive, mais ils décidèrent de le sanctionner par "l'incommunication" (c'est à dire aucun avocat ne devait lui parler sans autorisation).

Le *Mémoire* ainsi déféré aux gens du Roi fit l'objet d'un réquisitoire de l'avocat général Séguier, qui le stigmatisa en termes particulièrement durs, faisant l'apologie de l'ordonnance de 1670. A cette occasion, Séguier fut, sans doute, heureux de régler de vieux comptes académiques. Il n'avait pas oublié la séance du 6 septembre 1770, dans laquelle l'académicien Thomas l'avait attaqué pour la grande joie des philosophes. Séguier n'avait-il pas déjà dénoncé au Parlement en 1770 *le Systéme de la Nature* du Baron d'Holbach, et la Cour, élargissant le débat, avait fait un autodafé de cet ouvrage. Par 59 voix contre 39, le Mémoire fut condamné le 16 août 1786, sur l'avis due Président d'Ormesson, à être lacéré et brûlé par la main du Bourreau.[5] Une information en outre était ouverte contre ses auteurs et distributeurs. Dupaty et l'avocat Legrand de Laleu ne furent pas incarcérés grâce à la clémence du Roi. En effet, huit jours après ce jugement, le Parlement n'avait-il pas lancé contre Dupaty et Legrand de Laleu un décret de prise de corps?

Telle était donc la situation quand Condorcet intervient. Il le fait en 1786, quand le combat est à chaud. Quelques mois après, Lally-Tolendal – grâce à l'expérience qu'il a acquise de la procédure dans le procès en cassation de son père – étudiera[6] l'ensemble du problème, développant un véritable programme des réformes souhaitées dans son *Essai sur quelques changements qu'on pourrait faire dès à présent dans les Lois criminelles de la France par un honnête homme qui, depuis qu'il connaît ces Lois, n'est pas bien sûr de n'être pas pendu un jour.*[7] C'était à la fois une question de famille et aussi une question de principe. Condorcet fit bonne mesure – Il prît à son compte les critiques formulées alors contre la Justice par les Philosophes. Le prétexte de "L'affaire des trois hommes condamnés à la roue" ne pouvait être meilleur. Il suggéra à Condorcet ces observations:

1. Pas de constatations immédiates établissant le vol, l'effraction ou la violence, bien qu'un officier de la maréchaussée soit arrivé sur les lieux quelques heures après seulement. Rien ne peut remplacer cet acte judiciaire, "parce qu'il aurait pu "toujours en résulter une *preuve physique* de l'impossibilité "ou de la non existence du fait avancé par les témoins qui "ont pu se *tromper* ou *vouloir tromper.*"

Les constatations matérielles valent mieux que tous les témoignages. Condorcet se réfère à l'Histoire de Joli rapportée dans le 2ème volume des Mémoires du Cardinal de Retz et dans les autres Mémoires du Temps pour voir si le nombre des témoins peut dispenser de constater juridiquement le corps du délit.

2. Condorcet s'élève contre la fragilité du témoignage et en dénonce la partialité, quand les témoins sont intéressés. Dans l'espèce "tous les témoignages se bornent à ceux de Thomassin (le laboureur qui dit avoir été volé et maltraité). Condorcet remarque qu'ils ont varié dans leurs déclarations et "ont substitué des indécences à cet attentat si difficile à croire." Condorcet multiplie les preuves des variations des plaignants. Il s'élève contre le *secret* de l'instruction. Il indique en note: "On trouve chez les jurisconsultes romains plusieurs passages qui prouvent combien ils mettaient de différence entre les déclarations faites sur le champ et les déclarations méditées. Notre respect pour leurs opinions doit-il donc cesser quand ils leur arrivent d'être raisonnables et humains? D'ailleurs, la raison que nous alléguons ici contre la reconnaissance des Thomassin, est précisément la seule raison plausible que nos criminalistes puissent apporter en faveur du secret de la Procédure: cette raison cesserait-elle d'avoir quelque valeur à leurs yeux du moment qu'elle conduit à sauver des hommes et non à les faire condamner?"

3. Des deux cavaliers de la maréchaussée, un seul fut entendu au procès...Il a constamment désigné comme "vagabond" des gens qui se trouvaient dans le lieu

de leur domicile…D'un autre côté, le Juge de Chaumont laisse languir 26 mois les accusés dans les cachots, instruit leur procès en 7 jours, n'admet aucun fait justificatif et les condamne.

C'est au bout de *trente mois* que "le Juge" examine des armoires qu'on lui dit avoir été *forcées*, des cloisons qu'on lui dit avoir été brisées et qu'on dépose gravement à son greffe trois cordes dont on dit avoir autrefois été liées. L'exactitude de la procédure répond à ce qu'on devait attendre de cette négligence et de cette précipitation.

Il faut bien noter que Condorcet dénonce le non respect des dispositions prévues par l'Ordonnance de 1670 et invoque le texte même de l'Ordonnance pour établir la nullité de la *Procédure*.

"Par exemple," écrit-il, "le brigadier de la maréchaussée n'a pas été récolté,[8] ce qui est contraire à l'article 1er du titre XV de l'Ordonnence de 1670, disposition dont le Parlement de Paris a reconnu l'importance puisque par un arrêt du 24 *janvier* dernier (1786) il a ordonné aux juges de s'y conformer. Ainsi, le hasard ou la providence a voulu que le Parlement lui-même reconnût au mois de janvier la nullité de la procédure d'après laquelle il a jugé les accusés dans le mois *d'octobre* (1785)."

A cette occasion dans une note, Condorcet met en cause la toute puissance des Parlements. "Il n'est pas vraisemblable que Messieurs jugent à propos d'avancer que cet article de l'ordonnance de 1670 n'a force de Loi que depuis l'arrêt du 24 janvier 1786. Ils prétendent bien à la vérité ne devoir obéir qu'aux Lois qu'ils ont eu la politesse d'enregistrer, mais ils n'ont pas encore prétendu qu'il était nécessaire que chaque article en particulier eut été confirmé par un arrêt."

Aussi, les trois accusés ont été condamnés à la roue (peine conforme à l'usage et à la loi en cette matière) pour un délit qui n'est pas constaté, sans aucune preuve qu'ils l'aient commis, par une procédure nulle et inique.

Ce rappel des faits ayant été présenté par Condorcet, celui-ci aborda un certain nombre de questions qui posent le problème de la réforme de l'ordonnance de *1670*.

Première question:

Le témoignage des Thomassin était-il admissible ou non contre les accusés?
Pour répondre, Condorcet examine les points distincts qu'elle renferme.
1. Faut-il ainsi admettre certains témoins qui peuvent paraître suspects et qu'on nomme *"nécessaires,"* parce que l'on ne reçoit pas leur témoignage lorsqu'il y en a *d'autres*? Il est clair qu'il faut les *admettre* ou les *rejeter toujours*. Ce n'est pas sur *le besoin* que *l'on a d'un témoin* (sans lui pas de condamnation possible)[9] que l'on doit se décider à l'admettre ou à le rejeter, mais il doit *être admis quand on a lieu de croire que son témoignage est désintéressé et qu'on*

peut lui supposer assez de sens commun et de *bonne foi* pour mériter quelque croyance. *Une preuve ne devient pas meilleure parce qu'on n'en a pas d'autres.* Enfin, d'après le simple bon sens ce n'est pas lorsqu'il y a très peu de témoins, c'est lorsqu'il y en a beaucoup qu'on peut se rendre moins difficile sur les qualités qu'on exige d'eux.[10]

2. Mais le témoignage de l'homme qui se plaint peut-il être reçu contre l'homme duquel il dit avoir reçu l'injure?

Oui, sans doute, mais à deux conditions: la première, que l'injure soit constatée indépendamment de la déclaration. La seconde, que toutes les personnes parentes, domestiques, ou qui habitent ensemble ne soient regardées que comme un seul témoin, que ce témoignage entre dans la preuve, mais que jamais il ne suffise pour la faire. La première condition est nécessaire pour qu'on puisse supposer le témoin sans intérêt. La seconde, l'est encore plus parce que des gens qui vivent ensemble et qui ont souffert en commun une même injure ou seulement vu un même fait, et qui en ont parlé beaucoup entre eux, finissent par le raconter de même sans que cet accord rende leur récit plus probable. Ils ne peuvent donc valoir tout au plus qu'un seul témoin.

Autrement, il résulterait de l'admission *de pareils témoins que trois personnes ou même deux vivant dans la même maison pourraient avec un peu d'habileté envoyer au supplice qui elles voudraient.*

On répond qu'elles s'exposeraient à être punies de même supplice *si la fraude était découverte*: mais il nous paraît que le but de l'instruction criminelle est de chercher la vérité, de connaître avec assurance si un crime est prouvé, et *non de s'assurer que, quoi qu'il en puisse arriver, on aura toujours un homme à pendre.*

Seconde question:

On a demandé si le reproche fait au Parlement de Paris de ne pas rédiger par écrit l'interrogatoire sur la sellette était fondé, si cette omission était grave et devait être regardée comme une nullité.

Condorcet considère que ce reproche est fondé.

Le greffier reproduit cet interrogatoire: mais il n'est ni relu, ni signé par l'accusé. Sans doute, il ne peut faire charge contre lui…"Il n'en reste pas moins vrai que le refus de vérifier un fait…d'avoir égard à une réclamation fondée contre les premiers juges serait, de la part des juges supérieurs, une faute où la prévention, le désir d'expédier les affaires pourrait les entraîner, que ce serait un tort vis à vis de l'accusé." Sa "signature est nécessaire pour ce dernier interrogatoire, parce qu'elle constate à la fois que l'on n'a rien changé à ses réponses et que l'on n'a rien omis…Si cet interrogatoire n'influe pas sur la preuve légale, il peut influer sur l'opinion personnelle de chaque Juge.

L'ordonnance ne prescrit pas cette formalité d'une manière précise: elle est plutôt exigée par *l'esprit* de l'ordonnance que par le texte, mais elle l'est par *le droit naturel* qui est plus ancien, plus sacré que toutes les lois.

Condorcet—notons-le au passage—voit les questions sous un angle pratique. On s'aperçoit, en effet, que l'erreur provient le plus souvent de l'omission d'une formalité "pratique," qui constitue une sécurité pour *l'accusé*. La "cuisine" de l'audience est souvent plus importante, en effet, que l'énoncé des grands principes.

Troisième question:

Pourquoi des hommes auxquels il est physiquement impossible d'entendre la loi d'après laquelle on les juge, et par conséquent de réclamer à temps contre les dénis de justice qu'ils éprouvent, contre les irrégularités de la procédure, n'ont-ils pas le droit d'avoir un Conseil?

Pourquoi ce Conseil n'a-t-il pas le droit de connaître la procédure, de l'examiner; pourquoi tout se passe t-il dans l'ombre du secret comme si l'on craignait que l'accusé ne se défendît trop bien?

On a gémi, écrit Condorcet, de voir le Peuple où ont vécu les Montesquieu, les Voltaire, les Turgot, les Malesherbes, les d'Alembert, la nation obligée de solliciter encore non une législation digne d'un peuple éclairé, mais *la jouissance des premiers droits de l'Humanité*. (Ce droit élémentaire n'est-il pas encore souvent contesté aujourd'hui? Théoriquement reconnu, il es éliminé dans la pratique.[11])

Quatrième question:

Celle-ci est capitale. *Que faut-il penser de l'usage de condamner pour les cas résultant du procès?*

Nous répondons ici que cet usage en vertu duquel on termine par *un jugement secret, une procédure secrète*, est l'équivalent de la loi établie en Corse où le gouvernement gênois faisait tuer un homme ex "informata conscientia (*d'après la conscience informée*)."

Condorcet une fois de plus, en appelle au droit naturel. Il exige que tout homme qui emploie contre des membres de la société la force qu'elle lui a confiée, lui rende *compte des causes qui l'y ont déterminé*.

Voilà encore une observation *essentielle.* L'absence de motifs est la cause des plus graves abus et les Parlements—jugeant de droit divin, s'en dispensaient—ce qui permettait de juger sur des motifs inavoués parce qu'inavouables.[12]

Cinquième question:

C'est celle du Recours au Roi "ayant le droit de surseoir à l'exécution des arrêts, de faire examiner la Procédure, et de faire grâce." Ce droit est devenu illusoire puisque les Arrêts sont souvent exécutés, sans que le Roi ou le Ministère chargé du département de la Justice en ait eu, en aient pu avoir connaissance.

Condorcet souhaite qu'à l'exemple de la Prusse ou de l'Angleterre, *aucun homme* ne subît *la peine* de mort ni même une *flétrissure* sans la *signature*, sans l'aveu du Monarque...

Quel bien ne résulterait-il pas de cette institution?

D'abord les citoyens seraient assurés de ne jamais être opprimés par les Cours de Justice, et la sûreté publique exige cette précaution, partout où la justice criminelle est exercée par les tribunaux perpétuels, par des juges à vie, surtout dans les pays où les Tribunaux ayant ou prétendant avoir une portion de l'autorité souveraine *ont nécessairement des préjugés de corps, des intérêts séparés de l'intérêt général.*

Condorcet dénonce à cette occasion les risques de *précipitation*, de *négligence*, la contradiction si effrayante des jugements d'un même Tribunal, la dureté érigée en système. Par exemple, écrit-il, on fait brûler les ouvrages utiles, estimés dans l'Europe, de Rousseau et de l'Abbé Raynal, et on supprime au greffe les rapsodies au moins très inutiles de M. le Maître. On pend le Prêtre Ringuet[13] après lui *avoir donné la question* pour avoir mal parlé de Messieurs et on renvoie de toute accusation Mr le Maître qui a imprimé *des libellés contre les Ministres* etc...etc...Il est certain que les exemples de ce genre foisonnaient.

D'un autre côté, le Prince connaîtrait mieux les Lois qui gouvernent son peuple et les Magistrats auxquels il a confié une partie de son pouvoir.

A ce sujet, Condorcet fait le procès de la justice d'alors: "Il serait impossible que la dureté d'une instruction qui ne semble avoir pour but que de trouver un coupable, qui au lieu de chercher tous les moyens de connaître la vérité, semble s'être arrangée pour avoir nécessairement à punir ou l'accusé ou les témoins, et couvre d'un voile impénétrable pour les accusés la procédure de laquelle dépendent leur honneur et leur vie: il serait impossible que la cruauté de nos supplices si indigne d'une nation civilisée, si opposée à la douceur de moeurs qui *caractérisent les premières classes de la nation, que la manière dont la peine de mort est prodiguée pour le vol, décernée pour des délits imaginaires*, pour des fautes de moeurs, que tous ces vices de notre législation ne frappassent pas les yeux d'un monarque sage et humain."

Enfin, cette connaissance des jugements serait pour le Prince un moyen de connaître les hommes...Peut-être irait-on jusqu'à dire que trop de coupables seraient sauvés?...

Condorcet formule une critique sévère de la Justice telle qu'elle se pratique. Nous répondrons, écrit-il, que "tout coupable accrédité n'a besoin d'aucune institution nouvelle pour échapper au supplice: que tout homme qui a une famille riche, des protecteurs puissants, une grande fortune, trouve dans l'état actuel le moyen de solliciter un sursis ou une grâce[14] qu'on ne pourrait lui ôter cette possibilité sans une précipitation et des mesures qui, malgré la pureté des motifs des Magistrats, seraient une vraie prévarication, qu'enfin, toute la différence à cet égard serait de faire jouir les accusés pauvres et sans appui des ressources qui restent aux accusés riches ou protégés: en même temps l'on *ôterait à ceux-ci la facilité de surprendre la Justice ou la clémence du Prince, facilité qui est une suite nécessaire de la précipitation avec laquelle l'usage actuel oblige l'autorité souveraine de prononcer.*"

Faut-il le dire, tout l'inconvénient se trouverait à enlever aux Parlements la possibilité de faire pendre dans un moment d'humeur *un huissier du Conseil* ou *un employé des fermes*, et c'est un avantage que les citoyens, *ni même les magistrats* ne doivent regretter. Condorcet en revient à l'affaire des Trois Roués.

"Trois malheureux sont oubliés *vingt-six mois* dans les cachots parce que le juge n'a pas *le temps d'instruire le procès*: il les traîne enchaînés à sa suite, *parce qu'il trouve cette manière d'instruire le procès plus commode.* A peine daigne-t-on y faire attention, et l'Arrêt exagère encore par tant de souffrances auxquelles la Loi ne les condamnait pas à la sévérité déjà excessive de la Loi." Un homme généreux (Dupaty) prend leur défense et l'on s'attendrit sur le malheur de *M. Guillaume, assesseur de Chaumont dont le Mémoire ne parle pas avec assez de respect.*

Condorcet cite d'autres exemples, moins connus, mais aussi éloquents:

"A *Lyon*, deux hommes sont accusés de meurtre, un seul est arrêté. Il est condamné à la roue, son prétendu complice se présente, demande à être jugé, proteste de son innocence et de celle de son ami. Le Juge de Lyon refuse de suspendre l'exécution, et la suite du procès a prouvé l'entière innocence du malheureux exécuté..."

"A *Lyon*, deux hommes sont condamnés à la roue pour un assassinat. L'un d'eux est vraiment coupable, il l'avoue, mais son co-accusé nie constamment. Le coupable reconnu l'a d'abord déchargé de complicité, il a ensuite changé sa déposition. Il pouvait la changer encore. Cependant, c'est celui sur le crime duquel il pouvait rester quelque nuage qui a été exécuté le premier, et le testament de mort du coupable reconnu a renfermé un témoignage de l'innocence de son co-accusé, témoignage mendié peut-être, mais dont enfin une exécution précipitée ne permettait plus de se servir utilement pour celui en faveur duquel il était rendu."

Nous n'avons pas oublié ce mot d'un juge aux enfants de *Calas*: "Nous avons roué votre père, nous pourrons bien vous rouer aussi", ni *Lally* traîné dans un tombereau avec un baillon, ni le *Chevalier de la Barre* condamné à un supplice barbare comme convaincu d'avoir chanté des chansons trop libres, et *véhémentement suspecté* d'avoir mutilé une statue.

Nous apprenons de *Rouen* qu'on vient de condamner à la roue un homme *véhémentement suspecté* d'un assassinat, qu'il a subi la question et que les juges ont eu la barbarie de tenir la *femme et la fille* de ce malheureux dans une chambre voisine d'où, pendant six heures de torture, elles entendaient les cris *que la douleur lui arrachait*.[15] espèce de cruauté dont l'histoire des Caligula, des Néron, des Domitius n'offre point d'exemple...

D'après une procédure inique du juge de *Caen*, le même Parlement condamne une jeune fille à la question et à être brûlée vive. Elle a le bonheur d'obtenir de l'humanité du Roi un sursis et la révision. Le même Parlement ne peut s'empêcher de la trouver innocente: mais il abuse des formes pour la condamner contre la loi à une prison perpétuelle...

Condorcet se pose le problème de *la cause de ce mépris de l'homme*, mépris que le sang froid, l'indifférence qui l'accompagne, rendent plus *offensant* encore et plus *dangereux*. Tient-il uniquement à ce reste de nos institutions d'après lesquelles *on était quelque chose* comme *gentilhomme*, comme *Prêtre*, comme *gradué*, comme *bourgeois* même et *rien* quand *on n'était qu'un homme*? Non: et puisque ce mépris s'est affaibli dans les autres classes de la société et *qu'il subsiste encore tout entier parmi nos gens de loi*, nous devons le regarder comme la suite de nos Tribunaux, de l'étendue de leur ressort, du *secret* et de la *dureté* de l'instruction de la *sévérité* du Code Pénal.[16]

Restent deux questions particulières:

I. A-t-on bien fait d'imprimer le *Mémoire*? (Autrement dit, a-t-on le droit de porter le procès sur la place publique?).

Je crois que tout homme qui a plus à craindre *d'être mal jugé* qu'il n'a peur de laisser voir qu'il a mal jugé, n'hésitera pas à répondre *oui*, même pour *son intérêt personnel*. Or, cet intérêt *personnel* est ici l'intérêt *général* des citoyens, l'autre ne serait que celui de *l'intérêt des juges* qui en ce point serait *contraire à l'intérêt général*. D'ailleurs, tant que la procédure sera secrète, tant que les juges supérieurs auront pour les justices subalternes l'indulgence dont il ne s'agit pas ici d'examiner les *motifs* et les *effets funestes*, tant que ces juges supérieurs n'auront pas un Tribunal qui les juge, l'impression des Mémoires de cette espèce est un appui trop précieux pour ne pas louer les hommes dont la voix courageuse ose citer au Tribunal de l'opinion ceux qui ont l'orgueil de ne pas en reconnaître d'autre.

La formule est lancée. C'est au Tribunal de *l'opinion publique* qu'il convient de s'adresser en *dernière instance*. Ainsi l'appel à l'opinion publique confirme que pour Condorcet, déjà, la Justice appartient à toute la Nation et que son contrôle est l'oeuvre de chacun.

Condorcet approuve pleinement la position du *Conseiller Fréteau*.

"Mais." dira-t-on, "l'auteur du *Mémoire* doit à la complaisance d'un greffier et d'un juge la connaissance de la Procédure, et ce juge ne croyait pas d'abord les accusés si clairement *innocents*." *La réponse de Condorcet claque comme un coup de fouet.* "Que ce Magistrat ait été effrayé de l'arrêt dont il avait été témoin, qu'il s'est repenti de *n'en n'avoir pas senti toute l'injustice,* de ne pas *s'y être opposé* avec *assez de force* et qu'il a tout fait pour réparer une *faute involontaire.* Depuis, quand *le repentir,* et surtout le *repentir que répare* n'est-il pas une vertu? Quoi, le prix de la complaisance d'avoir laissé lire une procédure serait l'obligation de renoncer au droit de défendre les innocents qu'elle opprime...

"Gardons-nous d'avancer de pareilles maximes qui présenteraient aux yeux du peuple, tous les hommes de quelque autorité, de quelque crédit comme une troupe de brigands, ne connaissant, ne respectant d'autres devoirs que ceux qui les lient à leurs complices."

II. Quelle doit être la conduite du Parlement? *Le silence.*[17] Et Condorcet se livre à une diatribe violente contre le Parlement de *Paris.*

"*Le silence:* c'est le devoir de tout juge dont on attaque la décision. Il n'est ni de la dignité du Parlement, ni de son intérêt de combattre *l'opinion publique par des arrêts qui ne feraient que lui donner* plus de force. Punira-t-il des hommes qui ont pris la défense de l'infortuné sans autre intérêt que celui de l'Humanité, de *la gloire* si l'on veut, des hommes qu'il faudrait encore respecter quand même ils se seraient trompés, quand même l'amour de la célébrité les aurait seul conduits? S'obstinera-t-il à faire rouer les accusés? Il ne peut même en avoir l'idée..." Osera-t-il avouer qu'il regarde comme *une espèce de crime* dans les simples citoyens l'audace de juger sa conduite, qu'il veut *tenir nos opinions, nos idées dans l'esclavage, les forcer au moins au silence?*

Condorcet se tourne alors vers les avocats. *Oseront-ils rayer un confrère pour avoir rempli le premier devoir de leur état?* Les confrères de Maître Legrand de Laleu avaient dépassé les réquisitions de l'avocat général Séguier, particulièrement indulgentes à son égard. "Nous aimons à nous persuader," avait déclaré ce dernier dans son réquisitoire, "que Me Legrand de Laleu n'a pas connu le danger de sa complaisance...la modération dont nous usons envers lui, lui apprendra à se défier même de ses bonnes intention." Les avocats s'annonceront-ils comme de vils esclaves de la Magistrature, incapables de montrer de l'équité et du courage dès qu'ils peuvent craindre de lui déplaire? Se sont-ils emparés du privilège exclusif de nous défendre pour nous abandonner sans défense au despotisme des Tribunaux?[18]

Condorcet va alors conclure. Il procède à une attaque sans ménagement contre les Parlements. "Enfin croit-on que c'est l'intérêt de Bradier, de Simare et de Lardoise, que c'est l'éloquence de leur défense qui a produit cet effet prodigieux dont le Parlement est irrité et humilié? Non, sans doute: *que cette compagnie se rappelle ses jugements particuliers, sa conduite dans les affaires publiques, sa haine contre tous ceux qui ont voulu répandre des lumières, introduire des nouveautés utiles, réformer des abus:* elle verra dans l'intérêt que l'affaire des trois accusés a excité l'expression des sentiments que tous les hommes éclairés, sensibles, animés de zèle pour le bien public portaient au fond de leur coeur: elle verra qu'il est de son intérêt comme de son devoir de renoncer à des vues d'ambition odieuses aux bons citoyens, à des préjugés que la nation s'indigne de lui voir encore partager, à une intolérance qui la révolte, à un mépris pour les hommes, à une dureté de principes, à une négligence de ses devoirs, à une chaleur pour ses prétentions qui ont altéré notre confiance et détruit notre antique respect."

L'avocat général Séguier — on le comprend — ne ménagera pas Condorcet: "Ce nouvel individu dirigeant ses coups contre le corps entier de la Magistrature, jusque dans le sanctuaire de la Justice." Sans le nommer (car l'auteur des *Réflexions* était resté anonyme), il le traita "d'homme perfide tremblant d'attaquer à force ouverte et à visage découvert."

Condorcet n'avait-il pas ajouté une note à laquelle le Magistrat avait dû être particulièrement sensible…"Le magistrat qui a dénoncé au Parlement ce Mémoire en faveur des accusés après avoir supposé que tous les juges les avaient regardés comme coupables et n'avaient différé d'opinion que sur le supplice, ce qui n'est pas assez vrai même pour une dénonciation, a beaucoup insisté sur *l'aménité connue de l'âme de M. Le Rapporteur qui avait opiné à la roue. L'Aménité et la Roue.* Nous espérons qu'il voudra bien s'occuper de faire brûler ce petit écrit suivant l'heureuse invention de l'empereur *Tibère* dont il ne manqua pas de louer *l'aménité* et que notre diatribe obtiendra le même honneur que le *Cymbalum mundi*, les mandements de l'auteur de Marie à la Coque et le Voyage de Figaro…"

Condorcet avait tenu pour finir à faire suivre ses réflexions du Discours de Me Legrand de Laleu à la députation des Avocats, qui l'avait ajourné au 9 mars par le Ministère de Me Dand'Asne, Bâtonnier (son "dénonciateur").

Me Legrand de Laleu protestait avec noblesse contre le comportement de son Bâtonnier. "Suis-je avec mes confrères? Suis-je devant mes juges?"

"Avant que j'aie pu vous faire entendre ma défense, je suis déjà puni: par provision, mon état m'est enlevé."

"M. le Bâtonnier, dans la lettre que je reçus le mercredi 8 de ce mois, à 7 heures, pour comparaître le lendemain à votre assemblée. Il me refusait d'avance le titre de *confrère.*"

Après avoir reproduit la défense de Me Legrand de Laleu, Condorcet ajouta: "L'assemblée des avocats arrêta qu'ils attendraient pour prononcer, le jugement du Parlement et celui du Conseil, ce qui signifie qu'ils ne se permettent de persécuter leurs confrères que lorsqu'ils sont sûrs de pouvoir le faire *impunément* ou bien qu'il n'est permis à un avocat de défendre les opprimés que dans le cas où il est assuré de réussir, et de faire plaisir au Parlement. Ils ont de plus arrêté que M. de Laleu sera frappé de la peine qu'ils appellent *"Incommunication provisoire"*… Cela veut dire qu'aucun des avocats ne doit parler à M. de Laleu; rien n'est plus juste: car il est évident que M. de Laleu et ses confrères excommuniants ne parlent pas la même langue, et ne sont pas faits pour vivre ensemble.

Le jour où *"les Réflexions"* allaient sortir des Presses, le Conseil du Roi ordonnait l'apport des charges et informations, et admettait la requête des accusés: Les *Réflexions* sont une oeuvre de combat qui appelle trois observations:

1. L'intervention souhaitée du Monarque (droit de sursis et de grâce) démontre combien dans la période pré-révolutionnaire l'idée de renversement de la monarchie était éloignée des esprits éclairés, qui voyaient dans elle la garantie des droits du peuple, alors qu'au contraire, le peuple la voyait dans les Parlements.[19]

2. On retrouve, développées dans une forme pratique, toutes les réformes proposées par Lally Tolendal dans son "Essai sur quelques changements"... (cf: supra).

3. Condorcet, dans une forme, ignorant volontairement tout compromis, à l'occasion du procès de trois malheureux, a accepté de prendre parti pour déférer à la Place Publique, cette grande dame qu'est la Justice.

La pression de l'opinion est l'aiguillon indispensable pour que l'institution réponde du rôle qu'elle doit remplir. Il faut, en effet, que toute injustice soit débusquée: sinon l'atmosphère de la vie en société est "polluée."

Les peuples ont besoin de Justice autant que de l'air qu'ils respirent. Condorcet a eu le courage de sortir du rang pour faire entendre la voix des "non gradués." La Justice n'est, en effet, pas la propriété privée de personne: elle est à tous. La contribution de Condorcet dans "l'affaire des Trois Roués" est l'illustration de ce grand principe, qui veut que nous soyons tous des juges, à la conscience desquels il soit possible de faire appel. Condorcet est ainsi un des pères du journalisme réformateur moderne et toute l'Humanité doit lui en être reconnaissante.

P.S.—Le 15 février 1793, au nom du Comité de la Constitution, Condorcet exposa à la Tribune les règles de l'organisation judiciaire (cf: *Archives parlementaires*, t. LVIII—p. 538—*Moniteur* t. XV—p. 456 et suiv.). Il supprimait la peine de mort en matière privée et civile: le précédent de la condamnation de Louis XVI l'empêchait de le faire en matière politique. Cette distinction fut maintenue traditionellement: c'est ainsi que la peine de mort a survécu pour des besoins de gouvernement dans une matière où elle se justifie *le moins*.

Pierre Antoine Perrod

Notes

1. Francfort, 1786, 17 pages. A trouver dans le volume VII des *Oeuvres* de Condorcet, ed. O'Connor-Arago, (Paris 1847-1849).

2. Cf. *Recueil du Barreau Français*, 1ère séries, Tome troisième, (Paris 1822). Dupaty, *Mémoire justificatif pour trois condamnés à la roue*, pp. 77–276; et Seguier, *Requisitoire contre le Mémoire justificatif pour trois hommes condamnés à la roue*, p. 287–520.

3. A peine libéré, Lardoise fut condamné par le Bailliage de Meaux le 24 avril 1789 à un an de prison pour *vol*. Le Parlement de Paris qui tenait une premiere audience criminelle publique eut la satisfaction de confirmer partiellement cette decision, en la reduisant cependant à 6 mois.

4. Il est certain, soutenait la jurisprudence, que ces deux personnes qui concertent séparément un mensonge ne se reconnaîtront point d'une manière uniforme dans le construction de ce mensonge. C'est un piége que la nature tend perpétuellement aux imposteurs.

5. Cf. Louis-Sébastien Mercier, *Tableau de Paris*, (Paris 1781), 2 vols.: cf. Brûlement des ouvrages: "On allume un fagot en présence de quelques polissons oisifs qui se trouvent là par hasard, le greffier substitue une vieille Bible vermoulue au livre incriminé: le bourreau brûle le saint livre poudreux et le greffier place le livre anathèmatisé et recherché dans sa bibliothèque."

6. Cf. P. Antoine Perrod, *L'Affaire Lally Tolendal*, (Paris, Klincksieck, 1976)

7. Paris 1786 – 16-53p. B.N. F3 – 2436 et 80 – 8788; 1787 – 80-47p. B.N. F p. 1907 – analysé par Pierre Antoine Perrod – T II – service de reproduction des Thèses, Université de Lille III – 1876 – Appendice p. I a XXX.

8. Le Règlement à l'extraordinaire ordonne que les témoins seront recolés et confrontés à l'Accusé, si besoin est. L'ancien usage de faire dresser les informations par un Ministre subalterne a introduit dans la procédure une formalité de plus: *c'est le recolement*: la déposition des témoins se trouvait déjà rédigée, quoiqu'avec peu de solennité, et par conséquent peu de méthode sur la fidélité de la rédaction. C'était cette solennité qu'il s'agissait de suppléer. C'était cette fidélité qu'il s'agissait d'assurer. On y parvenait en faisant comparaître à nouveau les témoins devant le juge. Là, après un nouveau serment, on leur relit une déposition: on leur demande, s'ils la reconnaissent ou s'ils y persistent: on écrit tout ce qu'ils disent: et c'est là le véritable moment de leur témoignage, puisqu'il leur est permis d'y varier, et que passé ce recolement, un témoin qui varie doit être poursuivi comme faux témoin.

Plus spécialement, sur le cas qui nous occupe, on agitait encore lors de l'Ordonnance de 1670, la question de savoir si lorsque les informations avaient été reçues par le Juge lui-même, il y avait lieu d'ordonner un recolement qui paraissait dans ce cas, procédure superflue, un reste inutile d'un usage vicieux aboli. *L'ordonnance décide ce doute*, en ordonnant le recolement même dans ce cas: c'est un momument du voeu de l'ordre public en faveur de l'Innocent. (cf: *Code Pénal ou Recueil des principes, ordonnances, édits et déclarations sur les crimes et les délits* – Paris VM DCC – p. XXVII).

9. La parenthèse est de nous.

10. Cf. Voltaire dans le meme sens.

11. Note personelle.

12. Les Cours souveraines pouvaient se dispenser d'énoncer dans leurs arrêts les faits pour lesquels est condamné l'accusé. Il leur était même permis de ne pas le faire comparaître pour la derniere fois.

13. Jacques Ringuet, prêtre du diocèse de Cambray condamné à mort et exécuté en décembre 1762.

14. Ce ne fut pas vrai dans l'affaire du Comte de Lally. De nos jours, les erreurs judiciaires les plus graves sont nées de la rapidité des exécutions. Il est vrai que l'homme puissant, qui a perdu ses relations et ses appuis est condamné – pour l'exemple – plus qu'il ne le mérite!

15. Il est courant encore de mettre la *femme* ou la *maîtresse* en prison pour faire parler le mari ou l'amant.

16. N'en est-il pas de même aujourd'hui? Un juge d'Instruction frais émoulu de l'Ecole peut envoyer en prison n'importe qui. Comment ne pas comprendre qu'un tel pouvoir lui donne – en rien de temps – pour employer une expression à la mode "une grosse tête"?

17. Antoine-Louis Séguier, (1726-1794), avocat general au Parlement de Paris, dans son requisitoire, avait soutenu avec nuance le contraire. "Le Parlement ou Sénat dépositaire de

nos Rois, sans chercher à venger son injure personnelle, ne doit être affecté que de celle faite à la Loi et à son souverain."

18. Dupaty avait offert à Me Legrand de Laleu un dédommagement que ce jeune jurisconsulte a eu la noblesse de refuser.

19. Condorcet ne s'affirmera officiellement républicain qu'apres l'affaire de Varenne, dans un discours prononcé à l'assemblée des "Amis de la Vérité," au cirque du Palais-Royal, le 12 juillet 1791.

12
Condorcet as Constitutional Draftsman: Dimensions of Substantive Commitment and Procedural Implementation

Victor G. Rosenblum

Editor's Note

The literature on Condorcet and the French Revolution tells the story of the *Projet de Constitution*, which was substantially Condorcet's, the mature expression of his political views. He served as the *rédacteur* and the *rapporteur* to the nine-member Committee on the Constitution, which reported from February to May 1793 to the parent-body, the National Convention. Thomas Paine, serving as a delegate from Calais, was a member of that Committee. Danton and Barère were its Jacobins. The majority of the Committee being Girondins, Condorcet's Constitution became known as "la Girondine," although he belonged to neither group. Because of the animosity between them, and the crises, foreign and domestic, of 1793, Condrocet's eighty-page document was not even voted on. It was replaced by another version hastily drafted by the five-member *Comité de Salut public* headed by Héraut de Séchelles, who drew from Condorcet, but omitted constitutional review and other democratic provisions deemed essential by the *philosophe*. The Jacobin Constitution, adopted by the Convention on June 24, 1793, was never put into effect. Condorcet published an impassioned letter *Aux citoyens français, sur la nouvelle constitution*, attacking the new constitution and defending his own views. This led to the order for his arrest, July 8, and some months later his death, at the age of 50, in a prison cell.

Studying Condorcet's proposed constitution of 1793 for France from the vantage point of a teacher of U.S. constitutional law in the 1980s is at once enriching, challenging, and humbling. Commitments of the distinguished philosopher and mathematician to human dignity, social justice, and popular sovereignty pervaded the instrument he first presented to the National Convention on behalf of its Committee on the Constitution in February 1793; and his eloquent idealism and concern with operational details provided timeless models of democratic aspiration and expression.

Although differing in key respects with the concepts of federalism and checks and balances underlying the U.S. Constitution, he was a strong proponent of separation of powers and a relentless, meticulous advocate of individual freedom. Far more than the protection accorded Americans in the body of our Constitution and in the Bill of Rights, Condorcet's "projet de Déclaration des Droits Naturels, Civils et Politiques des Hommes" and his reiterations of individual rights in the text of the "projet de Constitution Française" endeavored to guarantee the safety, sanctity, and full and free exercise of human rights.

This chapter begins with detailed consideration of Condorcet's analysis of issues of rights, focusing especially on his recognition of the centrality of realistic protection of constitutionally defining citizenship. It then proceeds to explore and to compare with our own Constitution Condorcet's approaches to structuring and controlling the power to govern through his assessment of the functions and interactions of the national assembly, primary assemblies, national convention, administrative corps, executive council, and judiciary.

The Range and Scope of Individual Rights

Condorcet's constitutional provisions bearing on human rights were enlargements of his innate belief "qu'une constitution républicaine, ayant l'égalité pour base était le seule qui fût conforme à la nature, à la raison et à la justice; la seule qui pût conserver la liberté des citoyens et la dignité de l'espèce humaine" ("that a republican constitution based upon equality was the only one in accordance with nature, reason and justice; the only one that can protect the liberty of citizens and the dignity of the human race").[1] The predominant objective of society being to maintain the natural, civil, and political rights of man, Condorcet made it clear at the very outset of the "projet de Déclaration des Droits" that the constitution that guarantees the rights that are the foundation of the social compact must be preceded by the recognition and delineation of the contents of the rights. Consequently the first article of the thirty-three that comprise his declaration of rights stated forthrightly and succinctly that the natural, civil, and political rights of man are liberty, equality, security, property, resistance to oppression, and what he termed "la garantie sociale." He defined liberty, equality, security, and property but contented himself with illustrations of oppression and impairment of the social guarantee. Liberty was seen as the right to do all that does not contravene the rights of others; "thus the exercise of the natural rights of each man is limited only by those that assure to other members of society the enjoyment of these same rights."[2] The preservation of liberty was declared dependent on submission to law as the expression of the general will. Nothing that is not forbidden by law can be prohibited, and no one can be required to perform what the law does not ordain.

Included in the domain of liberty was the right to express one's thoughts and opinions and to exercise one's religion freely. A natural concomitant was freedom of the press and of any other means of publishing one's thoughts from prohibition, suspension, or limitation.

Equality was defined as the ability of each person to exercise the same rights as every other person. "The law must be equal for all, whether it redresses or punishes, whether it protects or reprimands."[3] Condorcet's conception of equal protection was given coordinate stature with liberty, in sharp contrast with the pre-Civil War U.S. Constitution that protected life, liberty, and property from incursions without due process by the federal government but did not address itself at all to equal protection. Every French citizen was deemed admissible to every public place and eligible to participate in every public function or employment. The only criteria for preferential treatment in choosing people for public employment were to be talent and virtue.

Security was defined as the protection accorded each citizen by society for the preservation of his person, goods, and rights. No one was to be accused, arrested, or detained except according to the forms and substance prescribed by the law. Any action against a citizen that was not pursuant to law was not only declared arbitrary and null; the perpetrator of such action was declared guilty and one who "must be punished." Legal process had to be applied prospectively and not retroactively. All persons were presumed innocent until proven guilty; and punishment for delicts, upon proof of guilt, were not to exceed what was strictly necessary for the general security of the community in relation to the nature of the offense.

Every citizen was obliged to obey the law as long as its forms and substance were observed by enforcing officials. The clear exception to this general obligation was found in Article 13 of the *Projet de Déclaration des Droits* which gave citizens the right to counter force with force when officials acted arbitrarily rather than pursuant to the strictures and structures of the law. The line of demarcation between official arbitrary acts that could trigger legitimate force by citizens in resistance and official acts under the authority and according to the forms of the law that require instant obedience was not made explicit, though Condorcet's illustrations of oppression in Article 32 struggled further with the problem. A dimension of circularity may unfortunately have entered the document at that point since a vital case of oppression was described as occurring "when arbitrary acts violate the rights of citizens contrary to law."

A further complication in drawing the line between official acts requiring instant obedience and those warranting forceful resistance stemmed from Condorcet's recognition that not every substantive and procedural act of the law is valid. For oppression occurs not only when public functionaries violate the law and tread arbitrarily on citizens' rights but also "when a law violates the natural, civil, and political rights that it is required to guarantee."[4] The obvious constitutional question left unresolved by Condorcet in the *Projet de Déclaration* is who has the authority to decide when a facially valid law, adopted in compliance with requisite forms and procedures, contravenes the constitutionally protected rights of the individual. Though he does not answer the question,

Condorcet does, nonetheless, establish the context for an answer in the last clause of Article 32, where he asserts that, in any free government, the mode of resistance to acts of oppression must be regulated by the constitution. Lest readers infer from his indorsement of the constitution's primacy as source of both the legitimacy of power and the legitimacy of resistance to power that Condorcet viewed his constitution as binding on present and future generations throughout time, he stressed in the concluding article of the Declaration, Article 33, that a people always has the right to re-examine, reform, and change its constitution. "One generation does not have the right to subject future generations to its laws," and any principle of heredity in constitutional functions is "absurd and tyrannical."[5]

Condorcet's treatment of property rights and of the right to social guarantees was cast within the same context of constitutional prescription tempered with ready potentiality for change. Property rights had explicit ownership and disposition entitlements and equally explicit limits. Every man was declared the master of his goods, capital, revenue, and industry. No type of work, trade, or cultural activity could be forbidden him; he could manufacture, sell, and transport all kinds of production. He was free to contract for his services and time. The emphasis upon one's own goods, revenues, and services was deliberate; for the individual had absolute authority to dispose of these at will.

No one could be deprived of the least portion of his property without his consent in the absence of public necessity and indemnification. But no individual could consent to sell himself. Article 20 conveyed its anti-slavery message in the clearest of terms: "il ne peut se vendre lui-même" ("he cannot sell himself"). One's person is not an alienable property.[6]

The issue of taxation was included for controls, too, in Condorcet's exploration of property rights. Taxes could be justified only to serve the general welfare and public need; no tax was valid without such justification. All citizens were given the right to participate personally or through their representatives, in the establishment of taxes.[7] The French philosopher took a more restrictive view of the government's taxing powers than did the framers of our constitution who simply allocated to Congress "the power to lay and collect taxes, duties, imposts and excises," requiring only that duties, imposts, and excises be uniform and that all bills for raising revenue originate in the House of Representatives.

Education was not designated a property right as such; but it is of more than passing interest that Condorcet included it as an explicit need of the people and obligation of the government. Placing the education article at the conclusion of his discussion of property, and before undertaking his section on social guarantees, Condorcet in 16 words would have resolved what U.S. lawyers, educators, and judges have agonized over for two centuries: whether education is a fundamental right in our constitutional system. To Condorcet, the answer was simple and compelling: "L'instruction est le besoin de tous; et la société la doit également à tous ses membres" ("Education is needed by all, and society owes it equally to all its members").[8]

Condorcet's conception of "la garantie sociale" of the rights of man was not a synonym for social security. If somewhat esoteric, amorphous, or even mystical, it was nonetheless formulated to relate national sovereignty to the general will. National sovereignty is declared the foundation for the social guarantee and described as "one, indivisible, unlimitable and inalienable." Sovereignty resides, not in any single individual or institution, but essentially in the entire people. Each citizen has an equal right to concur in its exercise,[9] though he cannot claim sovereign authority for himself. Essential to the operation of the social guarantee is clear determination by the law of the limits of public functions and the assurance of accountabilty of all public officials. All citizens must support this guarantee and enforce the law when they are called upon to do so in its name.[10] Once again, the quest for a line of demarcation between a proper and an oppressive invocation of law enforcement authority becomes essential here, but Condorcet goes no further than to balance the obligation of all citizens to concur in the social guarantee, in Article 30, with the recognition of Articles 31 and 32 that men united in society must have a legal means for resisting oppression by government.

Condorcet's "Projet de Déclaration des Droits Naturels, Civils et Politiques des Hommes" was deemed a prerequisite to any pact that brought people to unite in society. The declaration of rights had to precede the formulation of constitutional mechanisms since the latter were to provide the instruments for guaranteeing the sustenance of the former. Thus a critique of the declaration of rights for merely declaring the contents of rights but not prescribing the demarcations between legitimacy of enforcement and legitimacy of resistance would be premature at best. Clearly, Condorcet's Declaration of Rights provided a larger and stronger umbrella for individual protection than the Bill of Rights of our Constitution. For it applied to all throughout the land, not merely to particular units of government, and it dealt explicitly with such undeveloped areas of the U.S. Constitution of 1789 as equality under law, the right to public education, and the prohibition on human slavery. We proceed in the next section to analysis of the constitutional mechanisms for implementation.

Condorcet's Constitution

A Contrasting Description of Constitutional Objectives of the Framers of the U.S. Constitution and of Condorcet

In *The Federalist* No. 51, Alexander Hamilton, James Madison, and John Jay stated most candidly and powerfully the task undertaken by the drafters of the

U.S. Constitution. They proclaimed that government itself is "but the greatest of all reflections on human nature. If men were angels, no government would be necessary. If angels were to govern men, neither external nor internal controls on government would be necessary. In framing a government which is to be administered by men over men, the great difficulty lies in this: You must first enable the government to control the governed, and in the next place, oblige it to control itself."[11] The emphasis here was on the necessity for dual controls through government — control over the governed in the interests of union, justice, and liberty, and control over the government in the interests of preventing the abuses that unlimited power can generate. The ambition of one branch of officeholders was to be utilized to counteract the ambition of the others. The interior structures of the government were to be contrived "as that its several constituent parts may, by their mutual relations, be the means of keeping each other in their proper places."[12]

Condorcet focused less on interrelationships among the branches of the government than on reconciliation of the necessity for obedience to the law with the maintenance of popular sovereignty and natural rights of the individual. Condorcet's opening statement on his "Projet" to the National Convention in February 1793, summed up his view of the constitutional mission:

"To form, for a territory of 27,000 square leagues inhabited by 25 million persons, a constitution founded wholly upon the principles of reason and justice and securing each citizen in the enjoyment of his rights; to integrate the various parts of this constitution in such a way that the necessity for obedience to the law, and for submission of individual wills to the general will, shall leave popular sovereignty, civic equality and the exercise of natural freedom unimpaired: this is the problem we were given to solve."[13]

As noted in the previous section, Condorcet was sensitive to the capacities of officials and even the law itself to become oppressive and abusive. But whereas the framers of the U.S. Constitution found in federalism and in checks and balances the internal instruments through which government could be obliged to control itself, Condorcet would have relied on primary assemblies as major means for maintaining popular sovereignty and controlling governmental oppression. American federalism, as perceived by Condorcet, "threatened the success of their war against the enemy of their independence."[14] The division of power between the federal government and the states impaired the revolution to the extent that "every enlightened man, every patriot bewailed the lack of force in the General Congress and the lack of unified action among the various republics."[15] Far from being hostile to the U.S., Condorcet regarded us generally as "a people worthy of imitation." In this instance, with regard to federalism, however, France had to recognize that if she started with a diffusion of sovereign authority, she would be consigned to imitation of America's weakness. The Americans could not correct this structural evil, "so thoroughly, did they fear the effects of a great change executed under such dangerous circumstances." France should not attempt "what the prudence of the Americans dared not undertake in circumstances which served to require it."[16] Condorcet thus used his admiration for us to insist that France must, *ab initio*, establish the governmental system that would assure the capacity for unified actions that "every enlightened man, every patriot" in America knew to be unnecessary. "For these reasons it has of necessity been declared that France should form a republic, one and indivisible."[17]

While Condorcet saw federalism as a weakness that could threaten independence, his view of checks and balances was even less charitable. At its core, it was a dangerous sham. He recognized as one of two widely held opinions that "have hitherto divided theorists," the conviction that "certain independent forces should form a kind of balance, mutually serving to regulate one another; that each should become the defender of the general freedom against the other, so that each would oppose the usurpation of the others in order to defend its own authority."[18] Having summarized the underlying proposition of Hamilton, Madison, and Jay in *The Federalist*, Condorcet proceeded to attack it as unworkable and destructive. The public's tranquility would be threatened if opinions were divided and citizens split for and against particular units or authorities. The mechanism was deemed so complex and divisive that "either such complicated machines are destroyed by their own action, or, besides the system established by law, another is formed based on intrigue, corruption or public apathy."[19] Ultimately, two constitutions appear: one public, the other secret; one formally legal, the other real. Such complexity, productive of duplicity, must be avoided.

Condorcet believed he had an even more compelling reason for opposing checks and balances, and in his trenchant enunciation of that reason, he sharpened the dichotomy between his and U.S. framers' conceptions of constitutions. "Those constitutions founded on a balance of powers," Condorcet maintained, "suppose or lead to, the existence of two parties, and one of the most pressing needs of the French Republic is to be wholly free of party."[20]

The framers of the U.S. Constitution were as concerned as Condorcet about the evils of factional divisions in society, but the notion of being "totally free of party," while possible, was seen by them as coming at too high a price. In *The Federalist* No. 10, Madison first hailed the potentiality of a "well constructed Union" to tend "to break and control the violence of faction" and then went on to define the evil of faction as "a number of citizens, whether amounting to a majority or minority of the whole, who are united and actuated by some common impulse of passion, or of interest, adverse to the rights of other citizens or to the permanent and aggregate interests of the Community." Disturbing and destructive as a faction may be, "the spirit of party and faction" are involved "in the necessary and ordinary operations of government."[21] The mischief of factions could be cured by removing the causes of faction. But this would be "worse than the disease," for it would necessitate destruction of the liberty essential to its existence. "Liberty is to faction what air is to fire, an element without which it instantly expires." Since the causes of faction cannot be eliminated without destroying liberty, it is more prudent and sensible to focus on controlling faction's effects through emphasis on representative rather than pure democratic instruments of governance and through institutional separation of impulse to act from opportunity to take and implement action.

If Condorcet believed that France must be "wholly free of party" and that checks and balances exacerbated rather than mitigated the likelihood of such factionalism, what mechanism could be invoked to minimize politicization without denigrating popular sovereignty? What was required, he maintained, was "a single force" that would be "limited and regulated by law" as motivation for the social system. Should such a supreme authority attempt to impair the freedom or rights of citizens, the execution of the law against it "would be guaranteed by the general will of the people."[22] The major instrument for expression of the general will as a control of governmental abuse and incompetence as well as a spur to policy evaluation and reform was the primary assembly. The concept of the primary assembly was also made central to legal status of the person as citizen. This latter point warrants enlargement before we explore the functions assigned to primary assemblies by Condorcet.

Whereas the typical frame of reference for allocation or recognition of individual rights in the U.S. Constitution was to persons, Condorcet's constitution focused on "citizens" as those whose rights were protected. If citizenship were a rationed or restricted official status in Condorcet's system, his alleged faith in popular sovereignty would have turned out to be merely a facade for an authoritarian regime. The definition of citizenship in the constitution thus became the key to whether new hierarchies of status would be sanctioned, notwithstanding the stress on egalitarianism in the *Projet de Déclaration.* Title 2 of the constitution dealt with "the state of the citizens and the necessary conditions for exercise of rights." Any man who has reached the age of twenty-one, who has inscribed himself on the list of a primary assembly, and who has resided on French territory for a year without interruption was declared a citizen of the Republic. Once acquired, citizenship could be lost only as a consequence of punishment by law for "civic degradation" or of naturalization by a foreign country. The right to vote was conditioned on citizenship plus residence for three months without interruption in that sector of France in which the citizen wished to vote. In short, Condorcet disposed in three sentences of Title 2 of another facet of the slavery issue that tore the U.S. asunder, and was typified by the Supreme Court's 1857 ruling, in the Dred Scott case, that a black man who had been a slave could not be a citizen of his state or of the United States. Not until the adoption of the fourteenth amendment did we resolve the citizenship issue. Despite the openness of citizenship by Condorcet to all men over twenty-one, it must be noted that Condorcet's definition effectively excluded women and minors from explicit constitutional protection. His pro-feminist beliefs notwithstanding, Condorcet's constitution remained consistent with the sexism of its time.

The Central Role of the Primary Assemblies

Title 3 of Condorcet's constitution, consisting of five sections and a total of fifty-six Articles, presented meticulously detailed criteria for the selection and operation of the assemblies, broad declarations of their functions and powers, and yet, curiously enough, only minimum and maximum figures for their internal composition and only amorphous references to their interrelationships. It would thus be easy to criticize the drafting of this section both for preoccupation with details unsuited to constitution making, such as a reference to "reading in loud voices, the name of each voter and the names of the inscribed on their ballots,"[23] and for failure to deal with structural foundations at the core of constitutional promulgation, such as the number of primary assemblies in each of the eighty-five departments. But such criticism would miss the main thrust of citizen participation and control through the primary assemblies. At the outset of Title 3, Condorcet makes clear the function of the primary assemblies as the institutions "Où les Français doivent exercer leurs droits de citoyens" ("where the French shall exercise their rights as citizens").[24]

The breadth and detail of the Articles on the role of the citizen within the primary assemblies attests to the high priority Condorcet placed on local position and authority. The citizen could participate in local administrative functions as an elected member of the assembly's "bureau," vote in all elections as specified by the extensive guidelines in the 25 Articles of Section 3, and play an important role in stimulating and negating legislation through censure of the national legislature.

The "bureau" of each primary assembly was a popularly elected body of administrators which officially convoked the primary assembly, monitored citizenship qualifications, and communicated with other primary assemblies on common issues. Each primary assembly was to have not less than 450 members nor more than 900.[25] Its bureau had one member for every fifty members of the primary assembly; the top four vote-getters filled the roles of president, secretary, and election commissioners, respectively. Bureau seats were filled by plurality, rather than by majority as in the national election. The symbolic importance of the "bureau," like the primary assembly itself, was that of permitting a share of administrative control to be delegated directly to the localities. For instance, preliminary review of entitlement to citizenship was by the "bureau": "no person shall be permitted to vote in a primary assembly where he is not registered if he has not presented the proper credentials to the bureau eight days before the convocation of the assembly."[26] Given fulfillment of the "bureau" requirements, the primary assembly would then vote to confer citizenship officially. Re-election to bureau positions was permitted.[27]

Voting guidelines for the primary assemblies were minutely detailed. The "general rules for elections in the primary assemblies" were prescribed in 25 Articles of Chapter 3 of Title 3, belying in their specificity the ascription of "general." Everything from the two-stage election process[28] to the verification of the election outcome by the bureau "at four o'clock" was constitutionally ordained.[29] The same citizen could be nominated for several different offices, but, in recognizing "the incompatibility between public functions" that could arise, Condorcet required that "no citizen can accept a new public function without renouncing, by the very fact of his acceptance, the function he formerly exercised."[30] Conscious of the possibility that he might be charged with pre-occupation with minutiae, Condorcet had observed in a footnote at the outset of the *Projet de Constitution* that, "There are perhaps several articles in this project which, at first sight, will appear to be regulatory, but they are so essential to the general plan that reflection and discussion will come to recognize them as truly constitutional."[31] From a distance of 190 years and 3,000 miles, many of the details prescribed by Condorcet for the primary assemblies seem pedantic if not compulsive, but a focus of concern today on whether this phase of Condorcet's draft was constitutionally gauche would be at least as dysfunctional as his alleged preoccupation. The essential functions of the primary assemblies were stated with becoming brevity and with sufficient generality in the three Articles of Sections of Title 2 to make it clear beyond doubt that this was a Constitution Condorcet was expounding and not a prolix legal code.

Article I of Section 2 simply declared that French citizens will "convene in primary assemblies in order to proceed with the elections provided for by the Constitution." Article 2 added four examples of other deliberative and policy making responsibilities of the primary assemblies under the rubric of "objects which concern the general interest of the Republic." These were (1) accepting or refusing proposals for a new constitution or for amendments fo the accepted constitution; (2) calling for the convocation of a national convention; (3) expressing the views of the citizenry on issues raised by the legislature that interest the entire Republic; (4) and requiring the legislature to take new proposals into consideration or exercising over the actions of the national representatives, "the censure of the people" according to the manner and rules fixed by the Constitution. Finally, Article 3 declared null and void any actions of the primary assemblies not in conformance with this Constitution.

Although many of the thirteen Articles of Section 5 of Title 3, prescribing "the forms of deliberation in the primary assemblies," were open to the critique of over-specificity (it was constitutionally ordered, for example, that the room in which the primary assembly meets was to be open every Sunday of the year to citizens who wish to meet there),[32] the more salient point about them was that they attested to the vast national power of the primary assemblies acting in concern. Taken together with the primary assemblies, the vehicle for the exercise of the rights of citizenship, and the assignment, in Article 1, Section 2 of Title 3, of the functions of initiation of constitutional change and legislative censure to the primary assemblies, Condorcet's allocation to them in Article 9, Section 5 of Title 3 of authority to mobilize national opinion embodied the commitment to popular sovereignty of his constitutional plan.

Pursuant to Article 9 of Section 5, all the primary assemblies of the Republic could be convoked for deliberations on the same theme. In such cases the summary of the views of each department's citizens was to be forwarded to the national legislature, which would then have to publish within two weeks a national tabulation of citizen views. Nothing in Title 2 made such views binding on the national legislature, of course; and the legislature could, pursuant to the final Article of Title 3, rule definitively on claims that primary assemblies violated any constitutional requirements in the course of deliberations or in electing national legislators or public functionaries. Nonetheless, the instrumentation for official pulse-taking of the public in a manner more akin to that of a plebiscite than a polling sample was unequivocally set forth.

Emphasis on Public Participation

Condorcet may have underestimated the stimulus to party and faction that could be generated when public opinion was certified as in conflict with legislative policy, but his commitment to viable and robust public participation in the initiation and reform of national policy was pervasively evident in his structuring of the primary assemblies. Not only was Title 3 devoted profoundly and extensively to their establishment and delineation; a substantial portion of Title 8, which dealt with the right of petition and with censure by the people, focused on the primary assemblies as well. Any citizen, for example, had the right to require the bureau of his primary assembly to schedule a deliberation on any national issue the citizen believed "useful or necessary" involving the constitution or issues of legislation or administration under it.[33] All that was required as a precondition to agendaing was that the signature of 50 citizens of the district in which that primary assembly is situated support the petitioning citizen's request.[34] Title 8 implemented the procedures contemplated in Title 3, Section 5, Article 9, and added a sanction to public censure. If a majority of voices in all the primary assemblies called for revocation within a year of the adoption of a national legislative decree, members of the legislative corps who voted for such decree could not be re-elected to the legislature during the interval of one legislative term.[35]

The ultimate constitutional power of the primary assemblies was with regard to the convocation of new national constitutional conventions, and Title 9 of Condorcet's constitution dealt with the specifics. In the first place, it was emphasized again that the source of constitutional change was the people through their primary assemblies and not through any other representational mechanism. The sole vehicle of constitutional change was to be the national convention. Convocation of a national convention was the responsibility of the legislative corps, but performance of the responsibility was conditioned upon initiation or approval by the people. For example, the legislature itself could propose the convocation of a national convention, but the convention could only take place "when the majority of the French people will have approved this convocation."[36] By following the same procedure as for censure, any citizen could initiate a call for a new constitutional convention.[37] Once the majority of voters in the primary assemblies of any department call for convocation of a constitutional convention, the legislative corps would be obliged immediately to consult with all the Republic's citizens through their primary assemblies, and if the majority of voters in the assemblies vote in the affirmative, "the convention will take place without delay."[38]

Election of delegates to the constitutional convention was also a function of the primary assemblies, two delegates from each of the eighty-five departments to be selected in the same manner as the selection of members of the legislature. The convention had to complete its deliberations within a year's time, and all of its sessions had to be public.[39] The only situation in which the primary assemblies would not have a central role in convoking the constitutional convention would be when a constitution has been in effect for twenty years. In that unlikely circumstance, the legislature without more ado would call a convention to "re-examine and perfect the constitution."[40]

Convoking, electing, revising, rejecting, mobilizing, and expressing were all essential functions of the primary assemblies. Without a doubt, the allocation of such broad powers to an instrument of direct democracy by Condorcet went beyond the workable or the acceptable in the eyes of the framers of the U.S. Constitution. Although France was designated a republic rather than a democracy by Condorcet, his reliance upon direct democratic controls at the crunch points of governance contrasted sharply with the view of our framers that "theoretic politicians" who have patronized direct democracy "have erroneously supposed that by reducing mankind to a perfect equality in their political rights, they would at the same time be perfectly equalized and assimilated in their possessions, their opinions, and their passions." Our framers preferred mechanisms that could "refine and enlarge the public views, by passing them through the medium of a chosen body of citizens whose wisdom may best discern the true interest of their country."[41]

An Opening for Faction?

Whereas the framers of our Constitution opened themselves to charges of élitism for their total distrust and denigration of direct democracy and their insistence that it "can admit of no cure for the mischiefs of faction."[42] Condorcet's deep faith in democratic participation and control through the primary assemblies may have insulated him from recognition of the faction-supportive aspects of his draft. His constitution did not come to grips with the problem of how to establish separation of powers and still avoid the divisiveness of party and faction. His critique of checks and balances, concluding that it spawns rather than controls faction, makes one wish all the more that he had probed projected alternatives fully for their proneness to or immunity from faction. What, for example, would inhibit or prevent factional battles between or within primary assemblies over the propriety of particular legislative, administrative, executive or judicial acts? Surely it couldn't be just "the firm resolution of the people to obey the law"[43a] or the submission to them of questions "definitively and unalterably posed in such a way that they can be decided by a simple vote of affirmation or negation."[43b]

Condorcet's conception of separation of powers not only did not allow for checks and balances; it explicitly prohibited decisions by one branch of the government deemed to be within the competence of another. This would be bound to create special difficulties for the executive council of the new government and, even more so, for the judiciary.

Condorcet's executive council of the Republic, made up of seven ministers and a secretariat, was charged with responsibility for executing the laws and decrees of the legislative corps.[44] In carrying out its assigned functions, however, the council was "expressly forbidden to modify, extend or interpret the disposition of laws and decrees under whatever pretext."[45] The executive council was "expressly charged" with annulling the actions of administrators who act contrary to law "or who would compromise the public tranquility or security of the State,"[46] and it was required as well to initiate actions with the appellate judiciary, the "judicial censors," to correct abuses of power by judges.[47] But how the council could correct others' errors without interpreting the law was never enlarged upon.

The judiciary was even more sharply confined in performing its assigned functions. The judges who were elected for fixed terms were, on the one hand, insulated from interference with their judicial functions by the other branches. Performance of judicial functions was explicitly denied to the legislature, executive council, and administrative corps. On the other hand, judges and judicial tribunals were forbidden to do some of the very things inherent in the traditional performance of judicial functions. Condorcet prescribed that: "Les tribunaux et les juges ne peuvent s'immiscer dans l'exercice du pouvoir legislatif; ils ne peuvent interpréter les lois ni les étendre, en arretêr ou suspendre l'exécution; ils ne peuvent entreprendre sur les fonctions administratives, ni citer devant eux les administrateurs, pour raison de leurs fonctions. ("The courts and judges cannot interfere in the exercise of legislative power; they cannot interpret the laws, nor expand, terminate or suspend their execution; they cannot undertake administrative functions nor subject administrators to the legal process on issues concerning their functions.")[48]

How courts could apply law without interpreting it, how they could confront illegal actions without enjoining them are hard issues to understand; and Condorcet's prescriptions in these regards were not accompanied by explanations. In other respects, his judicial articles were far more perceptive than those of our framers on the need for arbitration and conciliation as alternatives to litigation in dispute resolution,[49] and more humane in their abolition of the death penalty for private delicts.[50] But the election of trial judges, juries, and appellate courts by the primary assemblies for limited terms, coupled with the confinement of the concept of judging and the subjection of judges to censure or worse for exceeding the limits of their power, could hardly be carried out at all without engendering factional disagreements and conflicts. Perhaps Condorcet's answer to this point would have been that it is more consonant with democratic principles to have the conflicts faced openly and directly in the people's forums, the primary assemblies and the national legislature, than to have them bargained away by élitist institutions only remotely subject to the public's scrutiny. In any event, his conception of the one-house national legislature was consistent with this hypothesized response.

Definitive Powers of the Legislature

The framers of our constitution granted "the executive power" to the President and "the judicial power" to the Supreme Court and such lower courts as Congress might establish; but to the national legislature they gave only "all legislative powers herein granted." The difference in terminology had to be deliberate for, as the authors of *The Federalist* No. 48 noted, there was concern over the danger of legislative usurpation of power. "The legislative department," Madison observed, "is everywhere extending the sphere of its activity, and drawing all power into its impetuous vortex."[51] By contrast, Condorcet's constitution, while subjecting legislative laws and decrees to the censuring power of the primary assemblies, nonetheless accorded to the national legislature more definitive powers than to any of the other branches. To the single house legislature, whose membership was to be renewed every year, was accorded the "full and entire legislative power" except for constitutional change.[52] All acts concerning civil, criminal, and police matters were included in the legislature's domain. Even extraordinary measures for "general security and public tranquility" were authorized as long as they were not in effect for more than six months at a time.[53] Although the "projet de Déclaration" and the section in Title 10 on "the means of guaranteeing civil liberty"[54] placed obvious limitations on legislative policies threatening individual freedom, the very inclusion of a provision for "extraordinary measures" suggested indorsement of legislative discretion to deal with emergencies in ways governed predominantly by perceptions of necessity.

Condorcet's speech to the convention, on behalf of its committee on the constitution in February 1793, was replete with rationales supporting the structure and powers of the legislature. By placing in the legislature as an assembly of popular representatives "the sole principle of social action," Condorcet declared, "we have seized the surest means of preserving unity and combining freedom and peace."[55] Recognizing that "enlightened friends of liberty" were wary of allocating to a single unit of government authority that "would have no other real limits than popular resistance," Condorcet simply reiterated to such "friends" his conviction that the channeling of popular resistance into forms and methods prescribed by the constitution would constitute an adequate and workable check on abuse.

When and How Can Resistance to Authority Be Justified?

The question of the right of resistance to a law that is evidently unjust, even though it has been instituted in legitimate fashion, was equally difficult in both politics and ethics, he acknowledged, since the further question it spawned was "who is to judge the reality of this injustice?"[56] The unequivocal decision of Condorcet's constitution was that the judge must be "the direct majority of the people." Not the courts, not the executive, but the people are "the first of political powers...beyond which one cannot go without destroying the integrity of the social compact and returning man to a state of nature...."[57] The two central components of Condorcet's constitution were thus the primary assemblies and the national legislature. The executive, as a council of national agents, was required between the legislature and the citizenry but was, nonetheless, "not to be considered as a true power." The executive must not "will" but must "watch." It must act so that the "national will," once expressed, "is executed with precision, order and certainty."[58] "True power" resided in the contents and interactions of decisions of the national legislature and the primary assemblies. The legislature was designed to be "an incessantly active authority"[59] that would never succumb to the fear of innovation, which fear was "one of the most fatal scourges of the human race."[60] The objective of the constitution was not to institutionalize inertia but to facilitate the expression and implementation of the general will through repair of the nation's losses, reformation of its laws, and creative and responsive use of its social power. Security against abuse lay not in fostering institutional stalemates but in assuring popular sovereignty. "The very frequent renewal of the legislative body, the remonstrances that the people will be able to make against laws it regards as contrary to its liberty, and the immediate dissolution of the assemblies that refuse to listen to its voice are sufficient guarantees against the schemes for the usurpation of power and the systems destructive of liberty that might otherwise be feared from a single assembly instituted as the only source of every social power."[61]

Condorcet was convinced that the procedures he prescribed for operation of the legislature facilitated unity while affording "the least pretext for division or for the creation of parties."[62] Policy issues, for example, were subject to two legislative discussions, the first to decide whether a proposal should receive consideration or be rejected or tabled, and the second—only after examination and report by an appropriate committee—to make the definitive determination about its adoption.[63]

It would be pointless to cavil over whether two considerations by a one-house legislature would prevent usurpation or stimulate creativity more than single deliberations by a two-house legislature. The point, rather, is that Condorcet, while mindful of the dangers of oppressive actions by government, was a partisan of channeled activism. He was certain that government must act affirmatively to meet social needs, and was equally confident that the functions and processes he assigned to the primary assemblies would assure accountability of policy to the general will within a workable and stable institutional framework hospitable to both protest and reform. Conflict that might erupt between the legislature and the primary assemblies over legislation would be resolved ultimately either by acquiescence of the primary assemblies in legislative policy or by formal disagreement with the legislature through majority vote of all the primary assemblies of the Republic, in which case the legislature would have lost the confidence of the nation and would have to be replaced with a new one. Through this institutionalization of protest and reform, "neither the will of the representatives of the people, nor that of a group of citizens, can ever escape the sovereignty of the general will."[64]

Conclusion

Charles Francis Adams, in his compilation of *The Life and Works of John Adams*, included several searing commentaries by our second President on Condorcet's constitutional views and provisions. Representative samples were:

> If the common people are advised to aim at collecting the whole
> sovereignty in single national assemblies as they are by...the Marquis de
> Condorcet...they will fail of their desired liberty as certainly as emula-
> tion and rivalry are founded in human nature, and inseparable from civil
> affairs....It is a sacred truth and as demonstrable as any proposition what-
> ever that a sovereignty in a single assembly must necessarily and will
> certainly be exercised by a majority as tyranically as any sovereignty was
> ever exercised by kings or nobles. And if a balance of passions and
> interests is not scientifically concerted, the present struggle in Europe will
> be little beneficial to mankind....[65]

> When a writer on government...argues against mixed governments or
> a balance in government, he instantly proves himself an ideologian. To
> reason against a balance because a perfect one cannot be composed or
> eternally preserved is just as good sense as to reason against all morality
> because no man has been perfectly virtuous.[66]

> I was personally acquainted with Mr. Turgot, the Duke de la Roche-
> foucauld, and Mr. Condorcet. They were as amiable, as learned, and as
> honest men as any in France. But such was their inexperience in all that
> relates to free government...that I should trust the most ignorant of our
> honest town meeting orators to make a Constitution sooner than any or
> all of them.[67]

Surely, the fate that befell Condorcet's constitution and Condorcet himself
contributed to Adams's superciliousness and smugness in evaluating Condorcet's
effort to establish viable democracy in France. But it must also be recalled that
Adams, as defender of the Alien and Sedition Acts of 1798, in repressing free
expression in the United States and potentially scuttling American democracy
in its formative era, exploited fears of contagion from the Jacobinism that had
engulfed France. Interestingly enough, it was not the checks and balances built
into our Constitution that rescued us from democratic collapse. Congress had
adopted the restrictive and punitive measures, the President had signed them,
and the Supreme Court lay fallow It was the elections of 1800 that spared us
from a Constitutional crisis. In short, it was a device closer to Condorcet's Constitutional faith than to Adams's that applied the corrective to keep American
democracy afloat at that time. From the vantage point of a 1980s observer, at
least, the tragedy of Condorcet's repudiation and premature death under the
most suspicious of circumstances lay not so much in the blatant personal injustice of the deeds as depriving the world of the opportunity to witness the testing
of his alternative constitutional premises for democratic governance.

Maybe Condorcet was naive and the framers of the U.S. Constitution sophisticated about the causes and controls of faction. But maybe our framers were

simply lucky that geographic expanse and separation from major world areas of conflict in our formative years reinforced and sustained a complex, amorphous, and vulnerable system. And maybe Condorcet's insights into the aspirations and capacities of ordinary citizens for channeled but authoritative participation in governance could have attained viability but for its birth in the ranging midst of revolution. The trite truth is that we don't yet have a way to proceed beyond musing and conjecture. Notwithstanding such deficiency of definitive appraisal, the premises and text of Condorcet's constitution deserve the closest attention of modern theorists and practitioners of democracy as they come to grips with interrelationships of traditional representational systems with burgeoning manifestations and utilizations of direct public opinion polling. Perhaps, on balance, Condorcet's only demonstrable fault was that his conceptions of popular sovereignty and human perfectibility through education and reason were not quite ready for prime time.

Notes

1. Condorcet, *Oeuvres*, 12:567. The text of the *Projet de Constitution* is found in Condorcet, *Oeuvres de Condorcet*, ed. Arthur C. O'Connor and Marie F. Arago, 12 vols. (Paris 1847–1849) 12:335–415.

2. "Projet de Déclaration des Droits Naturels, Civils, et Politiques des Hommes," Article 1.

3. Ibid., Article 8.

4. Ibid., Article 32.

5. Ibid., Article 33.

6. Ibid., Article 20.

7. Ibid., Article 22.

8. Ibid., Article 23.

9. Ibid., Article 27.

10. Ibid., Article 30.

11. Alexander Hamilton, James Madison, and John Jay, *The Federalist*, Jacob E. Cooke, ed. (Middletown, Connecticut, 1961), No. 51, 349.

12. Ibid., 347–48.

13. *Condorcet, Selected Writings*, Keith Michael Baker, ed. (Indianapolis, Indiana, 1976), 143.

14. Ibid., 146.

15. Ibid.

16. Ibid.

17. Ibid.

18. Ibid., 155.

19. Ibid., 155–56.

20. Ibid, p. 156.

21. *Federalist* No. 10, 57.

22. Ibid, 155.

23. "Projet de Déclaration des Droits Naturels, Civils, et Politiques des Hommes," Title 3, Section 3, Article 4.

24. "Projet de Déclaration des Droits Naturels, Civils, et Politiques des Hommes," Title 3, Section 1, Article 1.

25. Ibid.

26. Ibid., Title 3, Section 1, Article 2.
27. Ibid., Title 3, Section 1, Article 9.
28. Ibid., Title 3, Section 3, Article 1.
29. Ibid., Title 3, Section 3, Article 4.
30. Ibid., Title 3, Section 3, Article 25.
31. "Projet de Constitution Française," Footnote 1.
32. Ibid., Title 3, Section 5, Article 3.
33. Ibid., Title 8, Article 1.
34. Ibid., Title 8, Article 3.
35. Ibid., Title 8 Article 22, 23.
36. Ibid., Title 9, Article 7.
37. Ibid., Title 9, Article 5.
38. Ibid., Title 9, Article 6.
39. Ibid., Title 9, Articles 15, 16.
40. Ibid., Title 9, Article 4.
41. *Federalist* No. 10, 61–62.
42. Ibid., 61.
43a. *Condorcet, Selected Writings*, 144.
43b. Ibid., 148.
44. Title 5, Articles 1, 2, 4.
45. Title 5, Article 6.
46. Title 5, Article 8.
47. Title 5, Article 12.
48. Title 10, Section 1, Article 6.
49. Title 10, Section 2, Articles 1, 3, 6, 7.
50. Title 10, Section 3, Article 1.
51. *The Federalist* No. 48, 333.
52. Title 7, Section 2, Articles 1, 2.
53. Title 7, Section 2, Article 7.
54. Title 10, Section 6.
55. *Condorcet, Selected Writings*, 162.
56. Ibid.
57. Ibid.
58. Ibid., 163.
59. Ibid., 157.
60. Ibid.
61. Ibid.
62. Ibid., 159.
63. Title 7, Section 3, Article 5.
64. *Condorcet, Selected Writings*, Section 3, Article 5, 153.
65. Charles Francis Adams, *The Life and Works of John Adams* (Boston, 1856), 6:252.
66. Ibid., 10:257.
67. Ibid., 9:624.

About Our Contributors

MANUELA ALBERTONE has been a Fellow of the Fondazione Luigi Einaudi of Turino and now holds a fellowship from the Ecole normale supérieure of Pisa. She is the author of two books, *Una scuola per la Rivoluzione: Condorcet e il dibattito sul-l'istruzione, 1792-1794* (1979) and *Fisiocrati; istruzione e cultura* (1979). Dr. Albertone is currently engaged in research on Condorcet's pre-Revolutionary educational theory, and on the moral and religious ideas of Condorcet, Necker, and their wives. She has contributed a chapter to a forthcoming work, *French Women and the Age of Enlightenment.*

A. OWEN ALDRIDGE, Professor of French and Comparative Literature at the University of Illinois, Urbana-Champaign, has been visiting professor at the Universities of Toulouse, Clermont-Ferrand, Rio de Janeiro, and at Nihon University, Japan. Founder and editor of *Comparative Literature Studies*, he is on the Advisory Board of our professional journals. Among his ten books are *Man of Reason, the Life of Thomas Paine* (1959). One of his three books on Franklin, *Benjamin Franklin et ses contemporains*, appeared in Paris (1963). He is the author of *Voltaire and the Century of Light* (1975) and has contributed "Condorcet et Paine, leurs rapports intellectuels" to the *Revue de Littérature comparée* 32 (1958) and "Thomas Paine and the Ideologues" to *Studies on Voltaire and the Eighteenth Century* 151 (1976). He has played a leading role in the International Comparative Literature Association and the American Comparative Literature Association.

KEITH MICHAEL BAKER is Professor of History at the Morris Fishbein Center for the Study of the History of Science and Medicine and for the Committee on the Conceptual Foundations of Science at the University of Chicago. He worked at Princeton's Institute for Advanced Study, 1979-1980. *Condorcet. From Natural Philosophy to Social Mathematics* (1975) won him the Laing Prize of the University of Chicago Press and a citation from the History of Science Society. His *Condorcet. Selected Writings* (1976) made a good selection of Condorcet available in English. On Condorcet he has also written: "An Unpublished Essay of Condorcet on Technical Methods of Classification," *Annals of Science* 18 (1962) [1964]; "Condorcet," in Paul Edwards's *Encyclopedia of Philosophy* (1967): "Scientism, elitism and liberalism: the case of Condorcet," *Studies on Voltaire and the Eighteenth Century* 55 (1967); "Les Débuts de Condorcet au Secrétariat de l'Académie royale des Sciences, 1773-1776," *Revue d'histoire des sciences* 20 (1967); "Un éloge officieux de Condorcet: sa notice historique et critique sur Condillac," *Revue de Synthèse*, 3d series, 47-48 (1967); and "Condorcet's Notes for a Revised Edition of his Reception Speech to the Académie française," *Studies on Voltaire and the Eighteenth Century* 169 (1977).

CAROL BLUM, Associate Professor of French, State University of New York at Stony Brook, has been a Junior Fellow of the National Endowment for the Humanities, a Fellow of the French Government in Paris, and of the Guggenheim Foundation. She is the author of various studies of the literature and though of eighteenth-century France, including *Diderot: The Virtue of a Philosopher* (1974) and "Rousseau's Concept of Virtue and the French Revolution," in *Enlightenment Studies in Honor of Lester G. Crocker* (1979). She is currently completing a book on "virtue" in the French Revolution.

HILDA GREENBAUM is Research Associate (color vision), Department of Phsychology, Mt. Holyoke College. After a Harvard postdoctoral fellowship in psychophysics at the National Institute of Mental Health and one in psychoacoustics at the Laboratoire de Neurophysiologie Générale at the Collège de France, she served there as consultant in physiological acoustics. As research associate, lecturer, or consultant she has worked in the United States on brain mechanisms, experimental psychology, psychophysics, neurobiology, and child and human development. She has contributed to colloquia in Prague, Liège, Copenhagen, and Mexico City, published papers in French for the *Journal de Physiologie* and the *Journal de Psychologie*, and translated papers of her former associates at the Collège de France for the *Journal of the Acoustical Society of America*.

LOUIS S. GREENBAUM, Professor of History at the University of Massachusetts at Amherst, is the author of *Talleyrand, Statesman-Priest. The Agent-General of the Clergy and the Church of France at the End of the Old Régime* (1970). He has published numerous articles on the history of health-care and hospitals in eighteenth-century France, in *Clio Medica*, the *Revue d'Histoire des Sciences*, the *Archives internationales d'histoire des sciences*, the *Consortium on Revolutionary Europe, 1750-1850*, the *Bulletin of the History of Medicine*, and *Studies in Eighteenth-Century Culture*. His "Health-Care and Hospital-Building in Eighteenth-Century France: Reform Proposals of Du Pont de Nemours and Condorcet" appeared in *Studies on Voltaire and the Eighteenth Century* (1976). He has held fellowships from the French Government, the National Institutes of Health and the National Library of Medicine, among others, served on the White House Conference on Food, Nutrition and Health, and as Consultant on Historical Population Studies for the Harvard University School of Public Health.

JEAN A. PERKINS, Susan W. Lippincott Professor of French at Swarthmore College, is the author of *The Concept of Self in the French Enlightenment* (1969) and of articles in *Studies in Eighteenth-Century Culture, Diderot Studies*, and *Studies on Voltaire and the Eighteenth Century*. She was a Fellow of the American Council of Learned Societies and is preparing a book on the Physiocrats and the French Enlightenment. From 1973 to 1978 she served as treasurer of the American Society for Eighteenth-Century Studies, and in 1979 as President of the Modern Language Association.

PIERRE ANTOINE PERROD, a practicing attorney before the Court of Appeals in Lyon, France, directs the Commission for Liberty and the Reform of the Penal Code. Formerly President of the Bar Association of Lyon (*Bâtonnier*), he was named in 1976 Vice-President of the Conference of "Bâtonniers de France et d'Outre-Mer." A doctor of law, Professor Perrod taught at the law school of the University of Lyon from 1944 to 1972. He is also a docteur-ès-lettres of the Sorbonne. Four of his ten books have won prizes. In 1940 he was the recipient of the Prize for Theses in Comparative Law. His *L'Affaire Peytel* (1958) carried off the Prix Chazière of the Académie de Lyon. In 1963 his *L'Affaire Ledru*, crowned by the *Académie française*, was adapted to television, where it scored a hit. *Justice et Injustice* (1970) obtained the Prix du Palais Littéraire, and *L'Affaire LALLY-TOLENDAL* (1976) won the Prix Asie-Ecrivains d'Outre-Mer. Currently, Dr. Perrod is working on unpublished letters of Montesquieu. A member of the Comité d'Honneur de la Société d'Histoire Littéraire de la France, he has been since 1965 an Associate of the Academy of Moral and Political Sciences at the Institut de France, and since 1976 President of the Academy of Sciences, Belles-Lettres, and Arts of Lyon. He is a Commandeur des Palmes Académiques and Chevalier de la Légion d'honneur.

RICHARD H. POPKIN is Professor of Philosophy at Washington University in St. Louis. After advanced study in Holland, France, and England, he has become an *animateur* of studies in the history of ideas and philosophy in modern times. The numerous universities where he has taught include McGill University in Montreal, the Hebrew University of Jerusalem, and two others in Israel. He was Professor-in-Residence for 1981–1982 at the Wm. Andrew Clark Library in Los Angeles. His main fields include skepticism, millenarianism, Messianism, Christian Zionism, racism, Pierre Bayle, Isaac La Peyrère, Spinoza, and Hume. He was the founder in 1963 of the *Journal of the History of Philosophy* and is co-director with Professor Paul Dibon of the *Archives Internationales de l'Histoire des Idées* which since 1961 has brought out about 100 volumes. In addition, he has been the General Editor of encyclopedias and other series, including Texts in Early Modern Philosophy. Of his fourteen books, *The History of Skepticism from Erasmus to*

Spinoza has appeared in 1980 in an enlarged edition. His *The Second Oswald* had been translated into French and Portuguese. Forthcoming is his *Isaac La Peyrère*, as well as a volume of his articles on racism. The author of two hundred articles, and a contributor to many colloquia, he is with the late Giorgio Tonelli and Craig Walton, among others, one of the founders of the Society for the Study of the History of Philosophy. Columbia University in 1977 awarded him the Nicholas Murray Butler Medal in Philosophy.

VICTOR G. ROSENBLUM is a Professor of Law and Political Science at Northwestern University. Formerly President of Reed College, he has twice been Visiting Professor at the University of Louvain. He is also a lecturer at the Advanced Study Program of the Brookings Institute, and at the Legal Education Institute of the U.S. Office of Personnel Management. He has served on the Advisory Council for the University of Montenegro, and is a consultant for the Administrative Conference of the United States. He is active in various advisory committees and boards of directors for law enforcement, criminal justice, administrative law, etc., is on the Advisory Council of the Institute for Humanistic Studies, State University of New York at Albany, and is a trustee of the Law and Society Association. He has held key positions with the American Bar Association and the American Political Science Association. Studies of his have appeared on constitutional law, federal regulatory agencies, and on law and contemporary problems. See, for example, his article "A Place for Social Science along the Judiciary's Constitutional Law Frontier," 65 *Northwestern University Law Review* 445 (1971). A co-editor of *Constitutional Law: Political Roles of the Supreme Court* (1973), he has argued before the Supreme Court of the United States.

LEONORA COHEN ROSENFIELD, Editor of CONDORCET STUDIES I, and member of the Board of Directors of *International Studies in the History of Ideas*, was Professor Emeritus of French Literature at the University of Maryland. Two of her four books are *From Beast-Machine to Man-Machine, Animal Soul in French Letters from Descartes to La Mettrie* (with a Preface by Paul Hazard, 1940, 1941, 1968), and *Portrait of a Philosopher, Morris R. Cohen in Life and Letters* (1962). She contributed widely to books and journals in the United States and abroad and participated in American and international meetings. Of her essays, "The Rights of Women in the French Revolution" appeared in *Studies in Eighteenth-Century Culture* (1978), "La Mettrie and Quesnay, Physician-Philosophes of the Enlightenment" in *Enlightenment Studies in Honor of Lester G. Crocker* (1979). She has served as consultant-reader for the *Journal of the History of Philosophy, Eighteenth-Century Studies*, the *Studies in the Renaissance* issue of the *Renaissance Quarterly*, and *Studies in Eighteenth-Century Culture*.

CONSTANCE ROWE is Associate Professor Emeritus of French at Southeast Missouri State University. Her *Voltaire and the State*, first published by Columbia University Press (1955), was reprinted in 1967 by Octagon Books, Inc. She serves as president of the Writers' Guild of Cape Girardeau.

LOUIS TRENARD, Professor at the Université Lilloise des Sciences humaines, des Lettres et des Arts, is Director there of the Regional Center of Historical Studies. He is active on some fourteen Commissions of historical or cultural studies, president of some of them, and is Vice-President of the Société française d'Etudes du XVIIIe siècle. He has published a dozen or more books, including *Lyon, de l'Encyclopédie au préromantisme* (1958); *Histoire générale de la Presse française*, Tome 1, *Des origines à 1814* (1969); *De Douai à Lille, Une Université et son histoire* (1978), and has edited other works under his direction. One of his numerous regional studies was done in collaboration with his wife, Gabrielle Trenard. Currently he is editing works by Voltaire for the Voltaire Foundation. The Editor of *L'Information historique* since 1962, and of *La Revue du Nord*, he is a contributor to the *Annales historiques de la Révolution française, La Revue historique, La Revue belge de philologie et d'histoire*, to the *Revue XVIIe siècle*, and the *Revue du XVIIIe siècle*. Educational missions have taken him to Austria, Hungary, Poland, Florence, Cameroun, Cyrpus, Algeria, U.S.S.R, and to the Universities of Montreal, Geneva, Florida, and Ottawa. A member of the Académie des Sciences, Belles Lettres et Arts de Lyon and of several other academies he is Commandeur dans l'Ordre des Palmes Académiques, Officier de l'Ordre national de Mérite, and Chevalier de la Légion d'Honneur.

RENÉE WALDINGER is Professor of French at The City College and Graduate Center of The City University of New York. She is the author of *Voltaire and Reform in the Light of the French Revolution* (1959); "Voltaire and Medicine," *Studies on Voltaire and the Eighteenth Century*, vol. 58; "America: Another Link in Voltaire's Philosophic Campaign," *Kentucky Romance Quarterly*, vol. 16, no. 1 (1969); and "Diderot as Dramatist: Dramatic Prose? Dramatic Drama?," *Diderot Studies* 20. She has been active in colloquia in the United States and abroad and in learned societies. She has served as a Delegate for Pedagogical Concerns at the Assembly of the Modern Language Association. Her present duties include membership on the Board of Directors of the Metropolitan Branch of the American Association of Teachers of French, serving on the Fellowship Selection Committee of the American Council of Learned Societies, and acting as Consultant for the Panel on Research Tools of the National Endowment for the Humanities.

Subject Index